JONATHAN FREJUSTE

BRIDGE THE
GAPS

LESSONS ON SELF-AWARENESS,
SELF-DEVELOPMENT & SELF-CARE

Tools for Building a Life that Matters

Dedication

BRIDGE THE GAPS WAS WRITTEN to provide the next generation with vital tools for living out God's purpose for their lives. This book is dedicated to the following families, who are working hard to learn the lessons and overcome obstacles necessary for their children to reach their God-given destinies. May God give you the peace, grace, wisdom, and strength to raise them up in the way they should go, so when they are older, they will not depart. (Proverbs 22:6, NLT) God Bless You!

-Stephen Hayles and Savannah Hayles, whose parents are Maryann and Rupert Hayles

-Nathaniel Ron Francois and Nehemiah Hans Francois, whose parents are Tarana and Ronald Francois

-Elijah Joshua Chiedu and Faith Miciayah Chiedu, whose parents are Mimi and Emeka Chiedu

-Briana Iglesias, Cameron Campbell, Gabriel Iglesias, and Aaron Campbell (a/k/a "A-Town"), whose parents are Rosabel and Rohan Campbell

-Lilia Benisse Turenne, Benjamin Lotus Turenne, Lucy Brielle Turenne, and Brooklynn Louange Turenne, whose parents are Beatrice and Lotus Turenne

-Malcolm Reynolds, Grace Olivia Reynolds and Kaleena Reynolds, whose parents are Endgie and Kahreef Mikal Reynolds

-Julie Joseph, Jonathan Joseph, and Christian Joseph, whose parents are Cassandre and Jean Joseph

-Ari Jaxson Spears, whose parents are Myriam and Lewis Spears

-Andrew Arce, Aaron A. Jones, and Elijah A. Jones, whose parents are Diana J. and Cory A. Jones

-Christian Varghese and Dominic Varghese, whose parents are Siby and Don Varghese

-Stacey Desir and Stanley Desir, whose parents are Evna and Judson Desir

-Ruchama Casseus, whose parents are Ginette and Herve Casseus

-Carlynn Frejuste and Liam Frejuste, whose parents are Eurika and Romain Frejuste

Acknowledgments

MY GRANDMOTHER TURNED 92 ON February 19, 2017. She passed away the following morning. At her funeral, many people expressed their appreciation and gratitude for all that my grandmother had done for them when they were growing up in Haiti. As I reflected on the day's events, I realized that most of the people who had expressed their gratitude had never gotten the chance to tell my grandma how they felt about her or express their appreciation for her meaningful presence in their lives. I decided that I would give people their "flowers" while they were still here. I wouldn't wait for a tragic event to acknowledge someone's positive contribution in my life.

Mom and Dad, Julie and Romain Frejuste: Thank you for instilling in me the value of education, hard work, self-reliance, and perseverance. I would not have been able to do this without you. Thank you.

Pastor Charles Rejouis, Pastor Monel Fleurimond, Pastor Testar St. Victor, and Pastor Allrich Rejouis, Mount Olive Church of God (www.mont-desoliviers.com): Thank you for your leadership. I am very grateful for your work and sacrifice to build a community where our families could learn and grow together to pursue God's call for their lives.

Rupert Hayles, co-founder and president of the Center of Emotional Development (www.emotionalcenter.org): Thank you for the continual mentorship and for the opportunity to work with you in creating a path for people to bridge the gaps in their emotional and spiritual development. I am thankful to God for your guidance and unconditional support, especially through my foibles and mistakes as I stumbled to get on the path that God had for me. Thank you.

Robin Dougherty, executive director of the Greater Newark Conservancy: I will always appreciate what you did for us as young people who needed a safe place to find our way, personally and vocationally. You're a blessing. Thank you.

Brian H. Morrell, director of development at the Greater Newark Conservancy: Your work in mentoring me, when I was a teenaged intern—along with many other young people—to learn the ropes in the corporate world was instrumental in laying a foundation for my future. Thank you.

Pete and Geri Scazzero, founders of Emotionally Healthy Spirituality (www.emotionallyhealthy.org): Thank you for your leadership in creating Emotionally Healthy Spirituality, particularly with your leading out of vulnerability. It has set so many people free. This paradigm of spiritual formation has changed my life and continues to challenge me to grow as a man and a leader. Thank you.

Reverend Dee Verhagen, director and pastor of the Life Guidance Center, Calvary Temple: Thank you for your continued support, counsel, prayers, and encouraging words. You were absolutely right about Elijah House launching you into your destiny. I would not have been able to do this without you. Thank you.

Robert Porter, executive director of Employee Financial Services of Ernst and Young: Thank you for your support and counsel in helping me to carve out a career path that allowed me to serve my community and grow as a planner and a professional. I certainly have more hope that people in general, and people of color in particular, can find their way in corporate America with good men and culturally sensitive leaders like you. Thank you.

Sr. Maureen Crowley, former president and principal of Immaculate Conception High School, Montclair, NJ: Your work in making Immaculate a great place for people is remarkable. Thank you for your support in my life during and even after my high school years, particularly with the losses that I've faced. I appreciate your words of advice and encouragement, which helped me to have the courage to continue to take steps in my life and vocation. Thank you.

Mr. Patrick Dyer, assistant principal, advancement director/school security coordinator, Immaculate Conception High School, Montclair, NJ: Thank you for your commitment to Immaculate. I will never forget how you would lovingly confront all the students you encountered when they would get out of line. Your example of loving correction is one that I try to emulate with the young people I work with. You have certainly played a role in my growth and development as a man and a leader. Thank you.

Ms. Kathleen Badillo, assistant vice principal, Immaculate Conception High School, Montclair, NJ: Ms. B., You were my first English teacher. You were always down to earth and encouraging, but still tough and demanding of the best from your students. Your encouragement and guidance played a part in me doing this work today. Thank you for what you have done for me and for what you're doing for so many students.

Kristina Kersey, Assistant Deputy, Office of the Public Defender: Your dedication to serving young people and working tirelessly to give them tools to live their purpose is admirable and commendable. Thank you for your example and giving me an opportunity to serve. Thank you.

Albert Pastino, partner at Laud Collier Capital and alumnus of Saint Joseph's University: Because of your generosity, I was able to attend a great school, where I learned invaluable lessons and met amazing people who provided me with the guidance to find my calling. I will forever be grateful for your support and generosity. Thank you.

Reverend Malachia Brantley Jr., D.Min, Northern State Prison: You have one of the most challenging callings that I've seen yet you execute with grace, patience, humility, and a faithful confidence in God. Thank you for your words of encouragement and example of consistency and faithfulness in ministry.

Lawrence Evans, Vice Principal, Essex Regional Educational Services Commission: Your work with young people is a blessing and more than necessary. Thank you for your wisdom, humility and vulnerability in your service. Your example has been an encouragement to me whenever I get discouraged. Thank you.

Pastor Steve Gant, Pastor of Urban Family Life: Your gift is a perfect complement in our service in the prisons. I knew your passion with families would manifest into something tangible. Whether it's in prison or in a church, your gift resonates and will serve the healing of marriages and families. Thank you for putting work behind your words.

Mark Cheatam, manager, Pollack Financial Group LLC: The road to being great is paved by service and sacrifice. You have consistently exemplified that in your work in the community. Your words of advice and encouragement played a huge role in giving me the confidence to complete this book. Thank you for your example, guidance, and wisdom on my journey.

Pastor Dante Poole, MA, Principal of Aberdeen Elementary School: God set me up to meet you at a critical time in my life. Your words of encouragement and mentorship has been a blessing and a source of strength to me. Thank you.

Vera Nyajure, social worker and life skills coach, Somerset Home for Temporarily Displaced Children: Thank you for helping me think through some of the difficult issues that young people face. Your wisdom, counsel, and prayers are greatly appreciated. Thank you.

Chris Broussard, founder the KING Movement: Your work in building up men from all walks of life impressed upon me the desire to work to build up men on the margins. You helped to restore my confidence that black men who walk with Jesus can unapologetically exercise the strength and intelligence to face the misconceptions with integrity, courage, and wisdom. Thank you.

Maria Oquendo, assistant director for counseling services, NJIT: As a young intern in INROADS, you played a tremendous role in teaching me how to transition into being a young professional in corporate America. You know how to be tough and tender when necessary and that's why you're so effective at the work you do with young people until this day. You are another leader who I take a cue from in the work that I do with the people I'm privileged to serve. Thank you.

Lance McGraw, founder and CEO of Hustlelution (www.hustlelution. com): Your story is powerful and you work is needed more than ever. Thank you for being an example of the great things than can happen when you find your purpose. You embody humility, persistence, and consistency. Your work has blessed and inspired me and will do the same for many lives in the future. Thank you.

Saint Joseph's University: While I was at Saint Joe's, a number of administrators and professors played a major role in helping me navigate many of the challenges I faced and provided guidance and support, so that I could finish strong. Thank you Daniel Joyce, S.J., Dr. Shoshonna Edwards-Alexander, Miciah Yehudah, Professor Julie McDonald, Vernon Williams, Todd Krug, Timothy Lannon, S.J., Philip Florio, S.J., and Richard Malloy, S.J.

New Life Fellowship Family (www.newlifefellowship.org): Pastors Rich and Rosie Villodas, Pastors Peter and Myrna Rhodin, Redd and Aya De Leon Sevilla, Russell McLeod, Ruth Zsolnai, Silvett García-Tsuang, Jackie and David Snape, Kelly Ng, Rick and Pam Chowayou, Phil Varghese, Chris Wu, Dan Ports, Kizinga Fleming, Russ McLeod, The Latter Rain Community, Dr. Jay Feld, Thank you for making New Life Fellowship church a family for me.

Success in Motion (http://success-in-motioninc.tumblr.com/): Thank you Rebecca Benoit, Roosevelt Donat, Hans Pierre, Carl Fleurimond, Magdala Chery, Sondy Cadeau, Marline Francois, Samira Louis, Stephanie Eustache, Marlene Alcius, Monique Fleurimond, Ginie Milord, and David Pierre. We were a group of young leaders working to equip the next generation with the tools that we all had received along the way. I will always remember the times we spent preparing, planning, and working on events for the youth. I hope those times taught you as much as they taught me. I could not have asked to be around a more motivated and talented group of folks. Iron truly sharpens iron. Thank you.

Family and Friends: Chris Sanders, executive director of Wisdom Shapes Minds (www.wsmcdc.org); Uncle Eric and Aunt Lucienne Noziere; Rickaldo Noziere; Rick-kendy Noziere; Rocheny Noziere; Woodlain Brun; Mariane and Levy Bien-Aimé; Sebastian Bien-Aimé; Didier Bien-Aimé; Geoffrey Bien-Aimé; Zachary Bien-Aimé; Marvel St. Victor; Samuel

Belony; Dwight Phillips; Johnny Pierce; Darrius Harris; Alexander Exama; Bens Cherette; Gabriela Zamora-Porras; Moe Moore; Marie-Ange Renée (Nainain); Nyrva and Jason Redmond; Ralph Stainfil, Madje Piezema; Darlene Osit; Ariane Osit; Danielle Osit; Leo Faulk; Sean Allen; Todd Gorski; Kevin O'Brien; Jackie Cherry; Annie Scalora; Mickelang and Martine Montlouis; Jerome Wilson, Luqman Abdullateef, Kiecey Castle; Marcus Williams; Joseph Bodine; Wendy Pinos-Patiño; Samantha Ulysse; LaTanya Bynum; Norma Cherilus; Fritzner Alce; Portia Parker; Carlo Gantuah; Tevi Nouvi; Dorothy Antoine; Claudy Antoine; Carline Antoine, Irvin Antoine, Irva Antoine, Mikumari Caiyhe, Joshua Simone; Ted Smith; Kham and Summer Johnson, BassNewark, Thaddeus Price; Merhawy Worede; Kahlil Haynes; Dennis Rawls; Mahaadi Akbar, Nerly Lausier; Pastor Jasner Jacquet; Hassan Pierce; Jonah Laurore; Denise Brown; Michael Cooper; Moise Jean-Charles; Chris and Hope Soules; Nathaniel Cooke Jr – Founder of MRURBANSPORTS, LLC; Susan Ginsberg O'Sullivan; Bethlyn Brookes; Joseph Thomas; Esther Luna; Rosybel Luna; Alex Batista-Moulton; Ohnet Castor; Chris Winter; Tim Harris; Duke Alverna; Wanny Manasse; Pastor Lionel King; Pastor Ryan Faison; Al Hardy; Ian Winters; Andrew Clarke; Bernard Fan Fan; Brian Kim; Turron Kofi Alleyne; Pat Pearsall-Ramey; John Glasser; Ruth Joseph; Chyncia Smith; Edia Antoine; Gaby Antoine; Samantha Frejuste; Ranisha Frejuste; and last but not least, my baby sister, Belinda Frejuste (Proud of you, B.).

All of you have played a role at one point or another in my life, and so you had a part to play in this project—whether you realized it or not. Your presence in my life has helped to encourage, edify, and ignite hope in me to continue to serve others through your own personal examples of serving, living authentically and wholeheartedly, finding strength in your vulnerability, overcoming obstacles, demonstrating your heartfelt expressions of support, providing a stern rebuke when I veered off my path, and/or just giving me a listening ear during the very difficult seasons of my life. Thank you.

Table of Contents

Introduction

ONE OF THE BIGGEST CHALLENGES facing our communities today is the breakdown of the family.

Ideally, we all are raised in homes with loving parents who prepare us for every aspect of the journey we will face in life. They learn who we are. They help us identify our talents and provide opportunities to exercise them. They help us grow and develop as people, teach us how to take care of every aspect of our personhood, and facilitate the healing of the wounds we suffer.

Over the last few years of my life, I've served as a coach, speaker, and workshop facilitator in a variety of settings: schools, group homes, nonprofits, churches, prisons, and a substance abuse treatment center.

I've also had the privilege to serve as an emotional intelligence coach to individuals ranging from directors of law enforcement agencies to senior spiritual leaders. Many of the people I've worked with had a common denominator: the brokenness of the homes in which they were raised. They came from homes where there was mistreatment, abuse, and intentional or unintentional neglect. Their parents might have done the best they could, but they left areas of their children's development unattended.

Parenting is a skill that's learned on the job. Unfortunately, raising children doesn't come with a manual or a complete toolbox. When parents are not fully equipped, the children they raise suffer from gaps in their well-being and development, which also speak to the gaps in the parents' well-being and development.

Those gaps carry over into adulthood and affect nearly every dimension of life: relationships, economics, vocation, and subsequently involvement in the community. Children raised this way might grow up to be adults who make career missteps or poor life and relationship choices. Their lives might be marked by wasted time and continued emotional and mental pain—all of which could have been prevented if the necessary tools were available.

Many of us have learned these life lessons the hard way. If somehow, we never learned them at all, we might be living lost, confused, and disillusioned with life. If this is you, please have compassion for yourself. Remember, it's unloving and unkind to expect yourself to do something that you were never taught how to do.

Many of us have never been taught how to live. We might have been taught how to survive, how to get along without causing any trouble, and how to protect ourselves. But we've never been taught how to live wholeheartedly and abundantly.

Fortunately, there's hope that healing is possible. It's never too late to heal, grow, and reposition yourself to live your life wholeheartedly.

As a college student, I heard a quote that resonates with me until this day: Your greatest frustration is *a problem that you are here to solve.* It's frustrating to see talented people with great potential miss out on the opportunity to live out their callings and serve their communities.

I've taken time, over the last few years, to journal, reflect, and process all the personal experiences I've had as well as what I've learned from workshops, one-on-one conversations, and feedback from community leaders who work to help people build healthy and productive lives. This book is the fruit of that work. I wish I'd had a book like this when I was growing up.

I've received training over the years as a behavioral assistant and an emotional intelligence coach, but I would say that my most profound lessons came when I got close to people's lives, when I heard their stories and understood their concerns—experientially, not just academically.

One of the best aspects of being a coach is acquiring knowledge and information from people's life experiences.

With this book, I want to provide a structure and a set of tools and resources that people can use to bridge the gaps in their lives. I'll focus on three areas: self-awareness, self-development, and self-care. I'll tell you more about each area at the beginning of that section.

I believe many of the problems in our communities cannot be solved by money. People desperately need healthy relationships with others who inspire and facilitate hope, healing, compassion, and empathy through the example of their own lives.

My own life hasn't incorporated these lessons perfectly. There's always more to learn and to heal from. But I want to share with you the foundational lessons that I try to apply. The lessons in this material might not be new, but I do believe they are especially relevant to the condition of the world we are living in today.

You might read about lessons here that don't pertain to your current season of life, but they might apply to someone you know. As you hit new developmental stages, some of the lessons will become more relevant.

I want you to read these lessons, but also reflect on, talk about, and apply them. They are meant to provoke deep thinking and discussion. Such conversations can create fertile ground for change along with healthier choices, and stronger communities.

Some lessons might challenge you personally to improve. You might realize you need to think more on a subject, or work it into your life more deeply. If you have another point of view, that's great! Remember this adage: Chew the meat and spit out the bone. Take what is of benefit to you, and leave the rest behind.

Before you send me a message on social media or find me in person, please take a look at Chapter 35, where you'll find a discussion on clean fighting. Please also read Chapter 42 on listening. I've run into folks who love to debate ideas for a few hours, or even a few days! Healthy debate is constructive. It can sharpen our perspectives, provide new information, and create healthy communities. But unhealthy debates are destructive. They can tear people down and pit us against each other. So let's focus on cultivating healthy debate.

It's been said that children don't do well at obeying their parents, but they have no problem imitating them. As such, this guide is written to mentors and for mentees. Why? Because it's hard to teach the lessons that you don't live. I can't teach someone to be self-disciplined if I'm lazy and undisciplined. I can't teach someone to manage his or her money properly if I mismanage my money. And it's hard to teach someone to courageously pursue his or her calling if I'm not in courageous pursuit of mine.

I have to live and flesh out the messages in my life before I can speak with integrity. Integrity doesn't mean that you apply the lessons perfectly, but that you wrestle with them faithfully.

This guide is not meant to replace any teacher, therapist, or life coach. I can't take the place of good parents. But these words can be a supplemental resource and guide to help you identify your calling. I want to inspire you to be the best version of yourself, to achieve results in your life, and to facilitate healing for yourself and your community.

I want to see a better world. I hope this work can spark minds and motivate people to take actions. I hope you can go out and heal hearts that can change the world.

PART I
SELF-AWARENESS

You cannot be the best version of yourself if you don't know yourself.

Do you know who you are? Not just surface stuff, but deep down? How your brain reasons and responds? What makes you tick? Knowing who you are beneath the surface is the first step toward true self-awareness.

This section will give you a framework to develop a conscious knowledge of how you're wired—that is, your calling, talents, your dreams and visions, your values, your tribe, your ideal work style, and your beliefs. Growing in self-awareness is like digging for gold. How many tools should we use to find the gold of our authentic selves? The answer is, as many as possible—because you're investing in the most important thing in your life: yourself.

Getting to know yourself is one of the most difficult things to do, but also one of the most rewarding. I encourage you to keep doing the work, using the tools in this section and the resources given. It's going to take intentionality, time, focus, effort, and tenacity. The benefits of these tools will far outweigh the work you put into this project.

This journey of creating a life directed toward purpose requires mindful awareness and deliberate attention to your makeup, thoughts, emotions, and experiences. Over time, I've observed that the people who live wholeheartedly and love their work played a significant role in designing their life's path and creating the jobs they love. The bedrock of their fulfillment was self-awareness. A byproduct of knowing who you are is knowing what you want. That's how you can wake up every day and love what you do. To get there, you have to commit to doing the necessary work.

To give you an example, I'll share an email exchange with one of my college professors from ten years ago:

Jonathan:

We have spoken in the past about your interest in teaching. I would like to talk to you about the opportunity at a local school in Newark, New Jersey. It would offer you the opportunity to see if you like teaching. Given your knowledge of Newark and your success in high school and college, Jonathan, this is a real opportunity to make a difference in the lives of others.

My response:

I would like to know if I can meet with you to discuss this opportunity. There are several things that may keep me from pursuing it and I would like to have your insight.

His response:

Jonathan:

Sure on all accounts. I hear that you have a very nice job offer already. The hardest choices are when you have to choose between two or more good things. Nonetheless, offer God gratitude for the blessings of such choices.

After much reflection and unnecessary pain, I made a misguided choice to choose the "very nice job offer". My values and motivations were externally derived instead of personally discovered. At the time, I thought was doing the right thing. I was chasing money, social acceptance, and family approval. In the process, I betrayed one of my deepest values, which is service to my community and love for learning and facilitating learning for others.

I dishonored myself by settling for a life that didn't serve my highest and best use. However, no experience is wasted if the lessons are learned—and even less so if those lessons are shared. That's partly why I'm writing this book.

I'm not alone in making major life choices with poor self-awareness, misguided values, and the lack of courage to displease people who had agendas for my life that conflicted with my well-being. They may have meant well, but their counsel didn't serve me well. I am ultimately responsible for my choices and have no one to hold accountable but me. Though I managed to be relatively successful in my career, there were many parts of the journey where I felt weird, out of place, and downright miserable. Fortunately, what made me weird in those moments is what makes me unique at this moment.

I've had a lot of jobs in my life, including camp counselor, telemarketer, office manager, tax preparer, auditor, and behavioral assistant. Some were great experiences, and some were not so great, but I learned valuable lessons from them all.

In this season of my life, I feel most at home as a coach. I've developed skills in the area of life coaching because that's where I struggled the most and needed the most guidance. I especially needed help in discovering and uncovering the vocation that best suited my skills, values, beliefs, and passions.

Many of the lessons I'll share are ones that I've learned during my journey, but in no way have I fully arrived. I'm sharing what I've learned up until this point from my own experiences and those of others.

Someone might be saying, *But Jon, why is my self-awareness your problem?* It's my problem because it affects me. Every time I meet someone who spent much of their early, middle, or late career walking in the dark as it relates to their calling and living chronically unfulfilled, it grieves me. I feel a responsibility to help the next generation, to my generation, and even to the generation before mine to help them discover and own their calling. I want to help them use their visions, values, and talents to live with greater fulfillment and impact.

It's never too late to change and reposition yourself. Unfortunately, the Western world does not encourage people to be reflective. It encourages us to be distracted—Netflix, Amazon Prime, constant text messaging, Facebook, Instagram, Twitter, and a constant barrage of information and entertainment. They aren't always bad, but when we overindulge, they can distract us from what we are here to do.

To take advantage of this section, you need to commit to doing the work. You'll have to periodically go on a fast from all these forms of distractions. It doesn't have to be forever, though you might decide to make it permanent. It has to be long enough to get on, or back on, track to a state of mindful awareness of what you are here to be and do.

Yes, it's possible! Many people have done it, and they have enjoyed the benefits of taking a season of life to realign their focus. Many have taken the time to learn about themselves, how they have been wired, and what they are here to do. These exercises will give you a greater level of awareness that you can use to make major life choices about your career as well as your relationships, family, and other parts of your life.

I hope I've made a good case for loosening your grip on your phone or your remote control and committing to building, rebuilding, and repositioning your life, because you will not be able to sustain change without disciplined and intentional self-awareness. Just as a cruise ship needs ample time and effort from the crew to reposition and turn in a new direction, you will need to work to redirect your life.

Personal discovery and conversations with countless people have convinced me that most people need to take more time to learn about themselves and what they want for their lives. They need to be reintroduced to themselves, not just for excitement's sake but also for assignment's sake.

Most of what we do comes from social conditioning, proximity, and the expectations of work, church, and friends and/or family. In our culture, it's easy to get lost on the performance treadmill. We are not conditioned to slow down and ask ourselves if the way we are living comes from an authentic place of desire, or if we've settled for living out someone else's script for our lives. Most of us end up working *in* our lives instead of *on* our lives. We check things off the to-do list without checking to see if the items on that list are even important or relevant to our journey.

In this section, I want you to take the time to read, reflect on, and review these lessons. Try to focus less on what's going on in the world and more on what's going on in your heart and mind. Through these lessons, you will sharpen your lenses out of which you see yourself, the world, and the path you're called to walk. Then you can claim or reclaim your identity and integrity in a disciplined and deliberate way.

Every journey of self-discovery requires courage, persistence, and consistency. Consider me to be a fellow traveler. As we go on this journey, I want to encourage you to be open to the new roads this may take you on. Be brave enough to acknowledge if the path you're on right now just doesn't fit you. This is part of the necessary work of building and living a life that matters.

Word to the Mentors: These exercises can help you sharpen your perception of yourself, which also helps in mentoring young people. One of my core beliefs about mentoring is that you can't give what you don't have. The most impactful lessons you teach will be through your example. The change that you want to occur in those you work with won't happen until it happens within *you* first.

Before you talk about the lessons, be sure you commit to walking them out. This will make your mentoring even more effective.

I wish you well.

CHAPTER I

Your Calling Is Your Compass

Don't do things that you think will inspire hope.
Do the things that bring you hope, because those things can inspire hope in others.

"WHAT DO YOU WANT TO be when you grow up?"

I remember being asked this question for the first time when I was in middle school. My teacher had told us to stand up and tell the class what we wanted to be someday.

It's a great question to ask, because those conversations stir their hope and imagination, and get them thinking. The problem is that the follow-up to that question isn't always asked, *"Why* do you want to do that?"

The "why" is important, because it informs the journey. It motivates more powerfully than any position or career can. When the "why" is not established, there's a danger of a goal being driven by ego instead of a strong sense of purpose, mission, and calling.

Your *calling* is the overarching theme of your life. It encompasses the continuous task of responsibility that you are designed for, regardless of your current career or position.

The great thing about a calling is that it doesn't have to be static. It's actually very dynamic. Your calling can change, evolve, and grow in complexity or simplicity. I hope this lets you breathe a sigh of relief that you won't have to work in one job or career for your entire life. According to the Labor Department, the average person born in the later years of the Baby Boom held 10.5 jobs from age 18 to 40[1]. It's not uncommon to find your desired career has changed.

I recommend a calling-driven life rather than a career-driven life. Your calling might entail a particular career, but the career is not the goal or the focus. When you consider the underlying *why* of your life, it liberates you from being discouraged or derailed from your course in life if you're not able to obtain a particular career or position.

One of the steps to discovering your calling is inward. It involves learning who you are and how you're wired. People do sometimes admire a particular position, job, or career and chase that as their calling. As a child, I foolishly told my mom that I wanted to be an orthopedic surgeon. I said it not because I knew anything about it or cared about it, but because I felt like that answer would make her happy.

Fortunately, my interest in medicine was short-lived. I realized pretty quickly that I could never be a doctor, because I could barely stay awake in biology class. Some of my friends became doctors because they wanted to help people experience greater health, and they were also gifted at understanding biology and other sciences—but the latter wasn't the case for me.

Some doctors are empowered by a connection to assist an ailing parent or aid the communities in which they were raised. These are examples of a calling that informs the position—not the other way around.

The worst thing about having a career-driven life is the belief that you cannot feel fulfilled unless you get that career. Actually, you can live a meaningful life without a career more easily than you can live a meaningful life without a calling. When you don't discover your calling, it negatively impacts your life. When you do discover it, it can change your whole life.

I want to share with you a few statements from people I know who were courageous enough to discuss how they broke their connection with their calling and to discuss their journey:

1. "Law school sucked the life out of me. I realized halfway through school that I didn't want to be a lawyer, but it was too late to change."

2. "I'm only here because I have to make money. Most people don't want to work these crazy hours. They only do it because that's the conventional wisdom given to CPAs to be successful." (This personally resonates with me.)

3. "I know I chose the wrong career, but I'm a mid-level executive with a family. I can't make a change now. I need my salary to survive. I just take extra vacations to recharge."

4. "I never wanted to be a pastor. My father and grandfather were pastors. I have a few more courses before I get my Master's in Divinity, but I don't want to go into a church ministry. I haven't told my dad yet, but I just got an offer to be a teacher."

5. "I want to go back to school to be a nurse, but I feel like I'm too old. I know a lot of people go back to school later in life, but I am a little afraid."

6. "I ran the streets when I was young because I had no family. I spent 15 years of my life in prison. I used that time to find myself and to find my way. I might have ended up dead otherwise. It didn't have to be that way, but that's how it was, and I have to live with it."

7. "I was sexually abused as a child and never told anyone about it. After that experience, I felt a deep sense of shame and chronic low self-esteem. I never felt good enough or confident enough to be myself, so I just allowed other people's opinions to govern

my life and what I should do. I totally picked the wrong major in college, and I really don't like my life as it is."

Many people have experienced the emotions in these statements.

Lesson: When you do not pursue the mission for which you were designed and gifted, the substitute you find will inevitably lead to suffering.

If you are experiencing a tremendous lack of fulfillment, you might be alienated from your true potential. You probably already know someone who could have made the above statements. Why? Because it's easy to betray your innermost inclinations. Some cultures and some families encourage people to suppress their true paths. Most people are not coached or trained to discover their inclinations.

Society teaches us to be caught up in external pursuits and to ignore the inner motivation behind the jobs we take on. Fortunately, it's possible to change our perception. As an example: What is the difference between just piling sandbags on top of each other and building a dike to protect a city from a flood? The job is the same, but the perspective is different! Protecting a city is a new and more compelling motivation.

When you find your inner motivation, your sense of meaningless or undesired activity changes, because you can see your true path.

Remember: Your past missteps don't have to dictate your future.

What's the first step? You need to find out where you are in relation to finding your calling. Here's a tool you can use to get started. It's an acronym called DRILL.

Dig Deep Exercise – DRILL

"The purposes of a person's heart are deep waters, but one who has insight draws them out." (Proverbs 20:5, NLT)

Your calling is based on a careful consideration of your strengths and your deepest desires, as well as the future you want to have—but you need to DRILL to discover that calling and think about what's possible. You need to DRILL for a deeper awareness, because your calling requires a true perception of yourself.

Here's how you can discover the truth of who you are, how you're wired, and what you are here to do:

D – Desires. What made you come alive as a child? What did you enjoy doing? What movies or shows did you enjoy? What kinds of movies or shows do you like now? Who were your role models? What books did you like reading? Which classes in school did you enjoy the most? Did you even like school? When you're called to something, a desire is downloaded. You need to take the time to understand and name those desires and inclinations.

R – Risk Tolerance. Learn to evaluate risk based on your temperament and not the fears of others. Some people can take an extreme amount of risk and not be emotionally derailed. Other people are very cautious, prudent, and need extreme precision in their decision-making process. Some people are toe-dippers, while others like to jump right into the deep end. Neither way is right or wrong. Taken to their extremes, both approaches can be dangerous and costly. Ultimately, the steps you take to pursue your calling will involve a measure of risk. You want to be prudent, but you don't want to plan to the point where you don't take action because you're trying to mitigate every risk. Some people find fulfillment in a line of work where they do not know what each day will bring. Other people prefer work that is regimented and predictable. Everyone is different. Ultimately, how do you judge whether something is worth the risk? The simple answer is: the value of the goal. When you judge something as valuable enough, you'll make tremendous sacrifices and take relatively greater risks to obtain it.

I —Intuition. Avoid blindly following generic life advice or conventional wisdom. Look at the career you're considering and ask if the standard advice for this career applies to you. This will become clearer as you get a better understanding of your industry and your possible trajectory. This could also be called *faith*, which requires a spiritual leading from God. Oftentimes, everything isn't perfectly mapped out for us. One example is the Biblical figure Abraham. "It was by faith that Abraham obeyed when God called him to leave home and go to another land that God would give him as his inheritance. He went without knowing where he was going." (Hebrews 11:8, NLT) I believe the pursuit of a calling requires a measure of faith, because some things are uncertain. Trying to get assurances on everything might help you to be measured in your planning, but it will surely rob you of the greatness of the adventure of life and might even keep you in a state of paralysis. Do your due diligence, and then move confidently, in spite of the uncertainty. Give yourself permission to take chances.

L —Love. People who fulfill their calling have a connection to their gifts that surpasses the recognition they receive. They *love* what they do. Which activities do you have a passion and love for? What is it that you cannot live without doing? If the essence of the work is not remotely attractive, you probably are not called to the work. Imagine a doctor who doesn't want to be around sick people, an accountant who hates numbers, or a firefighter who doesn't like physical labor. You need a heart-connection to what you do. The work you're called to do is work you might get tired *from* but never get tired *of.* You'll find more in Chapter 8 to help you discover what you love.

L —Limits. Every calling comes with limits: time limits, physical limits, and intellectual limits. I know this is not a popular idea in today's culture. Many motivational speakers will tell you to "break past the limits." It's true that perseverance and tenacity are vital, but you can also recognize the limits. For example, I know I could not be a neurophysicist or a rocket scientist, even if I wanted to, because of my intellectual limits. I could not play in the NBA, because I'm vertically challenged and do not have enough game to be Muggsy Bogues or Nate Robinson.

When you continually go past your limits, it can affect your overall well-being. But if you can pursue something and do it in high volume *without* hurting your overall well-being—you might have discovered your calling. Always do your best – no more, and no less. When you try to push past your limits, you suffer. If you do less than your best, you don't maximize your effectiveness.

I have a great capacity to retain information relating to coaching and counseling. I stay within my limits, because that's where I'm effective. I can do a great deal in this area without becoming imbalanced in my life because I assess and respect my limits in the pursuit of my calling.

The Life of Rosa Parks

Rosa Parks is one of my heroes. She has become a prominent source of courage and inspiration in my life as I've learned more and more about her story. She was the woman who became famous for refusing to move to the back of a segregated bus after she sat in the white section on December 1, 1955.

It's been said that she commented, "I couldn't *not* do it." She was determined to remain seated, no matter what. That's the kind of resolve that's needed to pursue your calling.

The degree to which you fulfill your calling might be the degree to which you fight social pressure, so resoluteness is necessary. Many times, people ask themselves, "What do I want out of life?" Another question to ask is, "What is life asking of you? What are the circumstances of your life telling you about where you should be heading?"

Rosa Parks knew what she believed and what she loved. She trusted her intuition. If you study her life, you will see that she was prepared for that moment of destiny that transformed history. You must also work to discover your calling. Think of it as your assignment, sealed orders, mission, or purpose. It might work better to find a word that corresponds with the way you think.

Take some time to reflect and journal on the DRILL acronym above. Write whatever comes to mind. Don't feel any pressure to make something up.

Remember, this a beginning exercise to "prime the pump." Over the course of this section, as you read the chapters, I believe you'll start to dig deeper into discovering who you are and what your calling might be.

If you write this exercise and consider these questions enough times, your calling will naturally be revealed to you. Think of your calling as a funnel, and not a dot. Your interests start off wide and, over time—with knowledge and experience—things become more precisely focused. This tool will help to get you started.

DRILL

Several people have asked me why I stress writing exercises so much. I think the writing process helps us reflect and gives us clarity. Writing gets you to SLOW down, which is especially important in this fast-paced world. Here's a simple analogy to make clear why this is important.

A couple wants to go out for the evening. The man asks, "Where do you want to go?" The woman says, "I don't know. You pick a place." He names a restaurant, but she says, "I don't want to go there." Conclusion: She knows where she doesn't want to go, which means that she probably does know where she wants to go. She just needs to take the time to think about what kind of food she wants to eat and the ambiance she prefers.

This analogy might sound silly, but finding your calling works the same way. Innately, you *know* what you're called to do. You just need to take the time to reflect and then to put it into words.

As you go through life and garner knowledge and experience, you'll be able to define your calling more clearly.

Desires:

_____

_____

_____

Risk tolerance:

_____

_____

_____

Intuition:

_____

_____

_____

Love:

_____

_____

_____

Limits:

_____

_____

_____

Once you start this work, you'll be amazed at what you've been missing. The most often-named regret of people who are dying is that they didn't dare to live the life they wanted to live. Living your true calling takes courage. Why? Because people will question you. Your mom or your dad or your boss or coworkers or even your spouse might say:

"That doesn't make sense!"

"Why didn't you say something sooner?"

"I thought you loved what you did. Or at least that's what you've been saying."

"You're so talented at this job. Why would you want to leave?"

The truth is, many people live false lives because they're afraid of the opinions of others. They submit the ordering of their lives to the will of others, which is always dangerous.

You have to protect the calling on your life. You and you alone are responsible for its fulfillment. You must not confuse talent with purpose, walk to the beat of someone else's drum, or simply live unaware of who you are and where you want to go.

The good news is that, even if you feel like you've already been derailed, you can reposition yourself. It's never too late to be what you might have been—or at least some version of it.

Responding to and walking in your calling is like being in good physical shape. It requires a good plan, attentiveness, courage, self-awareness, and a commitment to protect yourself from anything that takes you away from being in peak condition. That's why I wrote this section of the book.

I have been a continuous learner, mainly through books. My mom was a major factor in this, because she didn't allow me to watch TV on school days, and I couldn't play outside until the weekend. Eventually, I found my calling through the love of learning.

I always had a lot of questions about various subjects, and books gave me the chance to explore these questions and find answers. My love of learning informed what I'm doing today. I found I enjoyed being a resource for people to facilitate the healing of their hurts. I liked bringing hope to their lives and tools to help them reach their destinies.

As I look back, I can see that my calling would be tied up in studying, listening to people's stories, and sharing what I learned with them. I landed on some career paths early on that just didn't fit me, including being an auditor—the worst possible job for me. I transitioned to being a financial planner, which certainly complements how I'm wired.

I really began to connect with a calling when I started working as a coach and workshop facilitator. I believe I'm here to restore hope, facilitate healing, and provide people with the tools to reach their God-given destinies—but it took me more than ten years to get to the point where I felt secure enough to say that was my calling.

If I'd known sooner, I could have saved a lot of time and stress. That's why this first chapter is so important.

Your calling will guide your life. Everyone is here to do something, and your job is to find out what that is. This first section is written to provide you with the tools to take the first steps of that journey.

Like all journeys, there will be starts, stops, delays, detours, accidents, roadkill, and roadblocks. It will not be perfect, nor will it always be easy—but the sooner you leave home, and the better you prepare, the sooner you can name your calling. Then you can chart a great course and create an impactful legacy. Let this first section provide you with the steps that you need to begin.

For some people, the highlight of their work is that they get to wear jeans on Friday. Some people enjoy working in an office space, sending/responding to emails, and sitting in front of a computer all day. But most people I know in these settings feel as if there is a greater calling and purpose for their lives.

Let me encourage you. What you start off doing might not be the thing that you were created to do, but it might lead to the thing that you were created to do. In other words, your first job or career might not be the *destination* but the *transportation*.

At different seasons of life, your sense of fulfillment with what you do from day to day can change. When you are dissatisfied, it means it's time to reflect and consider if a change is needed. Pay attention to your inner voice and honor it enough to follow its lead with courage, wisdom, sound counsel, grounded thinking, and diligent planning.

Finding your calling should not be something to make you arrogant or boastful. The purpose of identifying your calling is to inform your steps and help you find your place in the world in each season of your life. Your calling should strengthen you during difficult seasons, keep you from despair, and increase the significance of events in your life.

Shadow calling

A *shadow calling* is a calling that gets power from our temptations and selfishness. It's often closely related to our talents and gifts and it can be given tremendous social approval, which is why people fall prey to it. In the process of learning about who you are, you need to be aware of your temptations and your selfishness, which might cause you to betray your deepest values.

I know what my calling is, but I also know what my temptations are. I know my temptation tells me to make a lot of money without regard to ethics or morality, because many influential voices in my life had that mentality.

My selfishness tells me to only be concerned about my life and to avoid even becoming aware of people's issues—because I know that, once I do, my compassion and integrity will require that I do something to help them. My selfishness tells me to just ignore everyone and do what I must at all costs to "succeed."

This is a hard truth to come to terms with, but it's a reality. We are all sinners, and we can easily succumb to the temptation to betray our calling. You must do the hard work of finding your shadow calling and putting tools (Chapter 12 – Define Your Success) in place to combat it. This will help you to stay focused on your true calling.

CHAPTER 2

False Self

You lose resolution when you make copies.
Are you being you, or a second-class version of someone else?

IF YOU THINK YOU CAN please everybody, you guarantee yourself a life of burnout and constant frustration. It's tough trying to live up to everyone's expectations. If you manage to meet everyone's expectations, you have more than likely crafted a *false self*.

The false self is created through the gradual gathering of all the internalized messages and voices from people who want you to conform to their ideas of how you should be and what you should do. But living this way can make you lose touch with your true self.

The false self is the personality you construct that lives in response to what the outside world says instead of what naturally draws you. Being *who you are* is probably the hardest thing you'll ever have to do. You'll always find some conflict between your internal knowledge and social expectation.

Far too many people have their souls locked up in someone's tyrannical hold on their desires and wishes. They may have come from homes where their ideas were routinely dismissed or simply never validated. They might have been told to "shut up." Or their parents might have said,

"That's the dumbest thing I ever heard." Or even, "What do you mean you don't want to go to _____ or to be _____ or do _____? Of course you do!" You need tremendous discipline to be your true self.

The true self represents values and desires that come from your unique temperament, personality, and perspective. No two people's desires are the same, but many people give in to the social pressure to conform. They follow the pack and try to emulate other people, to help them determine what they should think and feel, and how they should behave. We are not conditioned to be our true selves. When we don't fit in, we might withdraw from social settings or try to see the world from a different point of view.

I firmly believe that each person is unique in his or her way of thinking, feeling, and seeing the world. When we minimize that uniqueness to fit in, we waste our potential and might miss our unique contribution to the world.

Below is an exercise that will help you get a sense of where you are on the journey to being your authentic self. We all project different versions of ourselves, based on the environment we're in. Sometimes, we just settle for being fake. We put on a mask and hide behind a persona, because we just don't know who we truly are or we're afraid to rock the boat by exposing our authentic selves.

Have you been putting on a mask so people accept you? Let's take an assessment to determine if there is a part of you that has become false. Take your time when reviewing this questionnaire. Don't feel rushed. Think about and reflect on the truth of each statement as it applies to you.

False Self Assessment[2]

1. I often need to be approved by others to feel good about myself.

2. I often remain silent in order to avoid conflict.

3. When I make mistakes, I feel like a failure.

4. At times, I compromise my own values and principles to avoid looking weak or foolish.

5. My self-image soars with compliments and is crushed by criticism.

6. I do for others, at times, what they can and should do for themselves.

7. I am fearful and reluctant to take risks or my fears often cause me to play it safe "just in case."

8. I often go along with what others want rather than "rock the boat."

9. I often compare myself to others.

10. My body feels tense and stressed more often than it feels relaxed.

11. I have difficulty speaking up when I disagree or prefer something different.

This assessment can reveal whether you are living out your true or false self. I think we are all guilty, at one point or another, of not living out what we believe or being who we are. Otherwise, we would be perfect. We can all breathe easy knowing that we are not alone in this: We want to be perfect, but we fall short.

The point of this assessment is to make you aware of ways that you might not have been keeping it real with yourself and with others. Part of the journey isn't about becoming something—it's about *unbecoming* everything that isn't you, so you can be who you were meant to be in the first place.

Becoming aware can sometimes be enough to make you want to change—but not always. If you've identified things that you are guilty of on this list, decide to do something about it today. This does not mean that you should break out in rants about how you don't want to be controlled by anyone or make major life-altering decisions impulsively. The assessment is meant to be a healthy self-reflection tool that will help you transition into the person you truly are.

A word of caution: GO SLOWLY AND THINK IT THROUGH BEFORE MAKING MAJOR DECISIONS! As a rule of thumb, anything that's done too fast is not good. "Desire without knowledge is not good—how much more will hasty feet miss the way!" (Proverbs 19:2, NIV) It took time to form your personality traits. It's going to take time to change the way you think, behave, and operate.

Be patient, but be intentionally patient. Review this list periodically as you go through life. One of the saddest things is to build your life portraying a certain image, only to find out you were being fake—and when too much time has passed, it's much harder to get back to discover who you really are. Don't let that happen. Decide today that you will choose to walk as your true self and live authentically.

When you live as your true self, you will be able to follow dreams and goals determined from within; state your beliefs calmly, without putting anyone down; and stay close to people without insisting that they see the world the same way you do.

When you're not being you, you lose out, and the world loses out, too—because you are robbing everyone of your unique self.

Most people don't live the life they were called to live because they are too busy living everyone else's. To live your life the way someone else wants, and to never do what you believe you are called to do, is a tragedy. True freedom comes when our acts proceed from our entire personality. Your decision to pursue a course of life should be based on a careful understanding of your strengths, deepest inclinations, and desires. Your course should align with your vision of the future.

Living authentically takes a lot of work and patience. Your path will be uncovered over time. Although we have all participated in inauthenticity at some point, it's hard to confront one's own hypocrisy. Yet looking at your true self is necessary if you're going to get back on the right road.

It's easy to veer off course. It usually starts out with small compromises of your integrity, but compromises can end up derailing your life.

Have you ever heard the saying: "Be yourself, because people who mind, don't matter, and the people who matter don't mind"? But what happens when the people who matter *do* mind? What if your parents and friends and even mentors cannot accept who you really are?

To live authentically, you need to be empowered to step away from being defined by people's opinions—even the opinions of those close to you. It's difficult to go against the dominant thinking of your friends and family, but it's liberating. Do your best to avoid doing anything that goes against how you're wired. Remember, you cannot live a brave life without disappointing some people.

You might find that the people who get disappointed ultimately *don't* matter, because they have their own agenda for your life that they forgot to tell you about.

THREE POWERFUL TEMPTATIONS

Three factors plague us as a culture and help to fortify the false self. Fighting these temptations is like swimming upstream. It's tough, but we have to do it.

1. Performance—I am what I do.

The devil said to him, "If you are the Son of God, tell this stone to become bread."
Luke 4:3, NIV

Our culture wants us to be concerned with resumes and titles. When people are introduced for the first time, the first question usually is, "What do you do?" The underlying message here often is, "What are you worth? How are you useful?" If you don't have the right answer, you might feel unvalued and worthless. But it's dangerous to think that your intrinsic value is determined by external success. It's unhealthy. Being productive and fruitful in your career is great, but it should not be a determining factor of who you are and what you're worth. You are *not* what you do. You are who you are, and you have value—even before you accomplish anything. Once you truly believe this, you can pursue your goals with less stress and anxiety, because you know your self-worth isn't attached to the work. Your true value is the fact that you are a child of God.

2. Possessions—I am what I have.

The devil led him up to a high place and showed him in an instant all the kingdoms of the world. And he said to him, "I will give you all their authority and splendor; it has been given to me, and I can give it to anyone I want to. If you worship me, it will all be yours."
Luke 4:5-7, NIV

If your identity is rooted in what you have, it is inevitable that your destiny will be off track. You can have things, but don't let things have you. Our culture measures success and security by what we own. One of my measures of success is who I am *apart from* my things. I am not validated by wealth. God validates me.

3. Popularity—I am what others think of me.

The devil led him to Jerusalem and had him stand on the highest point of the temple. "If you are the Son of God," he said, "throw yourself down from here. For it is written: 'He will command his angels concerning you to guard you carefully; they

will lift you up in their hands, so that you will not strike your foot against a stone.'
Luke 4:9-11, NIV

Maya Angelou had a saying: Don't pick it up and don't put it down. In other words, if you live for people's acceptance, you will die from their rejection. So don't pick up the praise you might receive, because then you'll have to pick up the criticism, too. One person said to me, "I've tried so hard to be who others wanted me to be that I've forgotten who I am." You will be free when you can be relaxed around anyone because you know you are a child of God. What people think of you is none of your business. What we believe other people are thinking is often just a reflection of our state of mind in that moment. Your business is to do the best that you can do, learn from your mistakes, and stay anchored in your values.

Resisting these cultural temptations will be tremendously hard for some folks. I know it's hard for me. I can hear people saying, "If I become myself, some people will be mad at me. If I become myself, I might lose money or even opportunities."

My answer is that any opportunity presented that tells you to not be yourself or to betray who God made you to be *isn't right for you*. Never do anything that requires you to be someone you're not. Resist the desire to be understood by everyone.

WAYS TO FORTIFY YOUR TRUE SELF

1. Find places that allow you to be authentic and the best version of that authentic self. When are you your best self? By "best self," I mean your most confident, self-assured, well-equipped, and centered self. For some people, it might be in some type of athletic arena. For others, it's in a classroom. For some people, it's in an office. For me, I'm my best self when I'm working with people in the role of a coach or workshop facilitator. I get to hold

space with people to clarify their situations and circumstances in order to help them find solutions for their problems and pursue their goals.

2. Every day, express a preference and find something that nurtures you. When you say what you prefer and choose activities that nurture you, you support a significant part of your true self.

3. Ask yourself this self-reflection question: Who is putting the pressure on me to be someone I'm not? What will be impacted if you don't have certain things, aren't perceived a certain way, or don't perform specific functions? Are you okay with just being you—or are you letting your performance, possessions, or popularity validate you?

CHAPTER 3

Values

Setting goals without clarifying values is like building a house without a foundation.

VALUES ARE VITAL. IN LIFE, you'll have to make some trade-offs; in order to do so, you must figure out what you assign ultimate importance to.

Pressures, demands, and expectations will push on you from all sides. We often find ourselves rushing through life. When we feel most stressed, our problem is not always the volume of demands or lack of scheduling skills—it's the fact that the demands and schedules are not consistent with our values.

Our values are reflected in how we use our resources: time, treasures, and talents. Values are the concepts, ideas, and beliefs that play a part in defining us. Values drive our behavior and govern our decisions.

When people are unhappy, it's often because they are living in conflict with their core values. Not organizing your life around your values would be like climbing a ladder only to realize that it's leaning against the wrong wall. If you are building a home but forget to tell the contractor what kind of home you want, don't be surprised if the house is built with the wrong number of bedrooms, the wrong lighting, and the wrong size kitchen. If you don't nail down the specifics, that house is probably not going to fit what you want. Your values should be the specifications of what you want in life.

We take on certain values because of conditioning and social expectation. The problem occurs when our uniqueness rubs against those systems. We all have different gifts, temperaments, and personalities. We have our own ways of operating and sets of priorities. We need to know what these are and express them, to end up with what we want.

Occasionally, after a movie, friends would ask where I'd like to eat. I'd say, "I don't know." They would suggest a restaurant, and I would say, "I don't want to go there." Then they'd say, "I thought you didn't know." The truth of the matter was, I *knew* where I wanted to go. I just hadn't taken the time to think about it and discover where that was.

Values work the same way. A value is a basic principle or standard that's important to you—something that you never want to live without. Values are not determined by what's *right* and *wrong*. Instead, they are about what's better and what's best to you. It's not always a matter of conscience. Sometimes, it's a matter of comfort and being the right fit.

Over the years, I've been fortunate to spend time with and work with different people from different walks of life. I've noticed a common haziness or instability around what people's values are. People often can't say what they hold most dear to them or what they believe are the most important things in their life. Just as I had to take the time to figure out which restaurant I wanted to go to, we all have to figure out and settle on a set of values that we will use to organize our life and define our success (See Chapter 12).

Your life plans should reflect your personal values. They become part of your compass. Once you have your compass, you can set goals and begin planning—weekly, and then daily—with a greater level of clarity. True success will often elude people who are not clear about what they hold most dear.

In the previous chapter, we discussed how the false self can make you spend your life focused on other people's wishes and wants. Parents, coaches, teachers, and leaders in the community exist to help you live the life that you are called to live. They should help equip you with the tools to do that.

I'm going to go on record and tell you that NO HUMAN BEING should tell you what you SHOULD want to do or be in life. That is something that you need to ultimately decide. You can be encouraged, motivated, and influenced by people, and you can even use their life as a framework to order your steps. But you need to make the final decision and come to the conclusion about how you will live your life. It's nice when what people want you to do or be is the same as what you want, but at the end of the day, your life is up to you.

I have lost count of how many people I know who wanted to do something different with their lives, whether it was their academic life or their professional career. Instead, they ended up following the direction of other well-intentioned but misguided or even manipulative people. As a result of bad advice, so many people have been influenced to stay in positions where they are miserable. They choose to live a life from which they want to escape.

This needs to stop. You have the chance to learn from the mistakes of so many other people. The first section of the book should have prompted you to begin drilling down to find your calling and discover your authentic self. Take the time to review the first section as often as you need to, so you can be as certain as possible about what your next steps will be.

Researchers have discovered that people who become successful and fulfilled in the path of life that they pursue have a *self-sustained motivation* and desire. In other words, the most successful people truly wanted to do what they did. For example, Kobe Bryant wanted to play basketball. Steve Jobs wanted to work with computers. Mark Zuckerberg wanted to be a computer programmer. People might have opened the door for these individuals, but they stepped through with self-determination and a clear sense of their values.

Your values help to light your way. Sometimes, you have to go deeper into the darkness to see the light. All successful individuals have had dark times in their lives on their journeys, but because they also had a clear set of values, they were able to respond to priority instead of circumstance. The more you care about your values, the stronger you can be. Your strength is not predicated on feelings, but upon acting on your values in spite of your feelings. The tests of your commitment to your values will come—and those moments will be the great revealer. If you respond courageously, you will find greater strength.

I have worked a lot of jobs that were not the right fit for me. I learned from those experiences, but I could have saved some time and trouble by knowing what was most important to me first. I want to save you the trouble by giving you the tools that I didn't have. If you don't have a set of values and principles to live by, you'll compromise when you are pressured.

On the next page, you'll see a list of values. It's not a complete list, but it's something to help you start your search for values. As you continue to do the work of figuring out what is most important to you, your self-awareness muscles will get stronger.

Accomplishment o Achievement o Accountability o Accuracy o Adventure o Positive Attitude o Beauty o Calm o Challenge o Change o Collaboration o Commitment o Communication o Community o Comfort o Compassion o Competence o Competition o Connection o Cooperation o Coordination o Creativity o Decisiveness o Delight of being, joy o Democracy o Discipline o Discovery o Diversity o Effectiveness o Efficiency Empowerment o Excellence o Fairness o Faith o Faithfulness o Family o Flair o Flexibility o Focus o Freedom o Friendship o Fun o Global view o Good health o Gratitude o Greatness o Growth o Happiness o Hard work o Harmony o Honesty o Improvement o Independence o Individuality o Inner peace o Innovation o Integrity o Intuitiveness o Justice o Knowledge o Leadership o Learning o Love o Loyalty o Management Maximum utilization (of time, resources) o

Meaning o Modeling o Money o Openness o Orderliness o Passion o Perfection Personal Choice o Pleasure o Power o Practicality o Preservation o Privacy o Progress o Prosperity o Punctuality Purpose o Recognition o Regularity o Relationships o Reliability o Resourcefulness o Respect for others o Responsibility o Results-oriented o Safety o Satisfaction o Security o Self-giving o Self-reliance o Self-thinking o Service (to others, society) o Simplicity o Skill o Solving Problems o Speed o Spontaneity o Standardization o Status o Structure o Succeed; A will to o Success o Teamwork o Techniques o Timeliness o Tolerance o Tradition Transformation o Tranquility o Trust o Truth o Unity o Variety o Wealth o Wisdom

EXERCISE:

From the list above, choose five values that are your top priority. If the most important values to you are not listed, you can choose your own. Then write a clarifying statement that makes your intent crystal clear. When you clarify your values, you can see your highest priorities clearly and can live your life with clear intention.

Make it a practice to regularly review your values and clarifying statements. This is a great exercise to guide you in deciding what you should make a priority, so that you can live a life that is personally meaningful.

Example
Value: Diversity
Clarifying Statement: I will seek out people who have different perspectives, opinions, and backgrounds from me.

Value:
Clarifying Statement:

Value:
Clarifying Statement:

Value:
Clarifying Statement:

Value:
Clarifying Statement:

Value:
Clarifying Statement:

How can you stay grounded in your values?

1. Read biographies and watch movies about people who stayed faithful to their values in spite of their pain. Recently, there was a remake of the 1970s mini-series *Roots,* the story of an enslaved African named Kunta Kinte who demonstrated tremendous courage during his enslavement in the United States. One particular scene shows his slave master beating him while telling him to recite his "new" name: Toby. He is repeatedly whipped while stating his true name, Kunta Kinte. He was strong enough to hold onto his identity. For him, the highest value was heritage and identity. I draw great strength and encouragement from this story. Where do you find yours?

2. Interview people you know who have the same strong and consistent values you admire. I love to speak with folks who demonstrate courage in how they pursue their values and even suffer difficult consequences for them. These people might be your family, friends, a leader in your community, or a public figure.

I have a friend who works at a prestigious company, earning about $150,000 a year. He was offered a promotion that would have paid $250,000 a year but required that he relocate his family to a different part of the country. He would have to leave the community where he's lived for many years. His kids would have to leave their school as well as their church, which is a pivotal part of their lives. A situation like this is a perfect opportunity to assess our values.

If money was his main priority, then leaving would be the best option. If family, stability, and his faith community were his main priorities, then staying would be his choice. If both values were equally important—but they were at odds in this situation—then he would need deep reflection about what was most important.

Do you see why this chapter is so important? You need to know your values because decisions like this aren't easy. People might disagree with you. You will have moments when you feel like quitting. You might feel confused about what is best.

But if you decide in advance what you want to assign importance to, you can strengthen yourself daily to remain firm in living out those values. You can figure out ways to be flexible while you remain committed to your values. If the nobility of your values is great enough, you will find a way to deal with the tough circumstances of life.

3. Pay attention to how you feel physically. Your body is a major prophet, not a minor prophet. Maybe you feel muscle tension, a headache, or knots in your stomach. If you stay attuned to it, your body will tell you when your values are being violated. Your body is an important part of the value assessment process. Take time, on a nightly basis, to ask yourself how your day went as you get in touch with your body. Which moments brought you tremendous joy, making your body feel relaxed and at peace—and which moments made you feel uncomfortable or uneasy, causing tension in your muscles? Journal your answers, and use them to reflect periodically. Your answers over time will give you an indication of what you find important and which frustrations you need to think about addressing more intentionally.

4. Remind yourself that you are the guardian of your values. You have to nourish and protect them. Historically, the people we remember most are the ones who paid a heavy price for their values: Nelson Mandela, Martin Luther King Jr., Rosa Parks, Steve Biko, etc. These are my heroes. Find some heroes of your own. List them below.

Chapter 4

Gifts, Talents, Skills, and Strengths

*If we are not doing what we are best equipped to do, we will lack soul fulfillment,
and it will get worse over the years.*

ONE OF MY FAVORITE SHOWS growing up was the *X-Men*. It was a cartoon about mutants who were a subspecies of humans with supernatural abilities. One thing I recently realized is that I've never seen a mutant who was jealous of another mutant's power. These heroes felt connected to and wanted to master their own talents. They did not need to envy another mutant's talent.

We need to be more like the *X-Men*. Far too many people are consumed with jealousy because they haven't taken the time to discover their own abilities, or their lack of confidence or awareness of their own abilities has held them back. Everyone has *gifts and talents*. A *gift* is something you do extraordinarily well with the least amount of effort. A *talent* is a natural way of thinking, feeling, or behaving that can be used creatively.

There are several types of gifts and talents.

- You might have the ability to sift through your world and observe things deeply. While others let things slip past unnoticed, you might have the talent of observation and analysis, which would make you a great researcher.

- You might have the ability to see through the clutter and find the best route to take. You're a strategist.

- You might have the ability to persuade other people to your point of view, using provocative speech and actions. You have the talent of speaking and leadership.

- You might have the ability to take in large amounts of data and research from books and lectures, and organize it coherently, so that it can be easily accessed. You are a teacher.

- You might have the ability to put people at ease when they're in crisis and help them navigate difficult situations. You are a coach and a counselor.

- You might have the ability to follow through on a plan that has been set into motion. You are an initiator and activator.

The above examples are different kinds of gifts and talents. With practice, these attributes can be turned into *skills* and *strengths*. A *skill* is the ability to perform fundamental steps of a process. A *strength* is the ability to provide an almost perfect performance of a talent. The most successful people invest their time discovering what their talents are, practicing them endlessly, and discovering how they might apply them.

Many people are disengaged from discovering their own abilities because they are too busy watching other people use their abilities, often on social media. They lose sight of who they are and what they are uniquely designed to do.

It's been said that there are 800,000 kinds of plants in the world, and the conditions required for growth vary. There are as many talents as there are plants—if not more. Keep that in mind as you to find your talent and its unique application. In my experience, most people are disengaged from their work. I believe this happens because they haven't identified their talent or made the connection between their talent and the work they are doing.

The key is finding a match between your talents and a calling. That's where a lot of the work is done. You can streamline the process by working with a quality system like the Strengths Finder (see information at the end of the chapter) or consulting with a career coach.

If you are not finding regular expression for your talents, something inside of you is being diminished. You might have to dig, because our talents are often buried. You might have to go looking for it. But it's important that you begin to take steps to discover your talents and also your interests, passions, and the causes that excite you.

Gifts and talents aren't something you earn; they are simply a part of who you are and how you're wired. When you make the best use of your gifts and talents, you'll find a greater level of fulfillment. You'll find you have the strength to put great effort into your work and find the tools needed to bring it to fruition.

This is how you begin creating meaningful work—and ultimately, a meaningful life.

EXERCISE

For this exercise, I want you to simplify your possible talents using verbs. This will take some time and reflection. I want you to select three verbs and three interests. This doesn't mean that you are limited to three, but for now, we want to identify the top three for each as a point of focus.

Verbs

Teach – Organize – Lead – Comfort – Counsel – Create – Change – Guide – Inform Consult – Entertain – Calculate – Search – Write– Speak – Listen – Sing – Act Guard – Protect – Research – Coach – Motivate – Compete – Plan

Interests

Politics – Studies of Culture – Business – Animal Life – Social Justice – Finance – Education – Travel – World History – Great Inventors– Family Health – Fitness – Airplanes – Faith – African American History – Music – Gospel – Mental Illness – Community Building – World Missions

My three verbs are teach, motivate, and listen. The way that I do that now is by being a financial planner, a coach, speaker, facilitator, and writer. The three subjects I care about most in this season of my life are family health, social justice, and community building.

You can brainstorm your own verbs or interests, if they are not listed here. Think about your experiences. Think about activities you do naturally. Think about what comes to your mind often. What stirs up your passion and leaves you with many questions?

It took years before I could land on something concrete and begin to put my skills and interests to use. It should not have taken that long. If I'd had the right tools and information, I could have started the exploration process sooner and not have wasted so much time.

I often see people working in a field simply because they are good at it, even if it doesn't resonate with them deeply. Ideally, you want to find a marriage between your talents and your passions. The combination of these things will put you on the road to your *calling*, as we discussed in Chapter 1.

What are your three verbs? What three interests resonate with you most deeply, and why? How might these verbs and subjects be present in your life now? If not present, what can you begin doing to use them?

Are there organizations you can join? In what professions can you see yourself using these gifts?

Even if you already have a good idea of what you want to do, let this exercise help you to be more concrete. There's power in naming your gifts and interests. Writing them down helps you to move out with a greater level of certainty and confidence. Your gifts and interests will unfold and evolve over time, so this isn't the last time you'll need this exercise. This is just a start.

Verbs

1) _____

2) _____

3) _____

Interests

1) _____

2) _____

3) _____

This exercise helps many people bring things to the surface—but others need a little more to prime the pump and get them reflecting and thinking. You are not what you do, but you will not be the best version of yourself until you begin using your gifts and talents and doing what you do well. Below are some strategies to use.

Strategies for Identifying Gifts And Talents

1. You might not know what you do well until you step out and try. Trying something new is scary, but it's worth it. You don't have to start in front of hundreds of people. You need a certain amount of privacy to have the courage to fail. Try using your gifts with a few close and trusted friends or a mentor, and let them give you feedback. You have talents, but they will never serve you if you don't use them. You want to do what you love to do. You may not find it on your first job, but don't give up until you do find it. You're never too old, and it's never too late to try something new. A great many people from their late 40s to their 80s and beyond have found new things that add value to their lives, and often to other people's lives in the process.

2. Ask the people close to you what they think you do well. This is probably one of the better ways to begin discovering your talents. Ironically, people who are talented often don't know they have a talent because it comes so naturally to them, while other people might see what they do as rare. Chapter 5 will address obtaining feedback from others.

3. Expose yourself to people who are incredibly talented and skilled at the activities that interest you. Listen to interviews. Watch movies or documentaries about them. Read their books or books about them. Watch their performances. Go to concerts. Attend their conferences or seminars. Observing people in their element can be inspiring because their enthusiasm is contagious. Examples: Allen Iverson watched Michael Jordan. Warren Buffett read Benjamin Graham. Denzel Washington watched Sidney Poitier. Exposure is the key.

4. Use the resources below to begin to discover your gifts and talents. For a small fee, you can take some of these assessments.

Resources

1. Strengths Finder – ages 26 and up – Go to www.strengthsfinder. com

2. Strengths Quest – ages 15 to 25 – Go to www.strengthsquest. com.

3. Strengths Explorer – ages 10 to 14 – Go to www.strengths-explorer.com.

4. Strong Interest Inventory – www.cpp.com   (Search for the "Strong Interest Inventory").

5. Visit www.onetcenter.org, which is a great site to start for your occupational search. You can browse the site by your abilities, interests, knowledge, skills, work styles, and context.

CHAPTER 5

What Do People See in You?

Few people have the understanding to take the feedback that would benefit them;
instead, they want the admiration that deceives them.

DO YOU HAVE SOMEONE IN your life who loves you enough to be truthful with you—no matter what? Have you ever asked that person to give you feedback about yourself?

I ask myself this every time I think of the show *American Idol* and recall contestants who thought it was a good idea to pursue a musical career. Unfortunately, many people don't have anyone around them who are willing to tell them the truth about themselves.

In finding out your specific gift, it's important to have someone in your life who can point out what you're great at and what you're not great at. There's a saying that "the eye can't see the eye." If there is a speck in your eye, it's best to have someone look in your eye to help you see what you can't. With gifts, it's the same way. Those who know you well are better at pointing out your best and worst qualities.

What would happen if you asked friends, family, peers, mentees, and managers/supervisors to give you feedback about yourself? What if you asked for their opinions on your opportunities for growth, areas of strength, and your conflict-resolution style?

It can be difficult to ask, and even harder to listen to their replies. Here are some of the results I received when I posed these questions to people in my life:

How can this individual grow as a leader?

- Ability to take the opinions of others into consideration and put his aside.

- I think there are times when Jon may be nervous about being the focal point of a project. This may not be something he is interested in. I think he is very good as a second in charge but perhaps could have some work on being the head of an organization if it is something he would like to do. I think the confidence to be the lead is something he questions at times.

- Jon has a very engaging personality, and I see him excelling as a motivational speaker giving words of encouragement to individuals in need of support.

What are the strengths of this individual?

- I think Jon has very sound judgment and is a hard worker. I think he understands people and knows himself. I believe he can network very well and is genuinely liked by those around him. He is a people person, and is good at conversations. He continually is looking to improve himself, which is a great thing to have in leadership positions.

- His ability to relate and connect with people.

- Humility and consciousness regarding the intersection of social identities and the importance of challenging the status quo when strategically appropriate. Values lead decisions ... leading to integrity in action. Ability to relate to youth and other men of color as well as be comfortable cross-culturally and in diverse settings.

Describe this individual's style of conflict resolution.

- He responds well to the situation in that he doesn't feel overwhelmed or overly stressed. He just sometimes needs more confidence, since more often than not he knows what to do.

- Jon is a critical thinker and approaches problems or conflicts with a great deal of thought.

- Jon is quite fixated on resolving conflicts with a "win/win" mentality. He likes to resolve conflicts with the least loss possible, whether it may be a loss of relationship or privileges. He often likes to consult with close and wise friends in an attempt to come with the best solution to his conflicts.

What should this individual do less of?

- Doubt himself. He is intelligent but sometimes lacks the confidence necessary for better execution.

- Keep internal emotional process inside. Put others first without leaving room for own needs/wants. Live for legacies from ancestors that don't support a more positive future.

- Jon should put less energy towards stressful and difficult situations as he faces them. I feel that he exerts too much energy toward stressful and difficult situations. I would like a more laid-back Jon in the face of stress.

- Argue when there are more sides to a story or argue when he loses.

Describe your understanding of this individual's purpose in life.

- My understanding is that the individual is pushing to fulfill God's purpose for his life. He is working in ministries to serve the community and the church. He is interested in helping people in many aspects of their lives, specifically financially, and may also be interested in becoming a Life Coach. He is definitely also a huge advocate for young men and helping them to become successful adults.

- Trying to find effective ways to be of service to others in his communities while following his values and faith. Trying to make a positive impact while finding fulfillment and satisfaction through personal growth, through overcoming challenges and fostering authentic relationships.

- Being able to apply his talents and knowledge in his career and everyday life. He enjoys helping others. Jon enjoys seeing his peers succeed.

This feedback helped me to see what I should continue to do and what I needed to work on. My level of awareness increased by reading what others observed about me. Without feedback, you can't be certain that you are going in the right direction and that you're maximizing your abilities. Take a chance today and ask for feedback from someone you know will tell you the truth. It is risky to be vulnerable with anyone, so the person you ask should have the following characteristics:

1. They love you and want nothing but the best for you.

2. They will promise to be honest with you, even if it hurts. "Wounds from a friend can be trusted, but an enemy multiplies kisses." (Proverbs 27:6, NIV)

3. You can trust them and feel safe being honest with them. (See Chapter 33 on Casual Friends.)

4. They won't tell you what to do unless you ask for advice. They are willing to tell you what they see and answer the questions you ask as honestly as possible.

You might ask a teacher, an older sibling, a mature friend, or your coach. Put your list together today and begin to ask the questions below. Give yourself time to unpack these questions and flesh out your answers.

QUESTIONS

How can this individual grow as a leader?

What are the strengths of this individual?

Describe this individual's style of conflict resolution.

What should this individual do less of?

Describe your understanding of this individual's purpose in life.

Chapter 6

Work Values

When creating your path, you want to determine your style of working and serving. This can help you organize your life in a way that's fulfilling and meaningful to you. It's been said that people spend more time choosing their clothes than choosing their job. In my experience, that is very true.

Here's a tool that can help you identify how you are wired to work, so you can move out in the world with a greater level of self-awareness and intention. Do you see yourself in any of these descriptions?

1. **CEO**—This type of person is an expert on their business or industry and wants to climb the corporate ladder. This person needs a lot of different skills: the ability to analyze and solve problems, work with many different types of people, and manage interpersonal conflict. They also enjoy dealing with every aspect of business, including marketing, finance, technology, etc.

2. **Surfer**—This type of person doesn't see work as a top priority. They are concerned about organizing their life around activities and people instead of work. They want their employers to understand that they prioritize family and personal concerns.

3. **Competitor**—These people are tough. They want to overcome tough obstacles and solve seemingly unsolvable problems—and to do it better than the next guy. Without challenges, these folks become bored and irritable.

4. **Freelancer**—This type of person wants flexibility. They don't want to be bound by anyone's rules, procedures, policies, dress code, or working hours. They don't want to be locked down. They tend to be self-reliant and independent. They hate close supervision. They despise golden shackles like pensions or 401ks that are not portable. They need to be masters of their own ships.

5. **Anchor**—This type of person needs safety and security. They want the future events to be predictable. They don't mind golden shackles. They don't mind being told what to do, as long as someone is there to take care of them. Once they have found security, they are satisfied with the heights they reach professionally and might find other ways to use their unused talents.

6. **Philanthropist**—This type of person is dedicated to the values of an organization. They are not concerned about stability but want to achieve the power to influence things. They want to serve humanity, improve the world, and work with people. They might overlook positions that offer more security if it inhibits them from having an impact.

7. **Nerd**—This type of person is concerned with pursuing the mastery of their talent. Their identity is based on their work and their expertise. They want unrestricted budgets and access to facilities. Steve Jobs is the perfect example of this kind of person. He was solely concerned with creating the best and most innovative technology.

8. **Creator**—Entrepreneurial Creativity – This type of person wants to create their own business by developing products and services. They will leave a pre-existing venture in a heartbeat once a new venture is created. They are obsessed with creating, and when they can't create, they get bored easily. They are more concerned with ownership and creative control than salary.

Once you know your values for pursuing work and service, you will have more mental and emotional freedom to pursue a career based on those values. Mentors and coaches often impose their own value systems without considering if their students are wired similarly. I've had significant people in my life seriously discourage the positive things I wanted to do, just because they didn't understand me. Their lack of understanding robbed me of the initiative to step out in unique ways.

Hopefully, this tool will give you the relief of knowing that you are not alone in how you choose to operate. You can be yourself. Most people are uncomfortable when others don't think like them, act like them, dress like them, vote like them, etc. This lack of acceptance and respect for individuality can harm individuals and even destroy communities.

Your work values can help you plan a career as well as help you identify role models. Take some time to write out your work values and motives.

Find Your Tribe

A *tribe* is a group of people connected to an idea or someone who represents the idea. People in a tribe have a common interest and a way of communicating to discuss ideas. As you discover your interests and passions, look for a tribe to connect with. They will help you find nourishment for these passions and interests.

Your tribe might consist of two people or two million people. It could be diverse. It could cross generations or cultures. Your tribe might even cross time, to include people who are no longer living. What ultimately defines a tribe is their shared passion. Here are a few suggestions.

- Talk to your teachers or mentors about ways to find people who share your passions.

- Join a club based on your talents, interests or desires. Most schools have different extracurricular activities and programs; use these to explore your gifts and interests. You might find a sports team, debate team, chess club, or student board that interests you. Explore what you like and don't like. If you're a professional, you can use networking groups for people in your industry.

- Find an interest-based group on Facebook, Twitter, or Instagram that fits your passion. Review their current and prior postings to learn more. They might have conferences, books, webinars, or courses you can take. I like working as a small-group facilitator and a coach. I wanted to find ways to serve, so I went online and looked up life coaching and counseling jobs. After a few weeks, I found an opportunity that fit my experience and my schedule. I took advantage of this opportunity and served as a part-time life-skills coach for a few years; the experience changed my life and informed much of the work that I do now. That opportunity helped lead me to more of the work that I love to do, coaching and motivating young people—but it started with that internet search.

Take the first step and see where it leads. When you take advantage of an opportunity, focus on learning as much as you can about what excites you and what doesn't. If one thing doesn't excite you, it's okay to move on to something else. Just take the step.

Michael Jordan says, "I don't care if I fail. As long as I did everything I could to succeed." Jordan's "do all that you can" attitude can help you pursue opportunities to learn about your interests and passions or to use your gifts. I've seen enough to know that people with this mentality do much better than those without it. Even if those closest to you can't or won't support your ambitions, you can get inspiration, affirmation, and encouragement from your tribe.

CHAPTER 7

Be Differentiated

One of the easiest ways to get derailed from your calling is to become someone you didn't want to become by saying yes to the wrong things and no to the right things.

IN MY EXPERIENCE, PEOPLE ARE more familiar with what other people think and believe than they are with their own thoughts and beliefs. They often fail to realize that every time you submit your will to someone else's opinion of what you should like or who you should be, a part of you dies. It takes courage to truly be yourself and think your own thoughts. To do this, you have to be *differentiated.*

Differentiation refers to a person's capacity to choose his or her own life's goals, beliefs, and values—apart from the pressures around them. Differentiation involves the ability to hold on to who you are and let go of who you are not. It means that we might not agree, but we can still stay connected.

When I was growing up, children usually didn't play a part in defining their own life goals, values, and beliefs. Values came from our culture, the school, our families, etc. Others decided what was best for us, and most of us followed blindly. Most of the people instructing us never took the time to determine what they wanted or even believed.

The advice we received might have been valid, but there was no moment during the maturation process into adolescence and adulthood when we could decide whether that advice fit our unique lives. It was almost as if young people were robots, doing the routine and expected thing.

Part of growing up is taking the time to decide on your own goals, values, and beliefs. It's been said that "you can take a person out of the ghetto, but you can't take the ghetto out of a person." Not true! While your upbringing played a huge role in who you have become, it doesn't have to determine the kind of future you can have. To subdue the ghetto spirit takes hard work and might involve being misunderstood by those around you. At this point in my life, my integrity is more important to me than being understood.

When social pressure tempts me to choose life goals or values that are not consistent with who I am, I remember my own role models, like Nelson Mandela. When Mandela saw the unfairness and oppressiveness of the apartheid regime of South Africa, he joined the struggle to put an end to it. The South African government did not take long to take note of this bold attorney; they arrested him and sentenced him to life in prison. Mandela spent the next 27 years imprisoned, until his release in 1990. He was deprived of his right to be with his family and friends. He lost more than two decades of his life. He was kept in isolation, and his human rights were violated. He had every right to be angry.

Mandela could have sought revenge, but when he got out of prison, he preached reconciliation and forgiveness. He genuinely felt that the white minority was an enemy to him and the struggle for his people—but he knew that if he did not forgive and work for reconciliation, his country would be in a constant state of violence and bloodshed. Mandela's mission became to work for a democratic, non-racial, non-sexist country, and that had to be done by eliminating all the negative and violent intentions in his soul and focus on the redemptive work.

Nelson Mandela is one of the strongest leaders I have ever seen. One of the most important aspects of his strength was his ability to define his goals, values, and the way he would go about pursuing them. He was opposed, not only by the South African government but also by people who shared his interests. Yet Mandela was able to stick to his guns because he was *differentiated*. The example of his life gives me strength and hope to land on my convictions after serious deliberation and to be willing to pay the price to follow through on them.

Find models of people who decided that they would be and do what they were motivated to be and do from an internal position. Martin Luther King, Jr.'s nonviolent resistance to racism, specifically segregation, in the South is another example. Mother Teresa demonstrated her differentiation with her request for exclaustration—a release from her vows as a nun in order to serve the poor of Calcutta, India. These individuals pursued their own life goals and defined their personal values and beliefs. This doesn't mean that they didn't have counselors and advisors helping them through it. It doesn't mean that there weren't times when they had to re-evaluate things or admit that they were stuck, or even wrong. It does mean that the final call for their life was theirs.

I believe that most people who are living for less than they were made for are in that position because of the boxes they've been placed in by themselves, society, or their culture. People who spend an extended period of time in prison often become "institutionalized." An institutionalized individual is unable to think or act independently of the institution they are in. Unfortunately, being institutionalized is not isolated to prison. A job, a school, a corporation, a culture, and even a family can institutionalize you. This doesn't always mean the institutions are bad, but it's unhealthy when you are defined by the institution's rules and have lost the knowledge and courage to step out and choose your own path.

To develop the strength to transcend that world and live out your calling, you have to differentiate. You would have to develop your own compass and not defer to others in the way you were taught. If you're going to be true to yourself, you must start by making one decision at a time as you pursue the life goals that you define.

Exercise – What Commandments Do You Live By?[3]

In light of the commentary on being differentiated, I want to invite you to do an exercise to concretely name the commandments from your culture or family of origin and then name your own rules for your life. This tool is here to help you learn to break the power of past unhealthy habits and behavior patterns by first identifying them. You can't change what you don't acknowledge. Culture is learned, and it can be unlearned in time.

I think this is one of the most valuable exercises in this guide. Our families of origin are probably the most influential group we will ever belong to. Sometimes, we have to do the work of going back to go forward with more confidence and determination to live out a new way, stand our ground for what we believe in, and change the culture for the better.

As you complete this exercise, try to separate what you think from what you have been told to believe. It takes courage to denounce the unhealthy ways of your family and culture, so it's important to stay committed to what *you* believe, even if you are met with parental, societal, or cultural disapproval. I want to guard against oversimplifying things, so I'll start with commandments to give you an example of the exercise.

Unhealthy Inherited Commandments[4]
Examples

Family: You owe your family until you die. You have a duty to family and culture that supersedes everything else. Never share your family's "dirty laundry" (flaws and problems), even if unhealthy and/or abusive things are taking place in the family.

Feelings: Feelings are not important. You are not allowed to have feelings. You can react based on how you feel without processing your emotions.

Attitudes about culture: Don't have friends from outside of your culture. Our culture is better than other cultures. Don't marry someone from outside your culture.

Money: The more money you have, the more security you have. The more money you have, the more important you are. Money and wealth prove you "made it."

Expressing anger and conflict: Anger is a bad and dangerous thing. Sarcasm is a way to show anger. Explode in anger to make a point.

Relationships: Don't trust anyone. They will hurt you. Never let yourself be vulnerable.

Grief and loss: Sadness is a sign of weakness. You are not allowed to be depressed. You need to get over losses quickly.

Conflict: Avoid conflict at all costs. Loud, angry, constant fighting is normal. Don't get people mad at you. Physical altercations are prime options to resolve a conflict.

Sex: Don't talk about it. Men can be promiscuous. Women have to be chaste. Women are only worthy of love if they are worthy of sexual desire.

Success: You must attend the "best schools" and make a lot of money. You must get married and have kids.

My Commandments

Family: Be thankful for the family I was raised in. Leave the dysfunctional ways of my family. Learn how to wisely live out the values I've chosen for myself while honoring the positive legacy of my family. Men have to respect and protect women and children.

Feelings: Pay attention to your emotions as a gift from God. Prayerfully and carefully think about your feelings before you act on them. Experience your emotions in order to love others well.

Attitudes about culture: No one culture is superior or inferior to another. Every culture has a redemptive gift to offer the world. There should be no sexism, racism, classism, or ethnocentrism in the family of God.

Money: We are stewards of God's money. We are to live below our means so we can be generous to others.

Expressing anger: Don't let the sun go down on your anger. Take time to discover the source of your anger. Use your anger to assert yourself instead of stuffing or projecting it. Explore the fear or the sadness behind your anger, because anger is usually a secondary emotion.

Relationships: Repair ruptured relationships to the degree that you can control. Receive God's love in order to love others well. Respect people's individuality.

Grief and loss: Pay attention to your losses and wait on God for understanding and comfort. Your losses are important to God. Grieving losses, instead of ignoring them, leads to maturity and compassion.

Conflict: Learn how to fight "clean" (See chapter 35). Allow God to mature you through conflicts. Don't run from or avoid conflicts, but use them to negotiate differences. Choose to resolve things peacefully. Take the time to cool down and think deeply before engaging in conflict resolutions.

Sex: You are to preserve the preciousness of sexual intimacy for marriage. Do not use people or let yourself be used.

Success: Learn from your mistakes. Become the person God intends and do His will. Live in brokenness, depending on God, and honor your deepest values. Put all your effort into becoming an asset to your community and influencing the world for the better.

The great news is that your family of origin doesn't determine your destiny. To a certain extent, your beliefs and choices do. You have control!

Take this time to reflect and think about what kind of life you want to create for yourself.

MY COMMANDMENTS

Family

Inherited:

Yours:

Feelings

Inherited:

Yours:

Attitudes about culture

Inherited:

Yours:

Money

Inherited: _____

Yours: _____

Expressing Anger and Conflict

Inherited: _____

Yours: _____

Relationships

Inherited: _____

Yours: _____

Grief and Loss

Inherited: _____

Yours: _____

Conflict

Inherited: _____

Yours:

Sex

Inherited:

Yours:

Success

Inherited:

Yours:

Last Word

At the end of your life, God is not going to ask you why you were not your mother or your father, or why you were not like the pastor or your other "successful" friends. He will ask you why you were not *you* and why you tried to live out someone else's life. Let's begin to organize life so that the answer will be that you were true to yourself.

CHAPTER 8

Visions and Dreams

It's hard to build a future if you can't see past today.

IN THE MOVIE *NOT EASILY Broken,* the main character, Dave Johnson, was a baseball coach who took some young boys under his wing and served as a father figure to them. One of the young boys' father, Darnell Gooden—who was not a fan of the coach—pulled his son out of practice. In a fit of rage, Darnell went on a rant about living in a heartless world. His final words to his son were to "wake up and stop dreaming!"

Unfortunately, I've seen and heard countless stories of well-meaning (or sometimes, ill-intentioned) people telling others to *stop dreaming.* While I do believe people should make plans that are grounded in reality, I believe it's just as important to acknowledge and pursue the reality of what's possible. That is where your dreams and visions come into play. One of the most dangerous and toxic things we can say to people is to stop dreaming.

What if someone had told Harriet Tubman to stop dreaming?

What if someone had told Dr. Martin Luther King, Jr. to stop dreaming?

What if someone had told Bill Gates to stop dreaming?

What if someone had told Barack Obama to stop dreaming?

These people were motivated by a dream, and to an extent, their dreams were realized because they fought to make them realities. The dream was the beginning of all of the work they did. People often associate dreamers with lazy and unmotivated people who don't work hard. That's untrue. Dreamers have a vision that motivates them to plan diligently and work hard. Lazy and unmotivated folks chase fantasies, not dreams. As Proverbs 28:19 (NIV) says, "those who work their land will have abundant food, but those who chase fantasies will have their fill of poverty."

A dream is based in the reality of what's possible. Fantasies are based on things that are removed from reality. With a dream, you don't need to have all the details perfectly pinned down. You simply need to have courage, work ethic, and patience to see it through to completion. Dreams are necessary to keep us motivated and moving forward. I believe everyone should take time to dream on a daily basis, to stay motivated on their path in life.

A dream could be a cherished aspiration, ambition, or ideal. A vision is a picture you have of that dream made manifest in the future that you desire. There might be a moral element to a vision, where one sees *what is* and thinks about *what should be*—or *what must be*. This kind of dream starts off as a burden or a concern and morphs into a vision.

One of the steps to creating a meaningful life is having a vision of what you want your future to be and what place in life you want to reach. At this point, you might already have a dream of what you want your future to be, but it might not be clear. The more you learn about yourself and about the world around you, the clearer that vision and dream will be and the farther out you will be able to see. Keep learning and paying attention to what excites you and what you see in the world around you, so that your vision becomes clearer.

Florence Chadwick was a long-distance swimmer and the first woman to swim the English Channel in both directions, setting a record each time. Following that, she was going to swim from the California Coastline to Catalina Island, a twenty-six-mile swim. On the day of the swim, it was very cold. The surf was rough, and conditions were foggy. After swimming for fifteen hours and fighting the surf and the cold, she turned to her coach and said, "I can't go any further. Pull me in the boat."

He asked, "Are you hurt?"

She said, "No."

He told her, "You don't know this, but your pace is really strong. You should keep going."

She did keep going, and she fought for another hour before asking to be pulled into the boat. As the boat departed, the fog lifted—and just a half-mile away was Catalina Island. She said, "If I could have seen it, I could have made it." The vision was fogged over.

Two months later, she tried again. The same thick fog set in, but this time, she reached the island by keeping a mental image of the shoreline as she swam. She said her vision of what was there kept her going.

PRACTICAL EXAMPLES OF DREAMS AND VISIONS

In this section of the book, I want to help you start thinking about some examples of a dream or vision.

Examples of a Dream

1. Having a solid financial foundation.
2. Restoring hope in the lives of people.
3. Bringing positive change to the justice system.
4. Reducing the high school dropout rates.

EXAMPLE OF A CORRESPONDING VISION

1. Having three to six months of emergency savings. Paying off all your debt. Saving consistently in your retirement account. Starting businesses with passive streams of income.

2. Hosting a block party and offering free healthcare to people in your community. Being a blessing to others by using your gifts and talents.

3. Working with your local legislators to change laws that harm your community. Working to build the bond between the community and the police department.

4. Starting literacy programs and obtaining funding to give after-school jobs to students in the school.

These are a few examples of a dream and the corresponding vision. Don't be limited to what you see here. At the end of this chapter, you will have an opportunity to write out your thoughts on your dreams and visions. Writing is a powerful way to begin transmitting thoughts into reality.

I want you to be excited about the journey that you are about to begin. Be intentional about the direction of your life. Take some time alone. Go for a walk. Go into a quiet room in the library. Sit in your car. Go to a place where you have peace and quiet, and take some time to think and write down some of your thoughts. If you're like me when I started, you might not have a lot to write down—but the more you learn, think, and plan, the more you'll be able to write.

Take the time now to write out your dreams and visions.

THINGS TO REMEMBER

1. A vision doesn't always require immediate action or action at all on your part. It will always require some form of patience. Something that was meant to be a blessing can be a curse if you get it too soon, so you have to let the vision mature in you. Even if you have a good idea, it might not be the best vision to invest in—because not everything that's a major concern today will be a major concern tomorrow. Or it might be someone else's vision that inspires you, and you might be called to support them without getting lost in their vision. Be patient and sort through all the emotions you experience. A genuine vision will eventually feel like a moral conviction and imperative. This can only be determined through patience and constant reflection. Remember, patience is evidence of wisdom. Patience will come from the strength of your vision.

REFLECTION QUESTION:

Has your vision become a moral imperative, or is it just something nice to see?

1. You have to mature to meet the vision. At first, your vision will probably be bigger than your ability to achieve it. You have to take the time to determine what your vision will require from you and how you'll need to grow in your skills and abilities. You might need to get additional education, read books on the topics, attend conferences, find a mentor, etc.

2. You are the guardian of your dreams and vision. You will need to affirm your vision every day. Don't measure the clarity of your vision by how others respond. As a matter of fact, sometimes opposition determines the legitimacy of your vision. Some of the

most successful and fulfilled people I've met have had the greatest opposition from their own friends and families as they pursued their dreams. The people closest to you might be the ones who either can't see or won't support your vision. Vision speaks to change, and some people simply don't want change, because it makes their life inconvenient. Be wise about sharing your dream and vision, because some people are small-minded and might be intimidated by someone with a big vision. They might even attempt to sabotage you. A vision won't stick without constant care and attention. There are times and even seasons when you won't feel passionate about your vision. These moments are never easy, but as you pursue your purpose, they're almost inevitable. Watch movies and read books that nurture your vision. Surround yourself with like-minded people who will help you focus on the vision. Find a story, a quote, or a Scripture that serves as a benchmark to help sustain you on the journey for the long haul.

3. When people are convinced that the vision has stuck with you, they will stick with the vision. If you are the person who has the vision and you want others to support you, you have to be the strongest champion of the vision. You will need tenacity before others will invest.

4. Having a vision helps you get back up after you fall down or encounter obstacles along the way. Also, having a vision will keep you from going back to unhealthy activities from your past.

5. Your vision doesn't have to be grandiose. Having a vision has nothing to do with being famous. It's about bringing into reality what's envisioned in your mind. Remember that everyone who is famous is not great, and everyone who is great is not famous.

6. We can never see our vision clearly if the trauma of the past blocks our perspective. I believe one of the dimensions of wholeness in someone's life is their vision. Part 3 will address emotional tools you might need to get unstuck or to free up the emotional energy to pursue your dreams. It's important to be free from the past, because if you can't visualize what you want your future to be, you'll likely become a victim of circumstance.

7. Be committed to your vision but flexible in your approach. Things won't be perfect on the journey. You will encounter challenges, so you have to grow in your ability to adapt to change (see Chapter 30). Problems are a part of the journey, but they are not the journey itself. Keep this in mind, so you can adjust your expectations.

CHAPTER 9

Models and Mentors

Success leaves clues. No one is self-made.

IT'S BEEN SAID THAT WE cannot choose our parents, but we can choose whose children we'd like to be. We can learn and extract principles from people we respect and admire.

Warren Buffett said the best thing you can do is choose the right heroes. A hero can help to propel you forward in your life. A hero is someone who represents what you would like to do or who you would like to be. A hero can help you discover the vastness of human possibility.

We need heroes and role models to help us normalize success and failure on the journey to living an impactful life. They are especially important in communities where positive role models might be scarce. Fortunately, those role models and heroes don't have to be people with whom you can speak. They can be authors of books you read or even great people portrayed in movies.

We can emulate particular virtues or qualities that a person possesses, even though each life is unique, and our directions and actions should reflect that uniqueness. The problems start when we lose sight of who we are and try to become exactly like someone else, instead of using them as a model.

I believe that children are like sponges. The first drop goes the deepest. I was fortunate enough to be raised in an environment that gave me access to cinema and literature that would forever shape the course of my life by giving me role models and heroes. I also was introduced to people who would give me the courage to follow my unique calling and help me find a structure for organizing my life. But I was influenced in both good ways and bad ways by what I saw. It's vital that young people begin to find people who are living overall positive lives to model themselves after.

The first three influential books I ever read were *Gifted Hands* by Ben Carson; *Rich Dad, Poor Dad* by Robert Kiyosaki; and *Race Matters* by Cornel West. The first three movies that I remember having a significant effect on me were *The Lion King, Amistad,* and *Malcolm X.* These books and films set the trajectory for my personal development, community engagement, and historical analysis of my life that I follow until this day.

There's a story about an eagle that was raised by a chicken. The eagle could soar high, but he chose to stay low to the ground, because all he could see were the chickens. The moment he saw another eagle fly in the sky, he realized that he was made for more than walking with the chickens, and from that day forth, he soared with the eagles.

Those movies and books help me to see how I should soar like the eagles instead of run with the chickens. There's power in learning about the journeys of others, because it can help you craft your own destiny.

In Chapter 12, you'll see a discussion about organizing your intentions on the different dimensions of life. Over time, you will need a combination of role models and mentors as sources of information, inspiration, and hope. These folks can help to influence productive thought in several different areas. Here are some of the people whose books I read and interviews I listen to for more insight:

1. Finances: Dave Ramsey, Suze Orman, Robert Kiyosaki

2. Social Change: Geoffrey Canada, Michelle Alexander, Steve Perry, Bryan Stevenson, Baz Dreisinger

3. Family and Relationships: Brene Brown, Henry Cloud, John Townsend

4. Motivation and Career: Eric Thomas, Les Brown, Jim Rohn, Zig Ziglar, Dan Miller

5. Wise and Brave Historical Figures: Nelson Mandela, Martin Luther King, Jr., Mother Teresa, Malcolm X, Rosa Parks

Many of the people we respect and revere would not have made it without the influence of a coach, advisor, or mentor along the way:

- Martin Luther King, Jr. had Mahatma Gandhi.

- Muhammad Ali had Angelo Dundee.

- Kobe Bryant and Michael Jordan had Coach Phil Jackson.

- Steve Jobs had Edwin Land.

- Mike Tyson has Cus D'Amato.

We must learn from not just one person, but several, because they are so many different and important lessons in this complex world. Begin today by looking for positive people who are doing what you would like and living in a way that you admire and would like to emulate.

Who do you have in your life that can help you along the way when you get stuck? Take some time to list them.

Make a list today of the people you look to in different areas of your life:

1) Finances

_____

_____

2) Family and Relationships

_____

_____

3) Motivation and Career

_____

_____

4) Historical Figures

_____

_____

_____

CHAPTER 10

Relax and Trust the Process

Persistent pursuit of destiny will ensure growth. You won't know when, but if you are persistent, it will happen eventually.

IF YOU HAVE READ THIS section and have done the exercises thoroughly, congratulations! You have just done some hard, interior work. If you continue to do the exercises in this section, you can move forward with a relaxed belief that you will find your way to your calling.

The journey to self-awareness is a continual process, and you will get out of the process what you put into it. You will experience some delays and detours. Consistency, commitment, and patience are essential in the process. Most people have room to improve their self-awareness. By this point, you should have a basic framework to start your journey and should be putting your newfound awareness to good use. I hope this section has given you emotional permission to step out and make the changes needed to be your best and most authentic self.

It can be scary, especially if you have lived conservatively. I know the feeling. The first time I gave a talk and led a workshop, when I stood up, my brain sat back down. I did a horrible job. I would have walked out if I weren't the one giving the talk! The key to living out your calling is that you get back up and try it again.

Don't fall victim to the trap of not wanting to be embarrassed. Don't focus on how "life is not fair and it shouldn't have to be this hard" or "It's not the right time" or "I tried this already, but it didn't work." Don't have the "I don't feel inspired" mentality. As Michael Jordan said, I don't care how many times I fail, as long as I did everything I could to succeed. Hold on to that mentality.

You don't need to be too specific too soon about how you will apply what you're learning. As you do the work in the exercises in this section, you'll find that your talents, beliefs, interests, and passions will begin to be revealed to you. Doing the work means doing what's necessary to know the truth of who you are and how you're wired. You cannot be at your best when you are in denial of who you are and how God made you.

There are so many voices calling you. Society calls. Self-interest calls. Family and culture call. As a rule, your *true* calling will be something that you are equipped to do, something that the world needs, and something you are passionate about. If you can find that combination sooner rather than later, you are one blessed individual.

There are no shortcuts. If you believe there are, you have already shortchanged yourself. Your biggest enemy will be your desire for an immediate result and unwillingness to stick with the process. Keep working. After all, the work of learning who you are and how you're wired takes a lifetime.

Have patience with the uncertain moments and unresolved questions in your life. Be excited about them, because they mean there is more to learn and you have more ways to grow. Give up on being perfect and work on becoming and loving your *true self.* As John 16:21 (NIV) says, "a woman giving birth to a child has pain because her time has come, but when her baby is born she forgets the anguish because of her joy that a child is born into the world." This process of discovering your calling is like giving birth to a new life. There will be times of stress, frustration, and uncertainty, but also excitement and joy when the process is complete. I wish you well.

PART 2
SELF-DEVELOPMENT

Your life is God's gift to you. Who you become is your gift to God.

ARE YOU THE VERY BEST version of yourself? There's a difference between having potential and performing at the level of your potential. Through self-development—the process by which your character and abilities are gradually developed—you can begin to be the best version of you. Then you can be effective in your calling and serve as an asset to your community.

Once, after I'd gotten an oil change for my car, I handed my debit card over to the cashier—who handed it right back to me. The card had been declined. I was surprised, because I'd just gotten the card in the mail. Then I noticed that I'd failed to read the label on the front.

The new card had to be *activated*. The potential was there, but the card hadn't been effectively "turned on." Activation is what turns potential into access and ultimately produces results. Like debit cards, we have the potential to do many great things, but that potential can never to be transformed into results if it's not activated. Your self-development is the activation.

It doesn't matter where you start, as long as you get started. One phrase I sometimes use to explain the importance of personal coaching is that, "You don't have to be sick to want to be better." Or I refer to the old saying: "Good, better, best. Never let it rest, until your good is better and your better is best."

In the pursuit of your calling, you should strive to be the best version of yourself. This section will provide you with a framework and structure to begin the journey of self-development. You will get out of this process exactly what you put into it, but remember, all the potential is there. Your job is to activate it.

Word to the Mentors: With these exercises, you'll be able to sharpen your perception of yourself, which will help you in mentoring young people. One of my core beliefs about mentoring is that you can't give what you don't have. The most impactful lessons you teach will be through your example.

If you want change to happen in those you work with, it must happen with you first. So before you talk about these lessons, commit to walking them out. When you review these lessons for yourself, your mentoring will become even more effective.

Why You Should Set Goals

You'd better plan your life, or someone else will.

BEFORE DISCUSSING HOW TO REACH goals, let's take the time for a definition:

> *A **goal** is a personally motivating vision of what you're commit-
> ted to achieving or doing, to contribute to your well-being and the
> well-being of others.*

If you have not yet worked through Part 1 of this book, I strongly recommend you stop here and complete that section before you start this one. Part 1 and its lessons about your calling are important, because it's hard to know where you're going and what you want if you're not in touch with who you are: your talents, your values, your beliefs, and your dreams and vision. Self-awareness helps to uncover that.

But after you have discovered your visions and dreams, you need to put a plan in place to pursue those dreams. Dreams without goals are just dreams, and ultimately, they lead to disappointment.

When I think about setting goals, I think about both *what I will get* and *who I will become* because of the lessons I learn in the process. The pursuit of goals helps you to refine your character, build toughness and durability, and sharpen your focus. That's why goals are so important: They help you to become a better person.

Having goals is one of the ways to take responsibility for your life and keep you focused. Your goals can help you decide what you will do and what you will not do. Instead of waiting for someone to save you or give you something, your goals will be something to wake up and chase on a daily basis. Whether it's big or small, your goal is YOURS. Don't allow anyone to tell you what to want. Take the time get really clear on WHAT you want and WHY.

The WHY is your major motivating force. More important than any goal is the motivation behind the goal. That's what gets you moving when you encounter difficulty and uncertainty. You'll need to dig deep to determine the results you want in your life and the reasons for those results.

It's important to note that, while goals can make your life more meaningful, they are not the meaning of life. If you get to the point where not reaching your goals feels like the equivalent to death, then your goal setting has become unhealthy and you need to take a step back to get some perspective. If not reaching your goals causes you to become hurtful, manipulative, physically sick, or emotionally broken, your goals have shifted from being healthy to toxic, and the toxic effect will be felt by other people around you. If this happens, it's possible that you have lost sight of who you are and why you're chasing your goals. Go back to Part 1 and review the exercises to get a clearer picture of your true direction.

Unless you're tempted to do something beyond what you have already mastered, you will never grow. An example for me is writing a book. It's new and challenging, and it pushes me to be better. I think everyone should have personally motivating reasons for why they want to achieve their goals. When you have a strong WHY for your goals, you can handle any HOW.

Four things keep my WHY sharp. I call them the "Four Fs." On any given day, one may be stronger than the other:

Faith

"Your life is God's gift to you. Who you become is your gift to God." My faith in God is an organizing principle in my life. When I reflect on this quote, I'm moved out of gratitude to make my life matter and to inspire others to do the same.

Future Family

A good person leaves an inheritance for their children's children. Proverbs 13:22 (NIV). One of my mentors would always say that great people leave something better than they found it. I interpret that statement to mean that I will make the legacy of my family better. To do that, I have to become better as a person, as a man, and as a leader. I set goals to continue the healthy traditions and break the negative cycles of my family concerning finances, relationships, emotional health, and spirituality.

Forefathers

Learning African-American and Haitian history continues to have a profound effect on me, as a Black man in America. Every time I watch movies like *12 Years a Slave, Amistad, Selma, Mandela, Malcolm X, Birth of a Nation*—or TV shows like *Underground* or *Roots*—I'm reminded of what my heroes have endured to achieve freedom for themselves and their families. Their inspiration moves me to sustain and build on what they've achieved.

Fear

I heard someone say that they have one thing to prove: that they can live their life without fear. I'm going to take that goal and make it mine. I want to live my life without—

- Fear of *criticism*
- Fear of *failure*
- Fear of *truth*
- Fear of *responsibility*

- And most importantly, the fear of *death*. If something really matters to me, I must be willing to die for it.

Your funeral might be the only time in your life when everyone will say nice things about you and reflect on all the great things you've been and done. In all likelihood, you'll be lying on your back and well-dressed while looking up; the preacher will be looking down, and everyone will be looking at you. At this time, you'll be able to say one of two things: I wish I had done (blank) or I'm glad I did (blank). I encourage you to live your life in such a way that you can say, "I'm glad I did."

Take some time to write out your major motivating force in life. What is your WHY? This exercise takes time, and answers might not come to you right away. Continue to ask yourself these questions. Know that your WHYs can be unlimited, and that some will be more important than others at any point in time.

Chapter 12

Define Your Success

Too many people sacrifice success in one area of life for success in another.

WHEN YOU THINK OF THE range of responsibilities and roles that people have in life, it's impossible to define success in a cookie-cutter way. How could there possibly be only *one* definition of success when people live in so many different circumstances?

You might be a social worker, a businessperson, an athlete, a home-maker, a student, an artist, an overseas mission worker, a retired crossing guard, or a police officer. The potential life paths are almost unlimited. It's important to take the time to find out precisely what success looks like for you right now, and know that it might look different later.

We must all live with the tension between our limits and our potential. We always have to weigh the cost of our decisions, particularly when it comes to finding success. We only have so much time, energy, money, and overall bandwidth to accomplish anything. When we see people who are considered "successful," we might imagine that their entire lives must be great—but that's not always the case. Many people have traded happiness in one area of their life for their success.

One of the philosophies that I live by is that I don't want anyone's "success" unless I'm willing to do what that person did, go through what that person went through, or sacrifice what that person had to sacrifice to obtain it. When I began applying this philosophy, I started to see that the people I thought were "successful" were only successful in parts of life. They privately experienced major failures in other areas, or their success was based on a set of values very different from mine.

I concluded that, before I would set out to pursue any goal, I would calculate the price. I'd decide what I would and wouldn't do, and what sacrifices I'd be willing to make in the pursuit of this goal. I'd begin with a clear set of values to guide me in the process. In Chapter 3, you'll find a great set of tools in naming your values.

Kobe Bryant, who was one of the greatest NBA players before he died in a plane crash in 2020, had an amazing, 20-year career filled with ups and downs. When he first came to the NBA, I was in the sixth grade. Following his career would teach me life lessons that I will carry with me for the rest of my life. Bryant ended his career with five championship rings and as an absolute a shoo-in for the NBA Hall of Fame—first ballot.

However, his career had not been perfect or without its share of bumps along the way. Poor decision-making might have destroyed his career. In 2003, a 19-year-old hotel employee in Eagle, Colorado accused him of sexual assault. He had checked into the hotel two days before he was scheduled to have surgery, and the day before surgery, he'd had an affair with this woman. Kobe admitted to the affair, but denied the sexual assault allegation. The case was later dropped, but that ONE night cost him more than he would ever imagine.

During the court proceedings, Kobe's wife, Vanessa, was pregnant. She miscarried the baby. There were those who told him that miscarriages are common, but he knew the stress from the media coverage had affected his wife's pregnancy. He later said he realized he had lost sight of what was most important: being the anchor of stability for his family. When reflecting on his childhood and the pain he'd endured in his career, he said he was not sure if he would have made the same decision.

I appreciate Kobe's honesty here. Most people see his glory, but don't know his story. His words can help us understand that what most people call "success" might not be comprehensive. We might need to re-imagine what success means to us.

If you haven't decided what your success looks like in every dimension of your life, then the one area you're not focused on could be the area that leads to trouble. Fortunately, Kobe's indiscretion didn't cost him his career—but he was an exception to the rule. I could tell you many stories where things went the other way. Poor decisions in the area of power, money, and sex have destroyed businesses, marriages, families, churches, organizations, and friendships. Bad decisions, even when they're not catastrophic, leave a lingering sadness around the mistake.

Today, ask yourself what your success looks like in every area of your life and what decisions you need to make about how you will live your life to prevent yourself from making a decision that will hurt you or others.

Toxic Success

Please know that some success is *toxic*. How can you identify a toxic form of success?

1. It requires you to be *someone you're not*. If you need to be inauthentic to be successful, that's a sure sign that you are on a path to toxic success. Yes, you sometimes will need to tone down certain aspects of our personality to be appropriate in a particular setting. But toxic success simply requires you to be fake.

2. It requires you to *compromise your core values* and what you hold dear to you. Ask yourself at every step, at what point would I walk away from an opportunity? This is part of naming your price in the beginning. It's easy to betray what you hold dear to you in a crucial moment if you are not grounded in your values. Do your homework (Chapter 3 – Values) in advance so you won't be

emotionally stuck when an opportunity comes your way. It can be harder to see what's right at the moment of decision, when your heart is exposed.

3. It requires you to *go against your purpose* and your calling in life. If a certain career pursuit requires you to do something that goes against your calling, you know you've messed up. It will probably be inconvenient to reposition yourself, but your career needs to align with the overarching theme of your life and calling. Being faithful to your purpose is greater than any individual accomplishment or accolade.

4. It requires that you *try to please EVERYONE.* That is impossible and an unhealthy way to live. We'll talk about people-pleasing in Chapter 36.

5. It requires you to *focus on the short term* to the detriment of the long term. Not all opportunities are good opportunities. You need to learn to say NO to instant gratification or easy fixes.

6. It requires you to engage in *negative or unethical* ways of thinking and acting. We live in a world where it sometimes seems you have to do a "deal with the devil" to be successful—but that's not true. You can be a person of integrity and stay honorable in your dealings. You need wisdom, counsel, and foresight to avoid getting caught up in unethical and illegal activities.

7. It bases your happiness on *one particular result,* instead of the fulfillment you get from knowing you gave your very best effort in your attempt. There's a mindset in this culture that says, "I'm only going to be happy if I win *this* award or if *this* person likes me or my work." Ultimately, it's dangerous to put your happiness in

the hands of anyone else. I believe simply being the best you can be will help you reach ultimate fulfillment. If you're positioned to use your genius-level talent, you'll also reach high levels of achievement. No one likes to lose, but the desperation that comes with the "succeed or else" mindset leads to unhealthy habits, fractured relationships, and a profound lack of fulfillment.

8. It requires you to move at a pace of life that is simply *unsustainable*. You cannot live your life at warp speed without warping your soul. I know that driving yourself hard is popular in this culture, but an unhealthy compulsion to succeed can lead to burnout, depression, and fractured relationships. If you decide to stand up to the beast of this fast-paced culture, you will need wisdom and courage. Try to find mentors and models who can guide you in evaluating your decisions about how to pursue success. See Chapter 9 on models and mentors.

9. It requires that you be more concerned about your *resume than your eulogy*, and more concerned about currency (dollars) than legacy (people).

A Note on Healthy Success:

Now that we've talked about toxic success, what does *healthy* success look like? The simplest way to know that your success is healthy is if you have the 3Cs: Calmness, Contentment, and Connection. Calmness is a sense of peace. Contentment is a state of mind that is satisfied with life. Connection is a state of being in mutually satisfying relationships that provide an openness and safety. See Chapter 33 on Safe People. Use the CASUAL tool in evaluating safe relationships.

Let me give you the high-level framework of success I use, which is based on seven areas. I have not arrived or reached a point of perfection with these standards, but I know these are the things I need to work toward and re-evaluate at every stage of life.

I've experienced times when my life was imbalanced, and I never want that to happen again. Sometimes you have to get burned to realize you don't want to touch the hot stove again. This lesson also serves as a reflection to not just work *in* your life but also *on* your life.

These are the seven areas of success, and the things I do to achieve them:

1. **Financial**: Living below your means, working to get out of debt, learning from past financial mistakes (such as not having or not sticking to a budget), establishing a plan of savings, and regularly reading and learning better ways to manage money. See Chapter 14.

2. **Family**: Working on building healthy relationships where we speak clearly, respectfully, and honestly. Learning how to listen and not just waiting to respond. Regularly expressing appreciation for family. (See Chapter 35 on assertiveness and Chapter 42 on listening.) Use the tools of emotional health to help build healthy bonds with family such as boundaries, forgiveness, grieving, shame, and assertiveness.

3. **Social**: Being a resource for friends to help them live wholeheartedly as they pursue their callings. Creating periods of uninterrupted time to spend with friends and family. (See Chapter 33 on CASUAL friends.)

4. **Spiritual**: Regularly reading the Word, devotionals, and inspirational materials. Spending time in prayer and meditation every day. Finding a way to serve using gifts and talents. Spending

designated periods of time in silence and solitude, and evaluating life regularly. Confessing failings to live out one's faith.

5. **Physical:** Going the gym regularly to engage in weight-lifting and cardio, creating a food plan that tracks calories, visiting the doctor regularly, drinking water, and staying away from sugars, sweets, and fast food.

6. **Personal Development**: Regularly engaging in personal development activities such as reading books, listening to audiobooks, taking classes, and attending workshops or seminars on topics that are relevant to life and work.

7. **Vocation**: Asking what the next five years will look like. I don't always like this question, because it tends to be accompanied by an unhealthy pressure to come up with a goal that's socially acceptable. When you ask yourself this question, don't feel pressured to come up with an answer right away. Just take the time to be more thoughtful and insightful about how you plan your future. Begin to ask the question and, if you feel comfortable, share your ideas with a trusted friend or coach who can hold space for you as you gain confidence and a sense of direction.

Take some time to write *your own definition* of success in each category, and think about what you do (or could be doing) to achieve them.

The objectives of this exercise are to:

1. **Help you find balance**. Get you to untangle your conflicting desires or adjust competing desires to achieve focus, clarity, and balance. *Balance* means you're giving the appropriate amount of time and effort to each area of life, creating overall stability. It

doesn't mean all things must be equal. Your balance will depend on the season of life you're in.

2. **Ensure that your desires are truly yours**. Many people's pursuit of success is driven by a need for parental approval, personal insecurities, feelings of inferiority, and shame. (See the Shame section in Chapter 34.) These are unhealthy motivations. Hopefully, after completing Part 1, you have the sharpened self-awareness to know which elements of success are truly important to you.

What would success mean to you in each of these categories?

1. **Financial:**

2. **Family:**

3. **Social:**

4. **Spiritual:**

5. **Physical:**

6. **Personal Development:**

7. **Vocational:**

CHAPTER 13

Self-Regard

Self-regard is the reputation we have for ourselves.

A MIDDLE SCHOOL STUDENT NAMED Malcolm was sitting at his desk, drawing a picture. His teacher walked by his desk and asked, "What are you doing, Malcolm?"

He said, "I'm drawing a picture of God."

The teacher said, "No one knows what God looks like."

Malcolm said, "You're about to in a minute."

While I don't endorse being conceited or boastful, there is a redemptive lesson in this story. Malcolm respected his own ability as an artist and had confidence in himself. I'm not sure he'll go on to be another Picasso, but he's definitely headed somewhere.

Many young people have confidence when they are around their peers in a comfortable setting, but when they're outside their comfort zone, they shut down. They have only developed the ability to be themselves and speak for themselves when they are completely comfortable and familiar with the environment.

A part of healthy maturation is knowing, accepting, and respecting who you are—including your strengths and your limitations or weaknesses. Eventually, we develop an inner strength and self-confidence called *self-regard*. Sometimes in life, you'll be in unfamiliar and uncomfortable settings. If you have a healthy self-regard, you'll be able to present yourself confidently in every situation.

Many people are not given the space as they grow up to develop self-confidence and a knowledge of their strengths and weaknesses. Some have the natural ability to know what they are good at and act on it, whether it's sports, music, chess, writing, speaking, etc. They can just step out. But other people need coaching and support to grow in confidence.

For example, I'm a good researcher, coach, and speaker. It took me a few years before I could begin to own these talents and say confidently what I could do well. I also know what I'm *not* good at. I am not good at analyzing extremely technical details, event planning, and more things than I can mention. I don't function well without having a sense of structure and order, while other people can perform well in the midst of chaos. I know I can learn how to develop the skills to perform in different environments, but it doesn't come naturally to me.

I want to offer a few ways to build your self-regard:

1. **Find the right environment**. Surround yourself with people who can help you develop confidence in who you are, apart from how well you perform. If you have low self-regard, find and place yourself in positive and encouraging environments where people affirm you instead of tearing you down. Sometimes you can lean on someone else's belief in you before your own belief kicks in. As much as you can, stay away from people who are negative or don't want you to succeed. Try to find an environment that offers you unconditional love. Ideally, this is your family. Family can provide a place that is safe. It doesn't have to be biological family. Find a place where it's okay to fail and to freely be who you are. You might find this place in church, with a few close friends, or in a support group of any kind. In a supportive environment, you can learn to feel good about yourself and appreciate yourself.

2. **Keep your word.** You can build up your self-regard by doing what you say you will do. When you fail to live up to what you say you will do, you now have information about your abilities and limitations, and you can make more informed decisions about what you will say going forward. You can't persuade yourself to have inner confidence. You have to earn it by putting in the work needed to accomplish your goals. It is built slowly.

3. **Keep working on yourself.** Continually work to discover your gifts and talents. Go to Chapter 4 for guidance on gifts and talents.

4. **Do your best in everything you do.** I love the movie Forrest Gump. It's a story about an athletic, kind-hearted, good-natured but slow-witted young man who witnesses and even influences some defining events in history. It doesn't matter what criticism you might have of Gump—in any activity he took on, he did his very best, and opportunities opened up for him as a result. That kind of success does a lot for your self-regard. To always do your best requires a strong will. It means doing something because of your love for it—not because you expect a reward. Doing your best will lead you to high self-regard. You won't need a participation trophy; the effort you put in is sufficient. Whether the circumstances are great or not, you will find that your self-esteem gets better when you do the best you can about your situation. As Kobe Bryant would say, you need Mamba mentality.

5. **Know who you are.** Evaluate how your self-image has been constructed. Study your history. Learning about yourself by studying your ancestors is empowering. As a black man in America who is the son of Haitian immigrants, I take pride in learning about my history. Movies like *Birth of a Nation, Roots,* and *Malcolm X*—and

people like Toussaint L'Ouverture and Jean-Jacques Dessalines—
helped to catapult my self-esteem. These strong, black men fought
for themselves, their families, and their people to achieve lib-
eration from oppression. While we need to be concerned about
how people of color are viewed, we should also consider how
people of color see themselves. For far too long, the images
of black people in this country have been negative, which had
perpetuated self-hatred and racial inferiority. American culture
is now working to reframe those images in cinema, writing, and
public circles. The way you are perceived is important, but how
you see yourself is vital. You can't always change other people's
perceptions, but how you see yourself is within your control and
will affect every area of your life.

Questions for Reflection

1. What habits can you commit to in order to increase your
   self-regard?

   _____

   _____

2. How would a higher self-regard help you at work, at school, at
   home, or in contact with others?

   _____

   _____

3. What are the internal benefits of having high self-regard?

_____

_____

CHAPTER 14

Money

*People buy things they don't need with money they don't have
to impress people they don't like.*

MONEY IS A RESOURCE THAT comes with no instructions included. Most
people I know have never been taught how to manage money. When I've
asked clients about their budgets – how much they make and how much
they spend—they usually look up at the sky and make a rough guess.
That's the extent of their financial planning analysis.

At that point, that I roll up my sleeves and force them to roll theirs
up as well.

For this lesson, we'll discuss how to manage your money by using
the acronym DEAL.

D — DETERMINE WHAT YOUR GOALS ARE

Without a vision for your finances, you will move without aim and intentionality, and you'll be vulnerable to making foolish financial decisions.
Many important decisions in your life have major financial implications,
including buying a car, getting married, buying a home, saving for college,
paying off debt, starting a career, travel, planning for retirement, or relo-
cation. I recommend speaking with/hiring a financial planner, preferably

someone with a designation Enrolled Agent, Chartered Financial Analyst, Certified Financial Planner, or Certified Public Accountant. These professionals can help you think through the implications of major purchases help you make a plan for spending your income. You can keep yourself safe by surrounding yourself with good counsel.

E — ESTABLISH AN EMERGENCY FUND

An emergency fund is an account in which money is set aside money for a financial emergency or unexpected, major expense, such as the loss of a job or a serious illness or injury. You need savings to cover about three to six months of necessary expenses (housing, food, transportation including maintenance, and any job-searching expenses that would be needed in the event of a layoff). Keep your emergency fund a savings or money market account. Keep this money liquid rather than investing in anything risky. Liquid funds can be accessed quickly, with little to no loss in value. Later in this chapter, you'll find a budget to help you determine what your monthly expenses are.

A — AUTOMATE YOUR FINANCES

If possible, set up your bank account so that money is taken directly out of your paycheck for your savings and your bills. The more automated your life becomes, the less work you have to do in figuring things out and the less risk you'll make financial decisions impulsively. For many people, the day a paycheck is deposited is a dangerous time. It can begin a battle between your practical side and your tendency to spend impulsively. Prepare for this battle in advance by automating your finances. Create a system using excel or a notepad, and arrange for your fixed bills and savings to be taken directly from your account each month. Most banks make this possible. If you are not able to automate, you'll need to follow your budget closely when you get your check.

L —LIVE BELOW YOUR MEANS

This might be one of the more difficult things to do in our culture. I want to give you two things to consider:

1. **Keep track**. Track your income and expenses using your budget. Cut back on your expenses if you can. See the conversation on budgeting, below.

2. **Buy less**. Don't fall victim to the culture of consumerism and materialism. Know the difference between a want and a need. Be sure all your needs are met first. See the conversation below.

MARKETING, MATERIALISM, AND CONSUMERISM

Instead of focusing on the mechanics of finance, we need to address the behavior patterns around money in our society. Many people don't understand the difference between a need and a want. A *need* is something that is necessary for survival. If the need is not met, you will not be able to function effectively and efficiently; you might even become vulnerable to disease or death. A *want* is an optional desire to have something, either immediately or in the future. The word *optional* means you have the ability to live without it. It's easy to get wants and needs mixed up when you have a strong desire for something.

How do you differentiate between a want and a need? Ask yourself:

1. Have I lived without this before?

2. Can I live without this now?

Marketing, in the form of commercials and internet ads, is a strong influence in our culture. Marketing constantly seduces us to feel that we will be unhappy or incomplete if we don't have this new product or that new upgrade in technology, transportation, or fashion. Every few months, there's a "new and improved" version of something. Marketing and advertising can make you crave things you didn't even know existed!

Companies with something to sell want you to be unhappy, because happy and content people don't buy things. I recently went to the Apple store to get a battery for my iPhone. The salesman looked at me like I had three heads. He was probably expecting me to buy a new phone, because that is the trend in the Apple store. Instead of walking out with an $800 phone, I walked out with an $80 battery. I chose function over form. Performance and purpose mean more to me in a phone than appearance.

Some people might think this decision was weird, but we have to make such decisions continuously in every area of life. If we choose to buy only what we actually need, the payoff will be substantial. It's hard to go against the grain unless you have a solid plan and a strong and motivating vision. My phone might not be as flashy, but it's saving me a great deal of money.

Unfortunately, most people are not aware of how deeply they are influenced to buy things they don't really need. The social pressure is too intense for them to go against it. Materialism and consumerism dominate our culture. *Materialism* occurs when you place material comforts and physical possessions above your values. *Consumerism* describes the condition when you become obsessed with the acquisition of goods. Materialism and consumerism in our culture are like undiagnosed diseases—even though most people won't call them that. Instead, they'll say things like:

- **"I like nice things."**

- **"Quality products are more expensive."** (Sometimes this is true, but overspending can also be a sign of financial mismanagement.)

- Here's the best one: **"You only live once."**

These statements are often code for, "I know I shouldn't be buying this, but I'm going to buy it anyway." I call this attitude a *disease* because it adversely affects our lives and it won't go away until you diagnose and treat it.

As a financial planner for the last several years, I've had the chance to witness the way many people—including friends, colleagues, and clients—manage their money. I've seen consumerism and materialism cause massive credit card debt, broken relationships due to unpaid personal loans, car repossessions, foreclosed homes, and even divorces from disagreement over the way to manage money.

For most people, it goes something like this: Money comes in. Money goes out until there is no more money left. Then bills come, and they wonder where the money went and run around looking for ways to pay the bills.

If this sounds like your finances, I have good news: YOU CAN CHANGE, if you have the courage.

BUDGETING MAKES THE DIFFERENCE

To be successful, you don't really need complex investment planning with stocks, bonds, mutual funds, real estate, currency exchange, bitcoin, commodities, or entrepreneurial endeavors. What you really need is one basic tool to get on the road to having a solid financial foundation: A BUDGET. An effective budget is about 10 percent technical and 90% behavioral. It's less about the money and more about your discipline and ability to commit to a plan.

Regardless of how much money they make, most people will feel a strong temptation to spend above their means. It's just human nature. Whatever we don't intentionally manage will tend to get out of control. You need knowledge and vision to manage money, but more than that, you need discipline.

In this section, I want to give you a framework to set up your budget. A budget can change your life. If you don't manage your expenses the right way, they will get out of control and keep you from saving for other goals. Whether you are a high school student or a CEO, everyone needs a budget to get a handle on their finances.

Someone told me that a budget would keep them from living flexibly. I told the person that, without a budget, they will probably lose their flexibility later on, when excessive debt and unpaid bills keep them from having peace. Life is so uncertain. The least we can do is precisely plan what can be made clear.

Learn the art of budgeting. Then you'll be telling your money where to go instead of wondering where it went. An intentional plan can direct your income and name your expenses. See the sample monthly budget.

Sample Monthly Budget

Take-Home Income (After taxes)

Source 1: Job	$2000
Source 2:	
Total Income:	**$2000**
Less: Tithes/Offerings	$200
Less: Savings	$200
Net Cash Available	**$1600**

Fixed Expenses

Rent/Mortgage	$500
Auto Loan/Bus Fare	
Auto Insurance	$50
Credit Card Payment	$400
Water/Gas	$50
Electricity	$50
Medical/Life Insurance	$50
Total Fixed Expenses	**$1,100**

Variable Expenses

Auto Repairs/Maintenance	$50
Lunches	
Groceries	$200
Recreation/Cable TV	
Laundry/Dry Cleaning	
Telephone	$100
Gasoline	$100
Clothing	
Grooming (Hair/Nails/Etc.)	$50
Vacation Reserve	
Other:	

Other:	_____
Other:	_____
Total Variable Expenses	**$500**
Total Expenses	**$1,600**
(Deficit) Cash	**$0**

Pick up your notebook and calculator or use Microsoft Excel and type it in so you can use this every month. Do what works best for you. Once you have no money left, you must STOP spending. This is called *zero-based budgeting*, and it calls for a little sacrifice—the ability to give up what you want in the short term to get something of greater value and significance.

Trust me, if you practice this consistently and diligently, you will be in a stable financial position when emergencies show up. If you don't follow a budget, one emergency can derail your life.

Choose today—whether you are in high school, college, or someone looking to improve their financial lives—to find financial stability. Know that it's never too late to start, as long as you are consistent. Just because you were disciplined yesterday doesn't mean you can be undisciplined tomorrow.

Most people have done dumb things with money, and I am no exception. You can learn from my mistakes and the mistakes of so many other people. Before you make your next financial decision, put a budget together and commit to sticking to it.

When I was in high school, I had a part-time job that I used to buy clothes and sneakers, and to put minutes on my phone (I know, I'm old). My mother would always tell me to save my money so that I could have some later on. I wish I would have listened. Saving my money would have helped me much more than wearing the latest fashion.

At this point, you should not worry about being the best-dressed person you know, but being the best-prepared for the next stage of life.

You can do this by saving money. Today's credit card society makes it so easy to "get now and pay later," but economic realities eventually set in. Then we regret the mistakes we made and live with a sense of shame.

Our unbalanced culture emphasizes acquiring more stuff without considering the price you pay. Debt takes a toll on your emotional, relational, physical, and mental health. Sometimes, money is just too expensive.

We need to come to terms with the fact that, if we concede to the demands of an imbalanced and sick culture, we also are sick. In light of this painful admission, the first thing I want you to do is to let go of the shame of past financial mistakes. Hold onto the *guilt*, because guilt signals that you made a mistake and need to learn a lesson. *Shame* signals that you are defective because of those decisions. You are not defective if you've made poor financial choices. You're human. The good news is that we usually remember the painful tuition we pay to the school of life, which helps us remember not to repeat the same mistakes.

Ultimately, we are made to be producers and not only consumers. If you produce more than you consume, your life will be better. If you only consume and don't produce, then you can only be proud of what you consume. I imagine a day when people are more apt to tell you about the business they just started than the new car or phone or shoes they bought. That would be a significant cultural shift!

If you want to steer clear of the harried, financially-based life that most people live, you have to decide that you will become a producer more than a consumer. I dream of and pray for the day when people are in positions where they can become self-sufficient to make major life decisions from a position of power instead of lack.

Reflection Questions

1. Do you struggle with materialism or consumerism? What are your shopping habits? Take a look at your closet. If you own

something that has lost its actual usefulness, but you cannot give it away, you don't own it. It owns you. Note: Because marketing has the power to make us suspend our reasoning, a good rule of thumb is to wait overnight before making a major purchase.

2. If everyone managed their money the way you do, would that be good or bad news for the community you live in? (Church, family, organization, etc.)

3. Who do you go to for financial advice? You will find a million talking heads on TV, podcasts, and YouTube. Decide for yourself which experts you will listen to and follow. Make sure their philosophies line up with your values and that they have a track record of success. It's easy to give an opinion, but it can be hard to find a qualified one.

4. Give yourself a grade.

    A – You stick to your budget 90% of the time
    B – You stick to your budget 80% of the time
    C - You stick to your budget 70% of the time
    D - You stick to your budget 60% of the time
    F – You don't have a budget.

Most people will fail this test, and it's not graded on a curve. The problem is, you can't get kicked out of this school because you will *always* be in a finance class. Money will always matter, because it controls your options. I firmly believe that many people can't pursue their calling because they are so swamped with the aftermath of financial chaos that it's a daily struggle to get moving.

Start today with a plan. Contact a certified financial planner for help, or take advantage of a financial planning course. I highly recommend

Dave Ramsey's Financial Peace University. Go to www.daveramsey.com to find a course in your area.

CHAPTER 15

SMART Goals

WHEREVER YOU ARE IN YOUR education or career, you need to find a structure to pursue your goals. Otherwise, your goals will most likely be wandering targets.

One of the tools you can use is called SMART goal-setting. Take the time to review the goals you have set for yourself academically, vocationally, or personally. A SMART goal is broken down into five factors.

1. **Specific** – Goals have to be clearly identified.

2. **Measurable** – You need to be able to measure your progress along the way.

3. **Authored** – In other words, they have to be written down on a piece of paper. Studies show that when goals are written down, they have a much higher chance of being achieved. Only 8% of the population can identify clear goals, and 3% write those goals down.

4. **Relevant** – These goals have to be YOUR goals, not your family's goals or your friend's goals. Take some time to reflect on this one. Review Chapter 12's exercise.

5. **Time-bound** – *When* will the goal be accomplished? Having a deadline helps to give you a sense of urgency regarding fulfilling a goal.

Let me mention that there are two types of goals: result-oriented and action-oriented. *Result-oriented goals* are focused on the end of the journey. They describe a picture of the desired future—your vision. *Action-oriented goals* are what you'll need to do to achieve the vision.

STUDENT EXAMPLES

SMART Result-Oriented Goals for a Student:
- Improve to a B+ in Algebra at the end of the marking period.
- To get a 3.5 GPA this semester.

SMART Action-Oriented Goals for a Student:
- Attend the study sessions offered by the teacher's assistant each week.
- List out the quizzes, homework assignments, and tests left for the marking period/semester and the grades needed to reach the desired final grade.
- Study three hours every night using the SQRRR study model (If you've never heard of this study method, Google it. SQRRR is Survey, Question, Read, Review, Recite.)
- Memorize key facts needed to pass the exam.
- Speak with your teacher weekly about any questions you have and ask for study tips.

PROFESSIONAL EXAMPLES

SMART Result-Oriented Goals for your Career:
- Obtain my teacher's certification by July 2017
- Earn a salary of $150,000 this year.
- Have a book published by the end of 2017
- Start my business by the end of 2018

SMART Action-Oriented Goals for your Career:
- Complete one section of bar review study material every week.
- After all modules have been completed, take practice exams and score a 90 and above every two weeks.
- Write one page a day for the next 90 days.
- Read three books in your profession each week.

On the next page, I've included some space where you can write out all of your current goals.

Jonathan Frejuste

CHAPTER 16

Personal Development

*You don't read to remember everything but to find the idea
that can change your life.*

ONE DAY, A MAN HAD a conversation with his mentor. His mentor asked
him how much he made for a living. The man showed the mentor his
paycheck and said, "This is all they pay." His mentor stopped him and
said, "This is all they pay you." The man asked, "What do you mean?" The
mentor said, "You don't get paid in life for your time. You get paid for
your value." This story is interesting because it shows the difference in
the way these two individuals defined value. The mentee was looking at
the dollar amount paid, while the mentor was looking at the value that
was brought to the time. If you need to make more money, you have to
ask this question: How do you increase your *value*? The answer is personal
development. The mentee did not have a personal plan for growth—in
fact, he seemed to not know he was supposed to have one. But the conversation caused a monumental shift in his thinking, because it revealed
one of the keys to change in life: You must change yourself through intentional plans for personal growth. Success is not something you chase,
but something that chases *you,* based on the person you become.

To increase your value, you must bring something to the table in every area of your life. Whether it's in your family, at your job, or in your church, we all can contribute something that serves to help other people. Some of the best ways to increase your value are to educate yourself. Read, take classes, listen to inspirational and informational audio recordings, get personal coaching, and attend conferences/workshops. It's been said that if you read an hour a day on a topic, in five years, you will become an expert on that topic. What better way is there to improve yourself and your community? It's been said that when times change, lifelong learners will ultimately succeed while the occasional learners might find themselves prepared to handle systems that are no longer relevant. We have to keep growing and changing. Otherwise, we'll be playing a new game by the same old rules.

Remember these two truths:

1. You will only think to the level of what you've been *exposed to.*

2. You can't learn what you think you *already know.*

Reading is probably the single most important thing you can do to keep your mind growing and expanding. As your vocabulary grows, your IQ increases. Reading will help you improve your mastery of words and also make you wiser in many ways. Part of guiding your destiny is controlling what goes into your own mind and committing to spending the time it takes to feed your mind things of value. Books and positive audio teachings are the place to start. Set a goal to read one book a month—or if you really want to improve, one book a week. There is not a problem that you have that someone hasn't discovered a solution for, and you'll find that solution in a book. If you're having a problem or you discover something you're curious about, read two or more books about that issue and then take another look at how you should approach it. I PROMISE you that if you pick up this reading habit, it WILL change your life.

If you think this will require some self-discipline, I am with you. I used to hear about successful people who read two books a week or even one book a day, and I was intimidated, because I knew that I was a slow reader. So let me encourage you to start at your own pace. I started reading one *page* a day. After a while, it got easier. I could read one chapter a week. Then I could read a few chapters a week and before you know it, I could read a lot in a little time. Reading is like a muscle; the more you use your reading skills, the easier it is to acquire more knowledge. So if you miss a day, just start again, one page a day. Then one chapter a day. Then a few chapters a week. Don't be overwhelmed. You can do it. Knowledge comes cumulatively. Just get started.

When I visit the homes of people I respect, who live their lives in a way that I admire, one of the common things I see is that they have a vast library. These people have made it a point to surround themselves with book titles in different areas of life: relationships, finances, business, spirituality, emotional health, career development, etc. These folks are lifelong learners, and their bookshelves are a reflection of their desire to continue to improve themselves. Here's my encouragement. Start thinking today about books that are important and personally meaningful to you, and begin building your own library. See the recommended resources at the end of this book for a list of the great books to begin with. Dust off your library card—or apply for one, if you need to—and take a trip to your local library. Walk through the aisles of your local bookstore; I visit these stores often. If you find a title that interests you, check amazon.com to learn more about it and to see what other readers thought. If you are often busy traveling or working out, consider audiobooks, which let you learn in the car, on the bus, or even at the gym. I have hundreds of audiobooks. Listening to books has been a life-changing habit for me. You can open an account at audible.com or even search YouTube for "personal development audiobooks." Reading can be the beginning of an exciting journey of personal development and can help you add value to your life and your community.

CHAPTER 17

One Major Focus

"It always seems impossible until it's done." Nelson Mandela

CHAPTERS 11 TO 16 SERVED as a starting point for your goal-setting. I hope you are getting excited and focused on a new goal: paying off debt, increasing your savings, improving your performance academically or vocationally, or putting together a personal development plan. Keep working hard to get focused on reaching those goals. This chapter will help you hone in on the season of life you're in and what your priorities should be.

I believe it's best to have one major focus in life. Having a single focus will help to keep you on task. This chapter is extremely important, because the things that matter most in your personal development might not always get the attention they deserve. You need intentionality, and that comes with singular focus. Trying to do two things with maximum effort is like trying to chase two rabbits. Both will get away.

Get comfortable with the fact that some things will have to wait for your attention. Your aim is to focus on what needs to be accomplished *now* and what perspective you need to cultivate *in this season*. Life will be much simpler and less hectic once you know your primary goal. Most great people who went on to accomplish many things had to establish a sole purpose.

Nelson Mandela's primary focus was to rid South Africa of *apartheid*—South Africa's form of institutionalized racial discrimination. Mandela became a world leader who set examples all over the world of the power of forgiveness and reconciliation.

Mother Theresa's main goal was to help the homeless people outside her convent learn to read and write. She later started a hospice for those who were sick and dying on the streets of Calcutta, India and became a global symbol of service and charity.

Kobe Bryant, the late basketball superstar, wanted to win an NBA championship. He also served as an inspiration to people all over the world by demonstrating how to recover from mistakes and stay focused on goals.

Not everyone will find the same kind of early clarity about their goals. Many of us stumble before we find that main focus. As your calling becomes clearer, prioritizing will get easier. Review Part 1 regularly to deepen your clarity about yourself and your calling. In this season of my life, my focus is writing, personal coaching, and facilitating workshops to promote positive change. My goal is to ignite hope and bring healing to my community. This represents a transition from what I've been doing for the last few years, but it has taken time for me to build the skillset, resources, and confidence to feel comfortable pursuing this goal. Like all of us, my life is a work in progress.

When I was in high school, I heard a motivational speaker say something that changed my life forever: "If you want to hide something from a black man, put it in a book." This speaker made the statement to help us, kids in a predominantly black school, become aware of the social perception of black people in America. I felt offended, sad, and angry all at once when I heard those words. He described how the enslaved Africans were hung for learning how to read—while like most modern-day Americans, I did not see the value of reading. We took the opportunity for granted.

That statement sent me on a quest for book titles that would help my knowledge about the world grow. That was 15 years ago, and I am forever grateful that I was in school that day. The message sparked something important in me. From that day on, reading and listening to audio teachings have changed my life and helped me to serve my community. Reading also became one of my favorite things to do!

The more you learn, the more you realize how much you don't know. I am forever on a mission to learn about the world around me. Social issues, health, finance, counseling, and history continue to fascinate me. As I read and learn, I grow and can share what I learn through speaking and writing.

I have compiled a list of thousands of book titles that I intend on reading over the next few years. Thinking about the information in those books keeps me excited and focused. I literally could spend all day with books.

What's your focus? When I asked a few people this question, here's some of what I heard:

- "What's bothering me is that I have to lose weight. I am overweight because I have not been eating right or exercising. It's affecting every aspect of my life. That's my focus right now. I've lost 10 pounds so far, and I'm committed to getting to a healthy weight. I feel better already, but I know I have more work to do."

- (**Focus**: *Physical health*)

- "I am focusing on getting out of debt. I got a credit card when I was in college, and because I never learned about money management, I ran up thousands of dollars in debt on nonsense. Now I'm working to change that so I can be financially free. I have to live frugally for now, and it's hard, but that's the sacrifice I need to make to get out of this debt in the next 12 months."

- (**Focus**: *Financial stability*)

- "I got divorced a year ago, and I feel like I'm starting all over again. I had to move out of my house, and now I'm doing better. I've been going to counseling weekly, going to the gym four times a week, and I'm taking one class every semester to finish up my degree. I see the light at the end of the tunnel."

(**Focus**: *Emotional and mental well-being after a major life transition*)

- "I just got out of prison, and my main focus is on getting a steady job and saving up for a car. Then I'm going to go back to school to get my truck driver's license."

- (**Focus**: *Successful reentry and obtaining employment*)

- "I struggle with an addiction, and I never went to get help. I am now going to counseling and my support group once a week. Every day is a battle, but I will never quit. I've been sober for the last four months."

- (**Focus**: *Sobriety*)

- "I want to open up a cleaning business where I can employ 10-12 people in the next year. I've been doing all the jobs with a few people, and the demands are great, so I'm excited about the possibilities."

- (**Focus**: *Entrepreneurial start-up*)

- "I got a 3.5 last semester, and I want to be on the Dean's List every semester until I graduate college. So these next few years will be focused on being the best student I can be."

(**Focus**: *Academic achievement*)

These examples show that everyone is different. Our priorities and individual challenges are different, so each person's focus must be different as well. Take some time to identify what your major focus should be at this point in your life. It might not be clear right away, so ask yourself this question often:

What should my priority be in this season of my life?

CHAPTER 18

Time

If you take care of the days, the years will take care of themselves.

ONE OF MY MENTORS TOLD me that if he looked at your daily schedule, he could tell how successful you would be in five years. He said that, for most people, their failure is not due to a lack of time but a lack of *direction*.

Hearing this was one of the most pivotal moments in my life. I realized that *time management* is an oxymoron. You cannot manage time. You can only manage priorities, and the amount of time you spend on completing the actions associated with your priorities determines your effectiveness.

Generally, the more you do something, the better you will get and the more effective you will be. The more you study, using effective study methods, the better student you will be. The more you practice your sport, the more skilled you'll be. The more you read about any topic, the more knowledgeable you will be.

In my observation, most people profoundly abuse their time. I know that it was very true in my life, and sometimes it still can be. I used to spend hours watching TV shows, surfing the web, going on social media, and playing games—all activities that added little to no value to my life and distracted me from what I really needed to do to improve myself vocationally, academically, physically, or spiritually.

I knew that if I wanted to accomplish my goals and end up living an impactful life, I needed to take an inventory of how I was spending my time. I needed to reduce or eliminate the time I spent doing unproductive things.

Here's a helpful activity management tool that I believe can assist you in assessing your activities and classifying them in the right way. It's called "the ABCD tool" and it requires that you sort out your activities in order of importance.

"A" activities are important and urgent. In other words, these are things you need to do by a certain time, or it will have immediate consequences. When you think of "A" activities, think of the word *deadline*. Something has to be done by a certain time, or you risk major consequences.

"B" activities are important but not urgent. These activities need to be accomplished eventually, but without a sense of urgency. If you don't do your "B" activities, there will be consequences over time, but nothing bad will happen immediately. "B" activities can fall under the category of *habits*.

"C" activities are urgent but not important. These activities have to happen at a certain time, but they do not have importance. They are opportunities that might or might not lead to anything of significance.

"D" activities are neither urgent nor important. Some of these activities could be considered dumb or dangerous, based on your goals and what kind of life you would like to lead, while others are just a waste of time.

Think of everything you do in a typical day, and assign it a letter based on its importance and urgency. Here's an example of ABCD activities that you may write out on a given day.

"A" Activities – Important and urgent

1. Write one chapter today to stay on track and reach my book submission deadline.

2. Start working on a paper that's due at the end of the week.

3. Pay the phone bill that is due tomorrow.

"B" Activities – Important but not urgent

1. Go to the gym four times a week. It's important to your health, but you can choose when you go.

2. Go food shopping. You have food enough for now, but because things will get busy for you in the next few weeks, it might be smart to stock up.

3. Organize your budget for the next month. For you to properly manage your finances, you want to set up a budget, so you don't overspend. You can certainly postpone it, but it makes sense to begin working on your financial goals as soon as possible.

"C" Activities – Urgent but not important

1. Watch the last episode of *The Voice* tonight instead of recording it to watch this weekend.

2. Go to the Lauryn Hill concert on Friday night.

"D" Activities – Neither important nor urgent

1. Shop for things you don't actually need.

2. Gossip on the phone with negative people.

3. Argue about petty things on social media.

Every morning, think about the things you plan to do and use this activity management tool to organize your day. At the end of the day, jot down all the things you did and ask yourself how important and urgent they were. How much total time did you spend on "A" activities? On "B" activities? On "C" activities? On "D" activities?

CHAPTER 19

Focus

Like billowing clouds that bring no rain is the person who talks big but never produces. Proverbs 25:14, MSG

IT'S SAFE TO SAY THAT the world we live in has become more and more filled with distractions. Social media platforms like Facebook, Instagram, and Twitter are addictive. Many of us become caught up in chronic texting via group chats—and there are always new things to watch on TV.

For many of us, life is simply too fast-paced and cluttered. This new American way of life leads many people to attempt to do too many things in too little time. Remember, if you want to be great at any profession, you need to be single-minded and focused.

Dealing with these modern life distractions is like being an NBA player who's trying to shoot a free throw while fans of the opposing teams are waving objects to distract you from making the shot. That's the way you need to look at life. You have to make a free throw to win the game, but there are forces that don't want you to succeed.

Whenever you decide to pursue something meaningful, you'll find people, events, and circumstances that will attempt to steal your focus, rendering you ineffective in accomplishing your task. Focus is a muscle that you will have to cultivate. Like any muscle, you'll use it or lose it.

Writing a book takes a tremendous amount of focus. It takes even more focus to write something good. Writers experience moments that are extremely painful and confusing. But one of the most liberating aspects of the process is when your focus becomes really clear, and the writing process flows smoothly. For me, this happens about 20 percent of the time. It's one of the best feelings in the world to be in this kind of zone. The other 80 percent of the time goes to research, organization, and the constant fight to keep my mind from wandering.

Distractions seem to get even more intense when you are determined to complete something of great importance to you. I've been blessed to meet many people over the course of my life who have learned not to allow most things to distract them. As someone who has faced a fair share of emergencies in my life, I certainly understand that life happens. Someone close to you might be suffering from a sickness and in need of help, your car has a flat tire, or you might be struggling with mental or emotional issues like depression (See Chapter 37). These factors require your time and attention, and make it harder to focus on your goals.

But when you're not in the midst of a crisis, try to take full of advantage of the relative peace to pursue your goals wholeheartedly, because you never know what card life may throw your way next. Over time, I've learned that what separates the people who are productive from those who are not is their ability to focus on what is most essential every time they can.

A time budget exercise can help you sharpen your focus so you will be more productive. This is a call for you to respond with a strong resolution. Learn how to lock in and not let yourself get derailed. Remember, FOCUS means Follow One Course Until Successful.

A. Time Budget Exercise

There are 168 hours in a week. Let's assume you sleep eight hours a day – 56 hours a week. That leaves 112 hours a week of waking time. Let's assume you work a 50-hour job (including commute). This leaves 62 hours a week. Let's say you go to the gym two hours each day. That's 14 hours a week. That leaves 48 hours a week that you have control over.

This is a sample scenario using conservative figures. You can create your own scenario by starting with 168 hours a week. Include your sleep, work/school, gym, family time, entertainment, and anything unique that I didn't mention.

Time Budget Exercise

Sleep	_____ hours
Work and commute	_____ hours
Gym	_____ hours
School	_____ hours
Church	_____ hours
Social Media	_____ hours
Goals	_____ hours
Other	_____ hours
Total	_____ hours

Make sure the total equals 168 hours. This is a simple way to do the hard work of figuring out where your focus and your time is going.

I'm sure someone will say that this is too simplistic. Sometimes unexpected things throw off our schedules. But the simplicity of the exercise is what gives it power. You need to know how your time is being spent before you can figure out how to spend it more efficiently. Breaking your waking hours down in this way will make you keenly aware of the hours you're spending in "D" activities.

B. SOME SUGGESTIONS TO STAY FOCUSED.

1. **Do the exercises!** Grab a sheet of paper and write some things down. Go back to Chapters 3, 4, 8, 9, 11, 15, and 17. Write and

reflect on your values, your talents, your vision, your role models, your Whys, your SMART Goal, and your major focus. If you have not done these exercises, go back and complete them now. Once you have done all the exercises, write them down on one piece of paper. Keeping this paper with you will help you organize your days and ultimately, your life. I've noticed that people who are constantly in crisis usually have a poor sense of priorities and are unorganized in multiple areas of their life. This will help you get organized, so you don't constantly cause your own crisis.

2. **Decide what *not* to do**. Knowing what your available options are and choosing not to participate in some is just as important as deciding what to do. Examples: I will not text anyone for the next four hours because of my work. I will not watch TV until I get work done up to a certain point. I will not attend any social events until I get a certain amount of my work done. You have to decide what *not* to do to put all your efforts into what you need to be doing.

3. **Learn to say NO**. Without sounding like a conspiracy theorist, I'll say that there are forces in the world that have a vested interest in keeping you distracted. You have to learn and practice the great skill of saying NO, because it will be necessary as you focus on accomplishing your goals. The more you say NO, the easier it will become. Go back to #1. What you have on that list gives you a strong YES, and that will make saying NO to other things easier. When we live by our priorities, we allow our calling to direct our lives rather than a crazy, insensitive culture.

Listen to me. You don't have to disappear forever. You have to disappear long enough to get some milestone accomplished. Whether it's earning your GED; passing the boards in medical or nursing school;

taking the LSAT; taking the bar exam; getting your CPA, CFP, or Series 6 or 65 or whatever number they have at this point; finishing your book, your CD, your movie, your website, your degree, or your certification program; or whatever you are working on—don't let other people tell you what you should consider to be important. You have to decide that for yourself. I hope you have a great support system that gives you the type of space and support you need, but if you don't, you have to put those other people at a distance.

4. Learn to delay pleasure and then take well-deserved breaks. Use your breaks to watch a show, play a game, or make a quick call to a friend or family member. Recognize the importance of rest periods—but if you can keep working, keep working.

C. BENEFITS OF FOCUS

1. Focus gives you a feeling of *alertness and clarity* of thought. It's known as "getting in the zone."

2. Focus gives you *confidence* that you can accomplish what you set your mind to by putting forth the necessary attention and time.

3. With focus, you can *take hold of your vision* and not let go until it becomes a reality.

4. Focus can make you *fearless* in the face of obstacles, because a focused mind doesn't have room for fear and anxiety.

CHAPTER 20

Self-Discipline

You lazy fool, look at an ant. Watch it closely; let it teach you a thing or two. Nobody has to tell it what to do. All summer it stores up food; at harvest it stockpiles provisions. So how long are you going to laze around doing nothing? How long before you get out of bed? A nap here, a nap there, a day off here, a day off there, sit back, take it easy—do you know what comes next? Just this: You can look forward to a dirt-poor life, poverty your permanent houseguest!
Proverbs 6:6-11, MSG

VERY SIMPLY, DISCIPLINE IS THE ability to do what you have decided to do, whether you feel like it or not. I believe that discipline is a byproduct of having a vision of the future that resonates deeply with your values and your beliefs and a sense of what matters to you, what you think about most, what disturbs you most, and what excites you most.

Discipline is a result of having priorities that are deeply planted in your heart and a vision of the future that inspires you to get your work done, regardless of what your emotions might be saying at that moment. Self-discipline also speaks to your commitment to keeping your life on schedule.

When people ask me how I learned to be disciplined in my work and studies over the years, I ask this question:

"If I tell you that for the next seven days, you need to fast from food, TV, and all other forms of technology (all you can do is drink water); you need to read four books and write a report on each book; and at the end of that period, I'll give you $2 million dollars—would you do it?"

This is a pretty ridiculous scenario, but I have yet to talk to someone who would say no. Why? Because they can see the value of that great sacrifice. If your effort is low, you're probably thinking about the obligation and not the opportunity. We can have great discipline for a great reward.

Self-discipline is something that I used to hate talking about. After some time, I realized that the key to discipline is motivation. You have to work *hard* to find something that you LOVE doing. It is something that you might get tired *from* doing, but not tired *of* doing – something that inspires and motivates you consistently, because motivation allows you to stay focused and get within striking distance of excellence. That's the trick. Once you find the activity you love that brings value to people's lives, hold onto it and let that be a source of motivation to follow through so you can become more self-disciplined.

Significant progress is made when discipline is sharp. We all have, at one time or another, hit a low point in life as it relates to discipline. Eventually, there comes a moment when we have to stop and say "no more." We cannot keep tolerating mediocrity—or even worse, totally becoming complacent. We have to get back up and get focused.

I hear a lot of talk today about being a boss. It refers to someone who is in charge. Remember, you can't be a boss of anyone if you're not your own boss first. Every time we fail to follow through with our disciplines, it weakens our character and confidence in our ability to reach our goals.

Hard work and discipline are the opposite of "chance." When you practice determination and discipline, you take your fate into your own hands. If you leave your fate in the hands of fortune and occasional work, you will succeed sometimes and fail sometimes.

The determined person refuses to surrender to the random winds of circumstance. The determined person adopts a consistent set of disciplines and work ethic, and finds that their self-discipline is critical to reaching their destiny.

If you want to be successful at something, you need to find the discipline to do things that bring value to your goal.

a. If you're a *basketball player*, you run drills, watch what you eat, take care of your body by stretching, work on your ball-handling, shoot many shots a day, and watch film of successful basketball players. Kobe Bryant would aim for 800 baskets a day just for PRE-SEASON SCRIMMAGES! His workouts during the season were even more intense.

b. If you're a *professional public speaker*, you read and research, practice your talks, and meditate on core values so you can speak from a place of substance. The legendary motivational speaker Zig Ziglar took up to six hours to prepare for a thirty-minute speech.

c. If you're a *golfer*, you go to the gym daily to stay in shape, practice your swings, and study the moves of great golfers. Tiger Woods would take 1,000 swings and run five miles every day.

d. If you're an *investor*, you read to stay up-to-date. Warren Buffett reads six hours a day to stay informed.

Being disciplined isn't exactly about being the best, but about being the most dedicated. You have to set goals for improvement and make discipline a lifestyle, not an occasional task. Discipline means these practices are a guaranteed part of your work habits, just like brushing your teeth is your habit of hygiene. You might not see the benefit of your daily work immediately, but the benefit will come if you are patient enough to work for it.

In the famous movie *Karate Kid,* a karate student named Daniel is being trained by a Karate master named Mr. Miyagi. Mr. Miyagi uses obscure hand motions from sanding and waxing the floor to teach Daniel how to defend himself in combat. Before Daniel understood how important the process was, he was extremely frustrated with the process and almost quit. His teacher knew that, at some point, it would all make sense. That's exactly what happened when Mr. Miyagi began to throw punches at him. Daniel was able to block every punch and kick.

The lesson here is that some of the activities you are doing might not have obvious value, but you have to stick with them anyway. Choose your activities and be consistent and diligent with them. It can be helpful to have a coach or mentor who understands your intended goal.

SELF-REFLECTION QUESTION:

Discipline is defined as the ability to do what you have decided, whether you feel like it or not. How disciplined are you in the following areas: financial, academic/professional, and health?

> **A** – You are disciplined 90 % of the time.
> **B** – You are disciplined 80% of the time
> **C** - You are disciplined 70% of the time
> **D** - You are disciplined 60% of the time
> **F** – You are very undisciplined.

Financial: Saving, spending, budgeting, and learning about money

Academic/Professional: Studying, preparing, and researching

_____

_____

Health: Food, exercise, and sleep

_____

_____

Review your past week, month, and year. How would your life have been different if you had been more disciplined?

_____

_____

What daily disciplines do you need to put in place to change your life? (Examples might be reading, exercising, or studying.)

_____

_____

CHAPTER 21

Character

If you take care of your character, your reputation will take care of itself.

BILL COSBY, BERNIE MADOFF, JOE Paterno: When I read these names, I can't help but think of people who could have gone down in history as successful people who lived great and impactful lives. Unfortunately, their legacies are permanently marred because of unethical things they did behind the scenes, leaving behind the emotional wreckage and many unanswered questions.

Each of these men had achieved success in their respective endeavors, but it was not good success. The foundation of all good success is *character*. Character is who you are when no one is looking. It is the sum total of your moral qualities, and it is the factor that determines what kind of effect you will have in the world. Character is about your moral firmness and your ability to stay strong and resolute so that you will do the right thing, regardless of the consequences.

Over the years, I've learned that every time you do something inconsistent with what you know to be right, you weaken your character, and that character is taken into every new situation you enter.

Almost a decade ago, I was arrested for a DUI (driving under the influence). Driving that night was probably was one of the dumbest choices

I've ever made. At the time of the arrest, I was on the board of trustees of my high school *alma mater*, the treasurer of a grassroots organization focused on community development, and a mentor to several young people. I had two choices: I could play the cover-up game or I could come clean with everyone I was accountable to. Covering up a stupid decision is very tempting, but I believe the long-term effects would have been detrimental. The right thing to do is usually the hardest. Coming clean might have tough consequences, but God determines the ultimate outcome.

To be honest, I was tempted to keep it to myself and never tell anyone. I thought about making it an issue where white officers wanted to arrest a black man, and some of that issue could have been—and most likely was— at play. But part of maturity is taking responsibility for your role in the situation. That's having character.

I tried to remember that, from everyone who has been given much, much will be demanded. (Luke 12:48, NIV) I have been blessed in my life in more ways than I can mention. Then I put myself in a position where I could have jeopardized my freedom, and even potentially put someone else's life at risk. I had let the people down who depended on me and looked up to me. So I chose to come clean.

As a result, contrary to my worst fears at the time, I was praised for my honesty and integrity. We live in a world where people are always covering up or twisting the truth to hide their mistakes—so much so that, when someone is honest, it's surprising and refreshing. I believe that our culture needs to shift from loving to see people "get caught" to loving to see people "come clean," because the truth is, no one is perfect. And once we all stop faking it, maybe we can give each other the safe space we need to change.

Now, I'm not suggesting that you go on social media and tell the world your deepest, darkest secrets or indiscretions. But you do need safe spaces where you can work through the issues in your life that are keeping you from being your best self with the utmost character and integrity. Here's the catch: The way of character has to be a way of *life*. If you are not going to commit to being the best possible person you can be in every moment, you might as well skip this chapter.

Cultivating character requires that you acknowledge the wrong ways of living and choose to change your life for the better (See Chapter 7). The way of character requires that you assess yourself and confront yourself wherever you fall short.

To change your life, you have to change your lifestyle. There's a spiritual teaching that says, "All things are permissible, but not everything is beneficial." (1 Corinthians 10:23, NIV) In other words, you may have the freedom to do anything morally permissible, but there are some things that are just not wise.

For me, drinking is one of those unwise choices. I have made a choice not to drink, not only because I got arrested, but because I knew it would not be wise for me in the long term. Something may be your right, but still not be the most constructive thing to do. The question we have to ask ourselves is not whether something is good or bad, but whether it's better or best.

Remember that everything matters when it comes to character. When you think about how the little things impact the big things, you'll begin to conclude that there are no little things. Leaders and successful people understand that, on the road to building a strong character, every element is important.

Maybe you don't like the kind of man or woman you have become. The good news is, you can change. Here are some questions to help search for cracks in your character, so that you can assess and, if need be, confront yourself.

Which parts of your character do you need to address?

Are you *judgmental and critical* of others, or are you someone who provides constructive feedback? **Note**: "Let the one who has never sinned throw the first stone!" (John 8:7, NLT) It is very easy to judge another person's weakness by your strength in that area. But we are all weak in some area of our life.

Do you *gossip* about other people, or do you keep confidences shared with you? The definition of gossip is bearing bad news behind someone's back. **Note:** "A gossip betrays a confidence; so avoid anyone who talks too much." Proverbs 20:19, NIV

Are you *lazy*, or do you spend time working on activities that can benefit you and the community? **Note:** "Lazy hands make for poverty, but diligent hands bring wealth." Proverbs 10:4, NIV

Do you *hold onto grudges* and find ways to get revenge on others, or do you forgive others and gain wisdom from the experience? **Note:** "Get rid of all bitterness, rage and anger, brawling and slander, along with every form of malice. Be kind and compassionate to one another, forgiving each other, just as in Christ God forgave you." Ephesian 4:31-32, NIV

Do you have any *unhealthy habits* or addictions that you need to stop? An addiction is meeting a legitimate need in an illegitimate way. It's only an addiction if you cannot stop. Have you found ways to get help in dealing with your issues, such as attending a support group or seeing a counselor? **Note:** "You say, 'I am allowed to do anything'—but not everything is good for you. And even though 'I am allowed to do anything,' I must not become a slave to anything." 1 Corinthians 6:12, NLT

Do you maintain a positive environment? Do you listen to music, watch movies or shows, or visit websites that offer *mostly negative* content? You become what you think about. Garbage in, garbage out. Do you spend too much time with information that will not help you to be wiser, more thoughtful, or better as a person? **Note:** "Summing it all up, friends, I'd say you'll do best by filling your minds and meditating on things true, noble, reputable, authentic, compelling, gracious—the best, not the worst; the beautiful, not the ugly; things to praise, not things to curse. Put into practice what you learned from me, what you heard and saw and realized. Do that, and God, who makes everything work together, will work you into his most excellent harmonies." Philippians 4:8-9, MSG

Do you set a good example? What kind of place would this world be if everybody in it was *just like you*? What if everyone worked like you or served like you or thought like you or forgave like you? Would the world be better or worse as a result? **Note:** Always let others see you behaving properly, even though they may still accuse you of doing wrong. Then on the day of judgment, they will honor God by telling the good things they saw you do. 1 Peter 2:12, CEV

Do you *keep your word*? Can people count on you to follow through on what you say, or do you talk about many things you will do without following through? **Note:** "Like clouds and wind without rain is one who boasts of gifts never given." Proverbs 25:14, NIV

Let this be a time when you can be honest with yourself. What's done in the dark will always come to the light. At the end of the day, the smartest thing to do is the right thing, especially at the beginning. It can be hard to confront your own hypocrisy. Bring it into the light, while the consequences of a poor character are minimal. The longer cracks in your character go unaddressed, the deeper and more destructive they get with time. This doesn't need to be something you share with everyone you know, but finding a safe and trusted friend or counselor may be helpful (See Chapter 33 on Boundaries and Safe People).

Use this self-reflection as a tool. Begin to ask yourself the hard questions about your character before it adversely affects your life and the lives of others. As a leader, you want to not only start well, but also finish well. One of the end goals for everyone's life is to be free of scandal, particularly in three areas: power, money, and sex. These are big areas of temptation that can derail anyone from doing great things.

I believe everyone needs to be acquainted with their moral weakness and put boundaries in place to protect them from themselves. Those who try to rush themselves on the journey to success might be doing a disservice to their calling, because they may be ready for the success they achieve but not the temptation that will come with that success. Your own strength and capabilities can become dangerous when they are used without reflection.

Meditation on your purpose is important, so your actions will be rooted and centered in a good mental and emotional space. To build character, we must devote time to acquiring knowledge and discipline, and then apply it to our lives—both public and private. Not everyone is going to have the same level of talent, but we can all choose to have consistency of character. If you are to strengthen your character, reflection must be part of your daily regimen.

Chapter 22

Environment

Do not be misled: Bad company corrupts good character.
1 Corinthians 15:33, NIV

PERSONAL DEVELOPMENT IS DIFFICULT TO sustain without a healthy environment. When your environment improves, or you find your way into a better environment, things will change for the better.

Your expectations for yourself and others change as you are exposed to new information. You'll find that when your environment changes, you will begin to see changes in how you feel, how you see things, and how you see yourself. These changes will affect how you perform. Think of your life like a plant. It's difficult for a seed to grow into a strong plant if the soil is contaminated.

I was born in Newark, New Jersey. I lived there until I was about sixteen years old, when my parents decided that it was time to move to a safer neighborhood where we would not be exposed to the gangs, violence, drug dealers, and addicts that were right in front of our doorstep. Sadly, for me, I had already grown accustomed to this environment. I felt bad leaving—as if I was betraying the friends I'd grown up with. But sometimes you have to leave in order learn. You can get better and come back to influence and help others in your old environment, because your healing is tied in with theirs.

That's what happened with George Jenkins, Sampson Davis, and Rameck Hunt. They are three doctors born and raised in Newark, New Jersey. Like me, they experienced the negative side of Newark. But unlike me, they had a great challenge: all three had grown up without fathers.

Jenkins, Davis, and Hunt grew up in public housing and came from low-income families. They first met at University High School, where they made a pact to get through college and medical school successfully, which they did. They attended the pre-medicine/pre-dental course at Seton Hall University on a scholarship program. All three are now serving their communities in different capacities. They wrote a book called *The Pact* chronicling their experiences growing up.

I can identify with this story. I've been in the corporate world for the last decade. I managed to do fairly well, but that would not have been possible without great programs like the Newark Youth Leadership Project.

This program gave me a great start. I was able to grow as a man and a leader, and I learned how to start my vocational journey: how to interview, complete a resume, tie a necktie, and speak in public, as well as a whole host of other skills that are paying dividends until this day. My mentors couldn't get mad at me for not knowing what I didn't know, but they couldn't let me off the hook, either. So what was left for them to do? They had to teach, support, encourage, and hold me accountable. This is the power of environment.

Environment lays a foundation for vision. It sets expectations and teaches you a value system. Many organizations serve the purpose of providing young people with the tools that they need to bridge the gaps in their vocational training and overall well-being. Most high schools, colleges, and universities should have systems in place to help you on your journey, if you want to know where to start. Here are a few other organizations to consider"

Boys and Girls Club of America – www.bgca.org
Mission: To enable all young people, especially those who need us most, to reach their full potential as productive, caring, responsible citizens.

Big Brother Big Sisters of America – www.bbbs.org
Mission: Big Brothers Big Sisters helps children realize their potential and build their futures. We nurture children and strengthen communities.

INROADS Organization – www.inroads.org
Mission: To take talented minority youth and place them in business and industry, to prepare them for corporate and community leadership.

I know many people who stay in environments where people are tearing them down by being pessimistic and abusive. If you are in an environment like that, or one that you know is not right for you, have the courage today to either remove yourself or do everything within your power to change it. Bad company will ultimately corrupt good character. Choose your environment wisely, as if choosing a greenhouse for a flower. Contact with the right elements is necessary for growth. Contact with the wrong elements does more damage.

Focus is contagious, but so is a lack of focus. Good ethics are contagious, but so is low character. Work ethic is contagious, but so is laziness. Emotional health is contagious, but so is emotional struggle.

Your environment should be one that respects your individuality; has core values that are reinforced and personally resonate with you; offers you high expectations that push you in a healthy way; gives you the motivation and tools to successfully live out your values; and has safe people you can trust.

Don't try to *fit in*. Try to *belong*. Fitting in requires that you change who you are to be accepted. Belonging requires that you be who you really are. Have the courage to find a place where you belong. Warning: No club, team, organization, or group of friends is going to be perfect. What you want to look for in any environment is *integrity*. Integrity means that the environment you're in lives up to the values that it claims. They don't have to be perfect in achieving those values, but they must demonstrate a commitment to their values.

In such an environment, the seeds you plant will bear forth beautiful fruits.

CHAPTER 23

Decisions

Sometimes we make decisions in life. Sometimes decisions make us.

IN MY LIFE, I CAN trace most of my failures and regrets to my ignorance about how to make good decisions. I want to give you a framework for making good decisions that I've learned over the years.

Some decisions in life are so monumental and destiny-shaping that you'll need a great deal of due diligence and preparation. The sooner you prepare, the better off you'll be. Examples of major decisions you will make over the course of your life include:

- Choosing a major in college
- Deciding on a new career
- Deciding where you will live.
- Starting a business and choosing the right industry
- Making a big purchase, like a car or a house.

Here's a framework that includes the vital steps of a decision-making process. To make it memorable, let's use the acronym SCORE.

1) **Study**: Do your research and obtain as much information as possible.

Nothing is worse than activity without insight. As a rule, the weightier and bigger the decision, the more time and effort you'll need for preparation and information-gathering. Some decisions are so important that you'll want to make them with as much certainty as possible. You might not be able to do all that you find, but at least find out all you can do. Here is a list of questions to help spark a few ideas about how to research:

- What books can you read?
- Which conferences or workshops can you attend to learn about the area of your decision?
- Which counselors or experts in the areas of your decision can you consult?
- Who is on your advisory team to help you work through the decision?

Note: Be careful who you allow to participate on this team. Be sure that the people you choose have your best interest at heart, have a track record of making quality and healthy choices, and are honest about the limits of their knowledge.

This step will help you think through all the information, so you have more ammunition for making a wise choice. It's not how much you *know* but how much you *ask* that arms you with the tools for decision-making. As a rule, try not to take a "leap of faith" when you can arm yourself with reliable information instead.

2) **Clear the way**: Get really clear on the decision to be made and remove any hurdles.

I believe that it's best to make big decisions when you are at your best emotionally. *Never* make a major life decision when you feel pressured, frustrated, angry, tired, fearful, or rushed.

Some of the worst decisions I've ever made were made in a state of fear, fatigue, and pressure when I had no time to process my thoughts and feelings. Remember, you are responsible for your life. Don't let anyone manipulate or force you to do something that you're not sure is right for you. Take some time to get away to sort out your thoughts, if you have to. If possible, enlist the help of a trusted and wise friend who can serve as a sounding board.

Both your head and your heart should come into play when making a major life decision. You need to look at the facts, but don't discount the feelings. We shouldn't be led by our feelings alone, but we shouldn't dismiss them, either. Your feelings about a particular decision can give you important information.

In 1977, a movie producer with some success had a big movie idea, but he didn't like the fact that the movie studio would have the final editing rights. Contrary to the popular advice within the movie industry at the time, he decided to take a pay cut to retain creative control. Instead of earning $500,000 or $1 million—which he could have gotten because of his early success—he accepted only the original director's fee of $150,000 along with merchandising rights, sequel rights, and most importantly, the ability to make the movie (and potential sequels) the way he wanted to.

That movie was *Star Wars*. George Lucas didn't let the lure of a big paycheck keep him from what he intrinsically knew was right, because for Lucas, it wasn't about money. It was about serving the work in the way that honored his vision. He was willing to bet on himself. Of course, Lucas's attorney disagreed with him vehemently—but he couldn't persuade Lucas to ignore his gut feeling.

Scientists who study the brain's function in decision-making say the best decisions take into account facts, statistics, and data analysis—but also life wisdom that can be felt in your body, specifically your gastrointestinal tract (your "gut"). The gut feeling can be valuable in the decision-making process. Sometimes, what your body "knows" can make you override the conventional wisdom of your brain.

George Lucas took a risk because it was consistent with what he inherently knew was right. Part of roadwork is knowing your values and knowing what really matters to you. I believe that having a strong sense of your values is the most important part of making key life decisions, and many people lack this in our culture. Go back to Chapter 3 to complete the values exercise, if you have not. Sometimes you have to go with the grain, but other times, it's best to go against it. Sometimes you have to follow conventional wisdom, but other times, you have to disregard it. This is part of the roadwork required in making major life choices.

3) **Know your options**: List your options and envision the future outcomes of each choice. After you have gone through the study and the clearing parts of this process, write down the options available to you. Complete a cost/benefit analysis. Here are a few basic questions to get you started:

- What are the options available to you?
- What are the pros/benefits of each choice?
- What are the cons/disadvantages of each choice?

Take some time to meditate on which choice is best. Remember, you want to look at both the hard data and the intangible internals. Keep your head *and* your heart involved in narrowing down your options, which is the next step. It's a good idea to journal your thoughts and feelings, or to sit with a counselor or coach as you think through your options.

Silence and solitude can also be useful. Silence is being absent to the external and internal voices, to discern which choice is best for you. Solitude is being absent to people and things. You might want to do many things, but the real question is, what are you *called* to do? Whatever you decide, you must stay true to yourself.

4) **Rank your choices**: Decide which choice is best, based on your value system (Chapter 3), and rank each of the other choices from best to worst. Is one option revealing itself as the one you should choose? When in doubt, go back and walk through the earlier steps in this process until you begin to get more clarity and confidence. The best solution might not appear immediately. Keep studying, clearing the way, and listing your options. Trust the process. If you do the work, the best answer will emerge.

5) **Evaluate:** Use hindsight to learn the lessons and keep moving forward.

When you ultimately make an important decision, it's not usual to experience regrets. If you have completed the process of studying, clearing the way, and listing options, you should have confidence in your choice— but regret is also common when the ultimate outcome is unknown. No process is perfect, and there will always be a level of risk and uncertainty in decision-making. Just making a choice doesn't guarantee that you've made the best choice.

The goal in this chapter is to provide you with a framework for decision-making and encourage you to do your due diligence with any decision you have to make. I want to invite you to reflect on all the destiny-shaping decisions you've made in your life up until this point. Please be honest with yourself about whether you went through a process like this and what lessons you learned.

Take some time to write down these lessons and what you would have done differently or what additional lessons served to help you in your decision-making process. What have you learned that can be useful to you now?

Jonathan Frejuste

CHAPTER 24

10,000 hours

Do you see someone skilled in their work? They will serve before kings; they will not serve before officials of low rank. Proverbs 22:29, NIV

A BOY AND HIS MOTHER used to walk past a piano shop in their small town every day after school. The shop owner played the piano loudly enough to be heard in the street. The boy was never allowed stop and listen because his mother had to rush him home so she could get back to work.

The little boy loved to hear the beautiful piano music. He longed to meet the person who played the piano and talk to him, in the hopes that he could learn how to play just like that. One day, the little boy pulled away from his mother and darted into the piano shop, running up to the man who sat playing the piano. The man turned very slowly. The boy was surprised to see that the man looked very old. The boy blurted out, "I've walked past this shop a lot, and I've always wanted to come see you play."

The man chuckled.

"I want to learn how to play, just like you," the boy said. "I would give my life to learn how to play like you."

The man replied, "I have given my life to play like me."

The story helps explain what talented people had to do to reach a high level of expertise in their field. Great coaches know that to become an expert at your craft, you have to put in "10,000 hours" of deliberate practice. Swedish psychologist K. Anders Ericsson's research concluded that was the approximate time it takes.

Deliberate practice is not about accomplishing a task using skills you already possess. It's not about *play*, which is partaking in an activity for the sake of enjoying the activity itself. Deliberate practice has the goal of improvement—becoming better at your talent. It requires total focus and is designed to stretch you. The great news is, if you want to improve and you have the ability to practice in some capacity, it's never too early or too late to start.

The story of the boy and the piano shop owner is encouraging because it shows that becoming truly skilled at something is not a miracle. It can be replicated. It takes hard work and deliberate practice. Your goal should be to reach this 10,000-hour mark of deliberate practice. If someone else accomplished this, you can do it, too—as long as you're willing to put in the work.

Sticking with a project through the first 10,000 hours requires persistence that is rooted in your love of your craft. I love seeing chefs in love with making great food, pilots in love with flying, teachers in love with teaching, and dentists in love with dentistry. People who are obsessed with being great at their craft can teach the world a great deal about the power of tenacity, persistence, and excellence.

Here are a few examples of great people who were in love with their craft enough to spend 10,000-plus hours working at it, and what we can learn from their journeys:

1. **Tiger Woods**, the legendary golfer, has been playing golf since he was two years old and began winning tournaments at an early age. He was motivated by his father's practice, but his family never forced him to play. Tiger Woods was self-motivated to do what he saw his father do. He is especially respected in sports because of his work ethic. Every day, Tiger wakes up at five a.m.,

throws his running shoes on, and jogs throughout his neighborhood. He goes to the gym three times a week to lift weights. He hits 1,000 golf balls at the club … EVERY DAY. This is how Tiger reached his 10,000-hour practice mark, which led to his subsequent achievements.

2. **Kobe Bryant** was a legendary basketball player until his death in a plane crash in 2020. Players throughout the league were afraid to compete against him because of his fierceness on the court. The players closest to him have said that he would call trainers up at four a.m. and ask them to meet him at the gym, to help him work on his shots. By the time the trainer arrived at the gym, Kobe was already there, drenched in sweat. The trainer would work with Kobe for about two hours and then leave, returning later that day to find Kobe just finishing up making 800 shots for a SCRIMMAGE! That was how Kobe got to his 10,000 hours.

3. When **Bill Gates** was a 13-year-old eighth grader, he joined a school computer club that gave him access to a time-sharing computer with a direct link to a mainframe computer in downtown Seattle. His interest in the computer turned into an obsession. He skipped athletics and worked every night, from eighth grade through high school, on computers. Some people will say that, without that work, he would not have achieved everything he did. I agree. He took advantage of the opportunity of a lifetime—but he still had to WORK.

What opportunities do you have in front of you that you're not taking advantage of? Are you wasting your 10,000 hours watching TV, text messaging, or doing things that won't benefit your future?

Great opportunities are not rare, but distractions can keep you from noticing them. Make up your mind today to stop doing things that detract from your future. Spend that time and energy focusing on improving your skills.

Four Keys to Practicing for 10,000 Hours

Let's discuss some things you can do to start your own journey to accumulating 10,000 hours of deliberate practice. This exercise can be done with a coach.

1. Deliberate practice needs to be highly personalized.
Your practice should be unique to your needs. Your personal plan for improvement will require in-depth knowledge of your talents, and it helps to have an experienced and perceptive teacher or coach. Find the exercises that will help you turn your talents into strengths. Be honest in your understanding of where you are in your proficiency of your craft and know where you should focus on improving.

2. Practice should push you just beyond your comfort zone.
You don't need to take huge leaps outside of your comfort zone to grow—just small steps. People who reach high levels of success find pleasure and satisfaction in small improvements. Work hard to find the enjoyment in being even a little bit better than you were before. Then it will be easier to give your gift time to mature.

3. Deliberate practice must be repeated at high volumes. Practice makes perfect. As you practice, your brain creates what is called "muscle memory." Anyone who's great has developed the circuitry in their brain that will allow them to excel in those well-practiced areas. Make it a point today to practice at a high volume so that you can build your circuitry.

4. Practice requires coaching and continual, specific feedback.
For your practice to be effective, you'll need feedback. If you don't see greatness in the rehearsal, you will not see it in the recital. It's hard to improve if you don't know how you're doing. You might need an expert coach or teacher to point out how you're doing. You might want to record yourself to see how you're performing relative to where you want to be. If you're learning some form of cognitive work, you'll need a benchmark or standard by which you can measure your performance.

Reflection Questions
Which hobbies, activities, or crafts would you say that you have a strong liking—or even a love—for?

_____

_____

What activities, projects, and exercises can you design for yourself to further your growth?

_____

_____

Who in your life could serve as a coach or teacher to help you improve?

_____

_____

You'll need to commit time to reach your 10,000 hours. To give you a sense of the time required:

- If you spend **two hours a day** working on your craft, you will hit your 10,000 hours in about fourteen years.

- If you spend **three hours a day** working on your craft, you will hit your 10,000 hours in about nine years.

- If you spend **four hours a day** working on your craft, you will hit your 10,000 hours in about seven years.

- If you spend **five hours a day** working on your craft, you will hit your 10,000 hours in about 5.5 years.

- If you spend **six hours a day** working on your craft, you will hit your 10,000 hours in about 4.5 years.

How many hours a day are you willing to commit to reaching the 10,000 hours you'll need to become great at your craft or profession? What could you spend less time doing, so that you'll have time to acquire those 10,000 hours?

CHAPTER 25

Habits and Systems

All of us are self-made, but only the successful will admit it.

A MAN WAS WALKING AND talking with his son. He asked his son, "Do you want to be successful?"

The son said, "Yes, dad."

They kept walking. The father stopped, looked him in the eye and said, "Do you *expect* to be successful?"

The son said, "I do."

The father sighed. "Given the fact that you decided not to go to college to further your education ... and you are very talented, but you are behind on your dreams and your bills ... based on your performance and what you've produced at this point in your life ... do you expect to be successful?"

The son said nothing.

After a time of silence, the father told the son, "Your wants and desires show up in your conversation. But your expectation shows up in your behavior. Ultimately, I can tell what you really want by what you are willing to do."

You can tell what someone expects to get out of life by what they do on a consistent basis. Whether you achieve your goals and live the life you want to live will largely be determined by the systems and habits you use. It's easy to push yourself hard when a goal is right in sight, but it can be hard to persevere during the long stretches in between.

I can recall different points in my life when things would be going well for me and I would reach the goals that I set for myself, either physically or financially or academically. It was a great feeling. But then I would stop doing those things that had brought me success, and all the progress I'd made would begin to disappear.

After reflecting on these ups and downs, I realized that my success and progress weren't due to good luck and that my failures weren't bad luck. The habits and systems that I had incorporated in my life had helped me to get ahead. Those same habits will help me sustain everything that I want to keep a reality in my life—and letting those habits slip will make my successes fade away. Realizing that my habits and practices could make or break my success was a major turning point for me.

Tony Dungy, the two-time Super Bowl winning NFL coach, knows about habits. He served as head coach of the Tampa Bay Buccaneers from 1996 to 2001. Dungy believed the best way to help the Buccaneers win was by changing the players' habits. It took a year to turn the team around using the philosophy that great habits determine victory. In Dungy's second season as coach, the team won the first five games and went to the playoffs for the first time in fifteen years.

The Buccaneers made it to the playoffs in 2001, but in critical moments, the team fell apart. They kept losing in big games. Coach Dungy could see what had happened. The players would try to do more than they were trained to do, or they would go back to old ways that they thought worked. They failed to understand that they had to maintain the system that had brought them success, or failure would follow.

This is an example of what happens when you don't stay committed to systems and habits that are tried and true. These systems and habits have been proven to work. If you work with them, things will improve.

When you run into obstacles, it's easy to abandon the system—but don't let the temptation lead you astray.

I'll list a few systems or habits that have helped people:

1. **Financial Stability** – Dave Ramsey's Financial Peace University (www.daveramsey.com) has helped millions of people get out of debt and stay out of debt. Many of us have our own philosophies on money management that DO NOT work, yet we refuse to change. Ramsey's system works. If you want to change your financial life, this system will help you. Also, see Chapter 14: Money.

2. **Sobriety** - Alcoholics Anonymous (www.aa.org) – This mutual aid fellowship was founded by Bill Wilson and Bob Smith in 1935. The primary purpose of the fellowship is to help former alcoholics stay sober and to help alcoholics achieve sobriety. I've known several people who have been regular members of AA for years, and I believe it's an effective system. People who have fully engaged in the process can achieve and maintain sobriety.

3. **Physical Health** – If you want to be physically healthier, there are a number of habit patterns that have been proven to work. You'll need to plan and prepare meals in advance, to avoid buying unhealthy fast food. You'll budget time to go to the gym several times a week. Drinking enough water, getting plenty of sleep, and staying away from processed foods can become habits that help you regain and maintain a healthy body.

I could mention other programs, but at this point, I hope you understand. Engaging in habit patterns and systems will help you get to the place that you want to be in your personal life, finances, your profession, or any other area. Others have discovered and proven effective ways to reach your goal. If you trust the process, eventually, you'll reach a high point.

Be careful. Sometimes after success, complacency sets in. Don't say, "I've worked hard and I've been disciplined. I deserve a break." That is a trap. Some of the things you did to achieve your goal will be the same things you'll need to do to maintain the place you reached. If you trust the proven habits, you can build on your successes instead of backsliding.

The quality of their rituals is what makes great people great. Their daily habits ensure that, when they need to perform, they are ready mentally, emotionally, and physically. The same applies to other areas of life. Whether you are an artist, teacher, lawyer, accountant, speaker, or student, certain habit patterns will help you shape your identity and stay on top of your game.

Often, people do not decide their futures. They decide their habits—and their habits decide their future.

Here are few tips that I recommend to everyone:

1. **Develop a morning ritual**. Identify those practices that you need to implement each morning to get your day started off right. It might include exercise, reading devotionals, listening to motivational tapes, or taking time to work before the day gets busy.

2. **Choose your routine**. Identify the habits you need to be the best at your profession. Your life is unique, and your habits must be tailor-made for that life. Will additional weekly or monthly reading help you most? Will attending professional development workshops or getting additional certifications be useful?

3. **Find a system**. Choose systems that are tried and true and have proven track records of success.

4. **Make changes gradually.** Make one small choice at a time, and keep at it until it becomes second nature.

In the next section, write down your current habits in three areas:

Financial: Saving, spending, budgeting, and learning about money

_____

_____

_____

_____

Academic/Professional: Studying, preparing, and researching

_____

_____

_____

_____

Health: Food, exercise, and sleep

_____

_____

_____

_____

CHAPTER 26

Problem Solving

"When you pray for rain, you have to deal with the mud."
Denzel Washington

FOR SOME PEOPLE, PLANNING AND problem solving comes naturally. If you are this kind of person, please be gracious to me as I lay out things that you may already know. Many natural problem-solvers rise to leadership roles because they easily find solutions, and others look to them for guidance. Others who have the ability to solve problems are not given guidance and instruction on the framework to solve a problem, so they fail to develop this skill. The good news is that problem solving is something you can learn.

Often, people spend more time being overwhelmed by a problem than working on solving it. They spend time expressing frustrations or worries about a problem, but never really deal with it. Excessive venting and complaining can actually make the problem seem bigger than a solution!

If we are to be effective in solving problems, we need to learn how to deal with them in a systematic and thorough way—from the most basic level to the most complex level. Our progress in life is largely determined by our ability to solve problems that arise.

Below you will see a list of steps you can take to deal with problems, and points to consider with each step.

1. Understand the problem and cause.
2. Generate and evaluate alternatives.
3. Choose the best option.
4. Implement the chosen option.
5. Reassess the problem.

UNDERSTAND THE PROBLEM AND CAUSE

To solve a problem, you have to accept it as it is and understand its cause as realistically as you can. Positive thinking is great, but if we're not careful, it can easily turn into the denial of reality. Resolve in advance to face the reality of a difficult situation, no matter how hard that might be. You'll be better for it.

Do everything you can to understand the issue you're facing. Just as you wouldn't be confident in a doctor's prescription if you did not trust her diagnosis, the key to good judgment in problem solving is first understanding the problem and its cause. Take the time to assess every aspect of the problem. It might help to explain your interpretation of the problem to at least two people, one who is connected closely to the problem and one who is a neutral third party, so you can get multiple perspectives. This step alone will help you focus. Accurate diagnosis is half the cure.

Depending on the complexity of the problem, you might need to consult with others who have more skill or experience assessing problems in this area. Speed rarely leads to careful thinking, so take your time.

GENERATE AND EVALUATE ALTERNATIVES

Now it's time to come up with alternatives. "Mind storming" is a great technique for creative problem solving. Its power comes from its simplicity. Take a sheet of paper and write your most pressing problem in the form of a question. The more specific the question, the better. You can do it on your own or with a group.

Now come up with a minimum of 20 answers. As you come up with the answers, ask yourself—what do you need to do more of and what do you need to do less of? The 20th answer might require the hardest work, but that could be the breakthrough answer. Don't worry about quality, just quantity. Loosen up and start making suggestions.

Next, evaluate these choices. Which choice is best on the basis of impact, costs, resources, and timing? Go the extra mile to ensure you have the reliable information you need to make a good choice. At the root of many failures lie false assumptions.

Pay attention to how each potential solution *feels* to you. Both intuition and logic are important. Intuition is about hunches and impressions. Logic involves using reasoning with a full view of reality. When you use both tools, you'll find a sense of clarity and resoluteness.

CHOOSE THE BEST OPTION

Eventually, you'll need to make a choice. Your confidence in the right choice will come from the knowledge that you are taking action based on information you gathered and going through an analytical process—either alone or with a team. You cannot predict whether anything will be 100% successful, but if you've worked through the first two steps thoroughly, you can be sure you've done all you can to mitigate the risks and move forward with confidence.

IMPLEMENT THE CHOSEN OPTION

The hard part of choosing an option is now done. Implement your decision with resolution, diligence, and follow-through. Once you've settled on an option, resist the temptation to get bogged down with the thoughts of going back and changing your mind. Give the chosen option a chance to work. You might have to make adjustments, but stay faithful to your choice.

One of the biggest obstacles to problem solving is indecision. Once you've gathered the reliable information and have made a choice, focus on the implementation and fight against indecision. Before you consider going back, consult Chapter 23 (Decision Making) for guidance on how to make a quality decision.

REASSESS THE PROBLEM

Has your problem been solved? If so, great! If not, start over. Take some time to write down the lessons learned over the course of this process, so you can become a better problem solver going forward.

TIPS FOR SOLVING PROBLEMS

1. **Set deadlines**. For complex issues, create a deadline for each stage of the problem-solving process. Deadlines help keep you efficient and less likely to put off a tough decision.

2. **Know your learning style**. Know your dominant learning or thinking style, and try other styles as well.

    a. **Auditory thinker/learner**: They need to *hear* ideas, discussions, sounds, or music. They might say, "That sounds good to me." Dialogue is helpful for an auditory thinker.

    b. **Kinesthetic thinker/learner**: They are more attuned to their feelings or emotions. They like to move around instead of sitting still during a conversation. They need to get a *feeling* for the problem or situation. They might say, "That feels right to me." They should move while thinking through a problem.

    c. **Visual thinker/learner**: They think in terms of pictures and written words. They might say, "I see what you mean."

Graphs and diagrams are a good way for a visual thinker to get insights or understand a problem in greater depth.

Try all of these styles when working to solve a problem and identify your dominant style. The more you can use all three thinking styles, the better your results will be. Also, learning the dominant thinking style other people use can help tremendously when collaborating with others.

3. **Plan ahead**. The more you plan and think ahead, anticipating problems, the more possibilities you have for success.

4. **Welcome challenges**. Think of problems as challenges or opportunities. If you frame a problem as a situation that might make you better or give you an edge, you can attack the problem with certainty and resolution. As the Scripture in James 1:2 (MSG) says, "Consider it a sheer gift, friends, when tests and challenges come at you from all sides. You know that under pressure, your faith-life is forced into the open and shows its true colors. So don't try to get out of anything prematurely. Let it do its work, so you become mature and well-developed, not deficient in any way."

What major problem or problems are you facing now or in the near future? Choose one and take some time and go through the steps below.

Problem and cause
Possible alternatives
Best option
Steps to implement
Reassessment

CHAPTER 27

Obstacles

Dear brothers and sisters, when troubles of any kind come your way, consider it an opportunity for great joy. For you know that when your faith is tested, your endurance has a chance to grow. So let it grow, for when your endurance is fully developed, you will be perfect and complete, needing nothing. James 1:2-4, NLT

RUBIN "HURRICANE" CARTER, A TOP black boxer at the height of his career, was wrongfully convicted of homicide in 1966. He was sentenced to three consecutive life terms. Although he reported to prison, Hurricane refused to surrender the freedoms that were innately his: his choices, beliefs, and attitude. He knew he would be freed at some point.

Instead of breaking down behind bars, he reaffirmed that he had choices. He would not let his anger rob him of perspective. He spent every available moment reading law and philosophy books, toughening his mind, and working on his case.

After 19 years and two trials, he overcame the verdict and was freed from prison in 1985. He took no action against the state, refusing to acknowledge that he'd been in prison and needed help. He had never let adversity control his thoughts or beliefs. His lack of power didn't make him powerless. In fact, the adversity made him tougher.

This story, though uncommon, offers many lessons that we can apply to the obstacles and difficulties that we will inevitably encounter in life as we pursue our goals and dreams. Each of us is bound to face money problems, relationship misunderstandings, issues at work, personal failures, etc. It's not wrong to wish that difficult and painful situations would end. It's wrong to avoid, deny, or blame your way out of dealing with those situations.

How you deal with and confront your obstacles will have a lot to do with how your future turns out. Your greatness will be measured to the degree that you can handle adversity without becoming discouraged to the point of ineffectiveness. You can't control the circumstances in the world, but you *can* control how you respond.

To be someone who accomplishes his or her goals, you need to decide in advance that you will not only fight through the pain and adversity that you experience on your journey in life, but you'll also use those obstacles to increase your resolve and wisdom. Remember that everything you go through in life is a chance to improve your character and practice a virtue or skill like resilience, forgiveness, flexibility, optimism, reality testing, assertiveness, independence, or teamwork. Far too many people go through painful situations and experiences mining them for the wealth of the lessons.

External factors might influence your path, but never let it influence your direction. Here are a couple of things to consider.

WAYS TO COPE WITH OBSTACLES AND ADVERSITY
Avoid negative self-talk. What you say *to* and *about* yourself during and after a tough moment determines how you get through it and what you get from it. Do yourself a favor by overriding negative self-talk with *reframing* talk. Here's a piece of advice from the good book:

Summing it all up, friends, I'd say you'll do best by filling your minds and medi-tating on things true, noble, reputable, authentic, compelling, gracious—the best, not the worst; the beautiful, not the ugly; things to praise, not things to curse.

Philippians 4:8, MSG

I incorporate this passage in my life through listening to powerful inspirational clips from sermons or motivational talks, watching uplifting movies, or keeping a set of quotes nearby that help give me perspective and provide me with wisdom to navigate through tough situations. Words pick me up when I'm down.

One of the ways of dealing with negative self-talk, especially when you begin believing things you have no evidence for, is the STOP technique. STOP is a tool that can be used to change how you look at any situation you're dealing with or gain perspective on a matter, instead of allowing your feelings to get the best of you.

Here's a simple example:

S – Situation
You are laid off from your job.

T – Thoughts and feelings
You believe that your future is ruined. You will never be of any use to anyone and can never go back to the market to bring value. People are probably laughing at you.

O – Outcome
You feel embarrassed, full of shame, and fearful about the future.

P – Personal Debate
You knew the company was having a hard time financially. You were aware that layoffs were possible. This might actually prove to be a blessing in disguise, because you did want a change in career. Now, the opportunity

is here. Sure, it's hard emotionally, but change is always uncomfortable. If you stop and learn the lessons, you can turn this situation around.

Exercise: Use this tool to evaluate any situation that you are facing, to ensure that your thinking is healthy.

S – Situation

T - Thoughts and feelings

O – Outcome

P – Personal debate

Cultivate optimism. Don't be pessimistic about the future. Greatness is not just about overcoming obstacles; it's also about not "crying over spilled milk" and sinking into a state of pessimistic thinking. Here are the three voices of pessimism:

- "Things will *never change*."
- "Everything in my life will *go wrong* now."
- "It's all *my fault*."

If you find yourself thinking like this, make a conscious decision to start thinking new thoughts.

"Tough times don't last, but tough people do."

"How you see the problem *is* the problem."

"The winds of adversity fill the sails of success."

"Although the world is full of suffering, it is also full of the overcoming of it."

Don't blame others. Taking responsibility for what you can control gives you back your power. Are you using blame to avoid taking responsibility? Here are six signs that you might be:

> 1. **"I'm unlucky."** You feel you have been dealt a "bad hand" in life.
>
> 2. **"I'm powerless."** You don't think you can change anything in your life for the better.
>
> 3. **"I can't fix this."** You view negative occurrences and relationships in your life as being out of your control.
>
> 4. **"I'm right about this!"** You rarely think you are wrong.
>
> 5. **"I'm not sorry."** You believe apologizing is a sign of weakness.
>
> 6. **"I remember ..."** You dwell on the past instead of looking to the future.

Embrace discomfort. On the road to pursuing your calling, you're likely to encounter seasons of discomfort. Clear the fog by clarifying your values, setting goals, and calculating how much longer you'll have to endure pain and difficulty before you reach your goal. Knowing the purpose of your pain and how much farther you have to go allows you to tolerate the discomfort. Go back to Chapters 3,12,15,16, and 17 and review the exercises.

Look to your heroes. Study the examples of people who overcame adversity. So many names come to mind, but some of my personal favorites are Nelson Mandela, Malcolm X, and Martin Luther King, Jr. Read biographies of these individuals. These books are available at www.amazon.com:

- *The Autobiography of Malcolm X: As Told to Alex Haley* by Malcolm X and Alex Haley

- *Long Walk to Freedom: The Autobiography of Nelson Mandela* by Nelson Mandela

- *The Autobiography of Martin Luther King, Jr.* by Claiborne Carson

Consider your history. Reflect on a time when you had a personal challenge or obstacle (financial, relationship, career, academic, etc.) in your life. On a scale of one to ten, how would you rate the way you handled the obstacle? What could you have done better? How could you prepare to make it easier to deal with the next challenge or obstacle?

CHAPTER 28

Failure

Sometimes, rejection is just redirection.

THE GREATEST LOS ANGELES LAKER, Kobe Bryant, retired in the 2016 – 2017 season. His career had included 33,643 points, eighteen All-Star appearances, and five NBA championships. His last game was a 60-point performance against the Utah Jazz.

Those who played with Kobe say that his greatest quality was his work ethic—and his most unusual quality was his tremendous work ethic *post-failure*. I will always remember one of the most important moments in his early career.

The Lakers made it to the playoffs in Kobe Bryant's rookie year. In Game 5 of the playoffs, the Lakers were playing the Utah Jazz, who led the series 3 -1. The game came down to the wire, tied at 89-89 with ten seconds left in the fourth quarter.

Kobe came down with the ball, drove to the foul line, pulled up and … AIRBALL! The shot completely missed the basket and backboard. The game went into overtime.

Kobe caught the ball on the wing and took another shot … another airball! Back-to-back airballs. With forty seconds left in overtime, another airball from Kobe Bryant. With four seconds left on the clock, Kobe shot *another* airball.

Can you imagine how he felt after those devastating misses? How would you feel? What would you do? Here's what Kobe did.

That same night, Kobe flew back to LA. He got the janitor to let him into his local high school and he shot baskets all day. He felt horrible for letting his fans down and feared that folks would dismiss him because of his failure. He kept practicing and returned the next season, determined to vindicate himself. That is exactly what he did.

This is a great example of how to handle failure. Devastating of losses can make you feel like life is over. But instead of allowing the failure to break you down, use it to break through. Kobe saw failure as an opportunity to reinvent himself and his game. He felt the embarrassment of his loss and used it to reenergize himself to succeed.

You don't have to be held hostage by the failures of yesterday. Instead, see failure as the price you pay to achieve progress and success. That perspective will lead to perseverance. Perseverance leads to longevity.

Every worthy goal includes some risk and uncertainty. You don't know what's going to happen. Before you take a risk, decide whether the goal is worth the risk. If it is, pull the trigger.

Sometimes, people won't try to get closer to their goal because they fall into certain mental traps. These traps that can keep you from taking the risks you need to get started. Here are the traps and how you can begin to think about them:

1. **"It will be embarrassing."** Yes, it can feel embarrassing when you fail. Many people avoid failure at all costs because they don't want to be humiliated. But the only way to be better is to take steps forward, even if those steps are small and shaky. You might fall. Don't be ashamed if you do, because the only real failure is in not trying. Remember that some of the greatest people endured

tremendous failure and embarrassment, but they didn't quit. They used failure to fuel greater effort.

2. **"It's not that important."** Some people second-guess everything they do. They tell themselves that success is not really important to them. The truth is, if you wait long enough, nothing is important. Unfortunately, you might well end up with regret in your mind and heart for never taking the chance. You can make amends for any mistakes you make, but you can do nothing about the attempts you never made.

3. **"It's too hard."** If you believe everything in life should be easy, and when you find out that achievement takes effort, you might give up. You must be willing to focus for the time it takes to reach your goal and do the hard work along the way.

4. **"It's not fair."** Life is not fair, but many people have trouble accepting that reality. They worry that others might have more advantages then they have instead of trying to take advantage of the opportunities in front of them. These people are always saying, "I shouldn't *have to* do this." Comparing their journeys to others' leads to discouragement and ultimately, quitting.

5. **"It's not the right time."** It will never be convenient to pursue a goal that's worthwhile. You'll have bills, family drama, obligations, and deadlines. Don't wait for all the lights to be green before you leave the house. I know your life is complicated, but I want you to do something. Even if you can't do it all, start doing *something* to get closer to your goals.

6. **"I don't feel inspired."** You don't have to be great to get started, but you have to get started to be great. Mediocre people do things

when they feel inspired. Great people do things regardless of what their emotions tell them. You need to be aware of your emotions, but not controlled by them.

I hope this list helps to eliminate some of the traps that have been hurting your progress or keeping you stuck. Do you see yourself in any of these ways of thinking? Which resonate with you the most? How can you begin to get out of the trap or traps you've identified?

CHAPTER 29

Fear of Success

The worst kind of sabotage is self-sabotage.

ONE OF MY FAVORITE MOVIES is *Good Will Hunting.* It's about a young genius named Will Hunting from "Southie" (the South Boston neighborhood in Massachusetts.) This young man has a photographic memory and amazing talent to solve complex math equations, but he refuses to take advantage of opportunities that will allow him to fully maximize his gifts and talents. He is guarded and doesn't trust people because of the abuse he experienced as a foster child.

As I reflect on the story line, I can't help but think of a phrase that many people struggle with: the fear of success.

Are you afraid of success? You might be, if you find yourself asking these questions:

- What if I'm not able to *maintain* my success?
- Will people think I'm a *fraud*?
- What if people have *higher expectations* of me than I do?
- What if I'm accused of being a *sellout* because I no longer have the same life struggles?
- What if I become *someone I never wanted to be*?

And one of the most intense and powerful questions I've ever heard: *What if people ONLY love me because of my success and not for who I am?*

I have asked myself these questions when I was on my way to accomplish a milestone, like graduating college or getting my CPA license, and even while writing this book. For some time, I thought I was the only one who worried about these things.

Then I began working as a life skills coach with young people, ages 16 to 21. One of my clients, a young man on his way to passing his GED and heading to college, intentionally failed the test. A social worker told me the young man had been in foster care his entire life and had formed bonds with the social workers and other homeless youth. These were the people who loved and accepted him unconditionally.

He and his peers often got in trouble and failed together. Their common bond was their struggle. He was afraid that, if he transitioned into a new life, he would no longer share that struggle and would lose fellowship with the people he considered his family.

When you spend all your time with people who are "losing," you normalize losing. By "losing," I'm talking about people who continually settle for being less than their best. When we become bonded around our struggles, the struggles might become more important than finding a way out. It's much healthier to normalize winning and succeeding, and to help others do the same.

This young man was terrified as he got closer to the point where he feared he would be independent and less connected to his peers. As I thought long and hard about this situation, I came to some conclusions about how our culture defines success and failure in terms of performance, popularity, and possessions. Sometimes failure isn't all bad, and success isn't always fun. Sometimes failure, as our culture defines it, helps you to see who is really on your side, while success can attract people who may not really care about you but only about what you can do for them.

We all have to acknowledge these realities, and sometimes, wrestle with them. But ultimately, we should try to be the best we can be. From a place of success, we can do the most good for ourselves and our peers.

To live well, we have to face our fears. Most of our fears are learned, including the fear of success. If it is learned, it can be unlearned.

Here are a few things that I believe we must do each time we struggle with those fears:

We must see success as a journey, not a destination. If we keep this perspective, we will be able to maintain emotional equilibrium. This might require a restructuring of your mental framework when it comes to success. When you succeed, see it as a springboard to the next achievement. Always work on improvement. Don't let the fear of success keep you from developing as a person. Success doesn't make you a "superstar," and failure doesn't make you the scum of the earth. Expect both successes and failures, take it all in stride, and keep moving forward.

We must know who's in the stadium. When you step out to do anything that makes you vulnerable, like chasing your goals, you're like a boxer entering the ring. There are four kinds of people that you have to keep in mind. In our society, most people's mantra is, "I don't care what you think." That's really not true. You do care, but you don't want them to know that, because it makes you vulnerable. If you want to stay connected to your community, you need to care about what people think—but not be defined by what people think. You might have to be unorthodox in the pursuit of your calling. That requires courage. I believe you should know who is in the stadium (people paying attention to your successes and failures) and classify them properly. These people are:

- **Cheap seats**: The people in the "nosebleed" seats haven't invested much time to get to know you, but they will voice their uninformed opinions and judgments. Acknowledge they exist, but don't invest much stock in their opinions.

- **Referees:** These people represent the rules of the fight and will hold you accountable when you violate the rules. Remember them, because you need them to maintain order.

- **Critics section**: These judges will let you know whether you passed or failed. They don't care about your feelings or your well-being—they only exist to keep score. Remember them, because you need their feedback.

- **Support section**: Your family members—those who love you unconditionally and will ride or die with you—are here. They care about your well-being. Some of them might tell you the truth, but at the right time and in the right way to help you improve.

Knowing who's in the stadium when you begin any endeavor will save you a lot of heartache. Classify them properly, because getting them mixed up can cause a heap of trouble and unnecessary pain.

We must know our WHYs. Continue to reaffirm and meditate on your major motivating forces, your "whys." These motivations will help to bring your mind, will, and emotions into alignment. That alignment will be a source of power to help you overcome your fears or keep them at bay when they show up.

In Chapter 11, I discussed my 4 "F" factors, the major motivating force for achieving goals. They are:

- **Faith in God** – Your life is God's gift to you. What you become is your gift to God.

- **Future Family** – "A good person leaves an inheritance for their children's children." Proverbs 13:22, NIV

- **Forefathers** – If history is your teacher, the future will be your friend. Honor the legacies of those who came before you.

- **Fears** – I have something to prove – that I can live my life without fear. The only thing we have to fear is fear.

If you have not yet done so, please go back to Chapter 11 and come up with your WHYs. This is not something you can rush. The number of your motivating factors can be unlimited.

It's also vital to know your limitations? What are yours—and have you imposed them on yourself? What specific things might you be doing that get in your way? Be honest here.

EXAMPLES:

1. Spending more than you've budgeted, once you're about to get out of debt.

2. Cheating on your diet when you've been eating right for two weeks.

3. Taking nights off from working on your goal (practicing your craft, studying for an important exam, etc.) when you know consistent work is key.

What are your WHYs? Go to Chapter 11.

_____

_____

_____

_____

_____

CHAPTER 30

Change and Transition

The only thing that won't change is change itself.

ABOUT A DECADE AGO, THERE was a competition between the cell phone brands Apple and Blackberry. One Blackberry executive is remembered for saying, "No one wants *apps*." Over two million apps later, it's safe to say he missed the mark.

Fast forward ten years, and competition wasn't even a conversation. Apps changed the way people used cell phones, and Blackberry didn't change soon enough to keep up. They're no longer discussed as a major player among cell phone companies.

Often, change is vital to continued progress towards reaching one's goals. Flexible people (and companies) are agile and able to respond to change. They can recognize when they are not on the right track and can make a course correction. They remain patient with the process of change and transition.

I believe that people who can't succeed in life have an underlying resistance to new ideas and new ways of doing things. They are not flexible, so they continue to practice old behaviors in new settings and are ultimately rendered ineffective. Opportunities slip through their fingers, which inevitably leads to regret.

Change is a part of life. If you don't prepare yourself for it, you will be doomed to a life of unnecessary frustration and stagnation. The degree to which you can embrace endings is the degree to which you can face new beginnings.

There is a story in the Bible about Moses and the people of Egypt. The Hebrew people were enslaved by the Egyptians. Moses, a Hebrew who was raised as an Egyptian, discovered his calling to deliver his people out of slavery in Egypt to take them to a "promised land" foretold by the prophets.

Talk about change! The Hebrews had spent hundreds of years in captivity, and now they had to change everything they knew about their way of life to adapt to the series of events in the desert and to make a long trek to a new land. They faced both change and transition: change in their circumstances, and a major transition in their thinking.

Change can show up in our lives in a lot of different ways. Often, it's not a choice—it's forced upon us by circumstances. Types of changes include:

- Going from high school to college.

- Going from college to starting your career.

- Being released from prison back into the world and getting back on your feet.

- Going from being an employee to starting your own business.

- Changing careers in your midlife and learning new skills.

- Going from unhealthy living (not sleeping, working out, and eating properly) to healthy living (getting enough sleep, eating right, and exercising).

- Going from spending money recklessly to living in a financially responsible way.

- Getting free from an unhealthy substance like drugs or alcohol.

- Leaving dysfunctional relationships and learning to be in healthy and safe relationships.

Most people are not taught how to handle change and transition in their lives. Without guidance, people often fumble through the process and experience needless pain or a sense that the wrong choice was made.

It's important to remember that life is full of different seasons and stages. To make it through these stages, you will have to grow as a person. That will inevitably bring about change, which is part of maturing. It's not possible to sustain anything forever, because change is necessary when you learn new information that's needed to support a new way of life. You cannot trust and rely on past knowledge, habits, and experience when you reach a new stage or season.

The people of Egypt had to endure three stages of the change: leaving their life in Egypt, the neutral zone of walking through the desert, and the beginning of a new life in their new land. Transitions in your own life are likely to encompass these three stages.

Here are a few considerations for the stages where change and transition occur. Understanding the process can help make change more manageable and ultimately result in a sense of completeness and health.

Stage 1—Ending things (Egypt):

While in the process of change in a particular area of your life, you have to recognize when something has come to an end. If you do not embrace the need for change, you will prolong the process of the transition and waste time and energy that could be put to better use. The quicker you let go of the idea that things have to stay the same, the sooner you can begin making a transition.

Ask yourself these questions at this stage:

1. *What is it time to let go of?* What activities are you doing that no longer serve a purpose in your life? What habits and relationships do you need to consider changing or even ending because they no longer serve you? Insanity has been defined as doing the same thing over and over and expecting a different result. Naming what has to end is a powerful way to make the transition to a new way of doing things. Here are two examples:

   a. Going to college means you have to let go of the way you thought and acted when you were in high school. In high school, there were probably more people who held you accountable and responsible for your actions. Now, you have to decide to end your dependency on others and take responsibility for your actions and their consequences. If you don't make this transition, you will have a hard time figuring things out in college and beyond. Get used to naming the things that have to end as you evaluate your changes.

   b. Learning how to spend your money wisely means changing reckless financial habits. It can be hard, especially if you've been living like that for a while. But you have to decide that you will put an end to spending sprees if you want to have a solid financial foundation in the future.

2. *What actions can you take now* that will help you with the transition? Most changes become harder if you wait to make them, but recognize that ending things can involve a certain amount of grief. If you're feeling this pain, talk with a coach or therapist, or

participate in a support group. Letting go is not always easy, but it's essential that you learn to end things well. Don't procrastinate, and don't leave things unresolved in your mind and heart. See Chapter 31 on Grieving.

Stage 2—Stuck in Neutral (The Desert):

When you begin to move in a new direction, you can give yourself the opportunity to make a smoother transition. In between an ending and a beginning something is the neutral zone, analogous to the "desert." This part of your journey can be pretty uncomfortable. You might feel boredom, restlessness, confusion, fear, panic, self-pity, and distress. The Hebrews leaving Egypt certainly did. But with energy and forethought, this stage can be a time of reinvention and repositioning for something great.

Transition can take months or sometimes years and most of the time will be spent in the neutral zone. You might feel like you're taking two steps forward and one step backward. I don't say that to discourage you. I say that so you can know what to expect and plan accordingly, because dealing with a hard truth right away helps you get adjusted more easily than learning it later on. Change can only surprise you when you don't expect it.

Expect that your anxiety will rise and motivation will fall. You're not weird or wrong. It is normal that with change and transition, you will feel disoriented and self-doubting. Get comfortable with being un-comfortable. When you stop letting fear and anxiety control your mind, it's like you release yourself from a self-imposed prison. What you are afraid of is rarely as bad as you imagine. Let your faith in God sustain you during this time.

Here are a few things to consider during this stage:

1. Holding onto a **vision** of where you will be is one way to make this time easier. Review the exercise in Chapter 8 to remind

yourself of your vision. For the change to stick, you have to see the advantage of changing yourself. Think about the kind of person you will be when this is done.

2. Know your **values**. During this time, anything that you were clear about can become unclear. It's important to know what holds ultimate importance in your life, so you can build your life from there. Review the exercise in Chapter 3.

3. Remember always to be **you**. Review Chapter 2's exercise on the false self. It's tempting to retreat to being what everyone thinks you should be during a discouraging time. The pressure of social acceptance isn't necessarily bad, unless it moves you away from your calling. Stick to your guns regarding who you are and how you want to be in the world. Over time, you will begin to regain your strength and confidence. Be patient with the process.

4. Think more about what can go **right** than what can go **wrong**. Watch your self-talk. Review Chapter 27 and use the STOP tool when needed. Much of your success during the transition will depend on what you choose to believe. When you change your beliefs, you change your actions.

5. Expect more **endings**. In this season, some things have to be allowed to die and some you'll have to end. Old systems of thought, old self-images, and old outlooks need to go so the new ones can be brought to life. What lessons do you need to learn during this season?

6. **Laugh** at yourself. Laughter is great medicine and is a valuable tool during these times. Don't take yourself too seriously. Don't

be afraid of your awkwardness in dealing with things. Simply laugh at it.

7. *Support* will help you. I always recommend a coach, counselor, trusted and wise friend, or a support group to help you during this time. Sharing your feelings in a safe place can help you process the emotions surrounding change in a healthy way.

STAGE 3—NEW BEGINNINGS (THE PROMISED LAND):

Once you've reached the point where the change in your life is complete, and the circumstances around the change are final, you might still feel some unresolved emotions around the change.

You got the new house. You changed careers. You started the business. You've been out of prison for a few months and started working again. But how you thought you would feel might not exactly be how you're feeling. The beginning of the change might not be as impressive as you thought it would be.

In most cases, it is totally normal and to be expected that your destination takes some getting used to. The true beginning of your new life will come when there is a re-alignment internally.

Here are a few things to consider that might help you finalize a transition:

1. **What will your new beginning require of you?** What new outlooks, habits, and systems of thoughts do you need to commit to? In the beginning, don't focus on the results of what you want to happen. Focus on the process to sustain the change you want. For example, when I first started leading workshops, I had to be more focused on preparing than I was with the idea that I was a facilitator. I've met folks who bought a new house and were so excited about the house that they neglected to factor in the maintenance work and cost to keep the house in order. Think

ahead to what you'll need to sustain success. Remember that maintenance takes just as much work as acquiring, if not more.

2. **What mental or emotional obstacles must you overcome** for this change to be complete? Is fear still a problem? Are you craving the comfort of your old ways? See Chapter 27 for methods to deal with adversity.

3. **Who can be a good example for you?** Study people who have gone through the type of change you're going through. Great people don't always show you the confusion or hardship they endured during their transitions. Learning their stories can help you stay encouraged and help you keep your eye on the result of a new beginning. Read their books, listen to their interviews, and watch their documentaries to get a blueprint of the perspective you need to cultivate as you survive change.

Use this section to process your thoughts and answer the questions listed above.

PART 3
SELF-CARE

Being your strongest—mentally, emotionally, and physically—depends upon three factors: sleep, exercise, and nutrition. Even under serious stress, your body can hold onto its energy if it's rested, fed correctly, and exercised properly.

THE TERM *SELF-CARE* DESCRIBES ACTIONS AN INDIVIDUAL might take to achieve optimal physical, mental, and emotional health and well-being. To be honest, this is not something that comes easily to me. I didn't get introduced to the concept until I started as a life skills coach at a home for temporarily displaced children (also known as a "group home").

If you know anything about social work, particularly in a residential crisis intervention center or a group home, life can be pretty hectic. If you're not careful, you will burn out, which happens pretty often. Self-care was a life-changing concept for me.

Prior to take off on an airplane, the flight attendant explains the emergency process: if an oxygen mask falls, you have to put the mask on yourself first before you can put it on anyone else. Trying to help others first can make you pass out, and then you won't be of any use. You cannot serve out of an empty vessel.

Those who know me and the way I work would always say, "Make sure you take care of yourself, Jon."

"I know. I am," was my usual response.

But the reality was, I didn't know how to take care of myself. I didn't sleep well, eat right, or exercise consistently. I didn't spend time cultivating healthy relationships or engage in the spiritual disciplines of my faith. I certainly stayed away from therapy, which was for "weak people," as far as I was concerned. I've made a number of improvements in self-care since those early days, but I certainly have not arrived. In every season of life, I recognize the need to come up with new and creative ways to meet my needs so I can be at my best.

The focus of self-care is usually sleep, exercise, and food. I want to add money to that list. One of the main sources of stress nowadays is financial. People fight about it and stay awake at night thinking about it. Taking good care of yourself must involve taking care of your finances.

Let's take a look at the basics:

SLEEP

Americans are more sleep-deprived today than ever in US history. I know this has been true in my life, starting in college, when I would write term papers at 3 a.m. Sleep experts will tell you that sleep is considered *ammunition* for the brain. Just as you should never go into battle without enough bullets, you shouldn't tackle your active life without adequate sleep.

Sleep helps you be fully engaged. It makes you more resilient to anxiety and stress and lets you recover from illnesses more quickly. When you're well-rested, you make better decisions, too.

Most people need between 7 and 9 hours of sleep each night, according to the experts, but you can experiment to find out how much sleep your body needs. Some day when you don't have to wake up at a specific time, go to sleep without setting an alarm and see what time you naturally wake up. You might need to try this experiment several times. Once you know how much sleep you really need, make it a priority. Do your best to organize your life around a healthy sleep schedule.

EXERCISE

It's important to regularly move your body in a way that raises your heart rate. Many people say they don't have time to work out. Let me assure you, you don't have time to *not* work out. Exercise not only strengthens your heart muscle, it helps you sleep better, improves your mental health, and lowers your risk of heart disease, stroke, and high blood pressure.

Yet so many people have a hard time making exercise a consistent practice. How can you make it consistent in your life? I have found that any activity has to be fun for you to stick with it. Some people enjoy weight-lifting, while others prefer to dance class or practice martial arts or play a sport. You have lots of choices! Just find something that you enjoy and can stick with on a regular basis – 3 – 4 times a week for 30 – 45 minutes.

Of course, talk to your doctor before starting an exercise program to ensure that it's right for you.

FOOD

As my nutrition-conscious friends tell me, America is a nation of "mindless eaters." The general rule when it comes to food says that, if you cannot pronounce more than one of the ingredients, you probably shouldn't eat it. I'm guilty at times of eating the wrong foods, which is why this is probably going to be the shortest paragraph in the book. But first, let me share some points to consider.

1.   **Learn about nutrition**. Get educated on what foods you should put in your body. We are surrounded by so many food options with fast food, the cafeteria at school or work, and restaurants, and we often don't take the time to shop for and prepare healthy food. We might not see the damage we're doing to our bodies by making unhealthy eating choices. Lack of knowledge can kill you when it comes to the food you consume. Should you be eating low fat, high fat, paleo, or vegan? Should you be fasting or juicing? Keep exploring and employ trial-and-error until you

find what's right for you. Consult a nutritionist if you can. Find an eating plan that helps you stay committed to lifelong health.

2. **Consider food as fuel**. Many times, we choose the foods we crave instead of the foods we need. Learn to distinguish between a craving and a need. Are your food choices governed by your emotions instead of an actual need for physical nourishment? Food should be fuel, not entertainment. (Confession: I get this backwards *all the time*.) It's okay to treat yourself sometimes; even professional bodybuilders have "cheat meals." The problem is, for many people, a cheat meal turns into a cheat day and a cheat week, and then they've completely derailed their healthy eating plan. Be honest with yourself about the quality of foods you are eating. Give yourself room to be imperfect, and don't beat yourself up if you cave in to a craving. We all mess up. But then do everything in your power to get back on track. Having an accountability system (through a program like Join Weight Watchers) can help you stay on track. Do certain emotions trigger you to start binge eating? Do you eat more unhealthy food after a bad day at work or when you're confronted with relationship issues, money problems, or overall stress and anxiety? It's important to learn to detach your hunger from your stress. Before you eat anything, ask yourself:

    •   Am I hungry, or is this just a craving?

    •   What happened that triggered my desire to eat?

    •   What emotions might be masquerading as the desire to eat?

Grab a journal and write out the answers every day if that's what it takes to regain control. Becoming more aware of your food intake and appetite triggers will give you a greater sense of control and accountability when it comes to healthy eating.

MONEY

Money is a practical tool to meet your needs, but sadly, it doesn't come with instructions. In my experience, most people have not been taught how to deal with money. If you're not careful, you can make bad financial choices with long-term repercussions.

It's been said that "money makes the world go round"—but that's not true. *Anxiety* makes the world go round, and for most people, money carries anxiety.

I know many people who struggle with financial problems. Some of them stay awake at night worrying about money. But if this is you, you're not stuck. Please go back to Chapter 14, where I've laid out a few principles to get you started on creating a financial plan. You will be amazed at how much your anxiety is reduced by simply having a plan and knowing there's a way to get out of your situation. Without a plan, all you'll be left with is anxiety.

To begin this section of the book, we will deal with issues of emotional self-care, particularly those areas that are not often discussed. Many people never learn to deal with loss and grief, forgiveness, boundaries, shame, and assertiveness. If properly addressed, emotional self-care in these areas could spark a wave of healing in people's lives and subsequently, their communities.

In the second half of this section, I want to address patterns that I've encountered personally that also affect many communities in our nation. These issues include mental health, fatherlessness, colorism, sexual abuse, and mass incarceration. I want to unpack these issues to remove the stigma. I will also provide the tools to begin the process of healing from these experiences.

As you build your self-care practice and learn the tools needed to deal effectively with whatever issues arise, you'll be challenging long-held beliefs, changing relationship dynamics, and shifting the way you understand and interact with the world. It's like you're that boxer, back in that ring again! And just as we did before, when we step into the ring of life, we need to know who is there. Here are three types of people you're likely to have in your arena:

1. **Encouragers**: These people support you wholeheartedly and encourage and affirm you. They are your cheerleaders. You can turn to them when you need a sounding board. They let you be vulnerable, and they help you with your personal development and other issues you encounter along the way.

2. **Examples**: These are your role models, whether you know them or have only heard of them. Maybe you've read their books or watched their interviews. They are proof that it's possible to live authentically. These are information-bringers and way-showers. They connect, refer, and direct you to resources or people who can help you on your journey.

3. **Enemies**: These people are your critics, and they belong to three sub-categories:

   a. The critics are those who are against you embracing a healthy lifestyle, where personal care precedes service.

   b. Those who don't know who you really are, your calling, and the values that motivate you. They simply judge, slander, and gossip from a distance with no empathy or compassion.

   c. Those in the box seats who expect you to conform to their expectations, ideals, and wishes. They might pretend to agree with you, but really just want to reinforce their own views.

They might use blame, judgment, or criticism to manipulate and suppress your efforts.

Another word for enemies can be *haters*. I've never liked to use this word, but as I continued to live life, I realized the haters are real. They invest their time in destroying others through dysfunctional behaviors, manipulation, and even sabotage—both overt and covert. Ultimately, haters are bad investors because they don't understand God's economy for those who trust in Him. Here are two things to consider when you encounter haters:

1. *"You intended to harm me, but God intended it for good to accomplish what is now being done, the saving of many lives."* Genesis 50:20, NIV

2. *"And we know that in all things God works for the good of those who love him, who have been called according to his purpose."* Romans 8:28, NIV

God is *for* you, no matter who decides to stand against you. If God wants you to do something, He will see you through. These verses show that anyone's plans to hurt you cannot overrule what God ultimately determines will happen. Trust in Him.

Haters might treat you poorly, but don't let them make you stoop to the level of hating them back. In fact, *love* your haters. They make you better and help you refine your character by telling you things that you might need to hear, things that your #1 supporter won't say. Again, *love* the haters. The victory of fulfilling your calling is stronger when you face opposition.

Ultimately, I see self-care as a matter of life and death, because the foundation of your choices and life decisions are rooted in your overall well-being. To live at a high level, you have to be at your best emotionally, physically, and psychologically. Yes, we all have—and will continue to have—work to do in this area. I hope and pray that you decide in advance to approach these topics with pure motivations, an honest heart, and a willingness to change for the better, for your sake and the sake of our communities.

Far too many people are living lives that are unmanageable. The goal of this section is to raise awareness about self-care and to give people the tools and motivation to make healthier choices in life.

A Word to the Mentors: With these exercises, you'll be able to sharpen your perception of yourself, which will help you in mentoring young people. One of my core beliefs about mentoring is that you can't give what you don't have. The most impactful lessons you teach will be through your example. The change that you want to occur in those you work with won't happen until it happens with you first. Before you talk about the lessons, make sure you commit to walking them out. When you review these lessons for yourself, your mentoring will be even more effective. I wish you well.

CHAPTER 31

Grieving

Grief doesn't play by the rules.

I KNOW WHAT IT'S LIKE to face loss. In the process of writing this book, my grandma passed away. She turned 92 on February 19, 2017, and passed away the following morning. She arrived here from Haiti when I was eight years old and played a big part in raising me.

I saw her physically decline for a month before her passing and was intentional about spending time with her and preparing for her loss. They call it "anticipatory grief." The problem was, I wasn't aware of how strongly the loss would affect me after her passing.

About two months after her funeral, I called my parent's home, where she had been living. I expected my grandma to pick up the phone, as usual—but she didn't. That's when the grief of her loss hit me. I began crying, and for the first time, I knew it was the right thing to do. Growing up, I was taught that men aren't allowed to cry. I can recall a Haitian funeral where one man started crying, and other men told him to stop crying and to "be a man." That was the common phrase.

I know now that real men do cry. There's no shame in it. It's a normal and healthy way to process the pain of a loss. Unfortunately, many cultures and societies teach otherwise.

All of us face losses that we might not acknowledge, but that deserve attention. In addition to losing a loved one through death, we might lose a job, break up a relationship or marriage, or lose our health. We might come to terms with childhood abuse or lose our national identity, as well as our routines and stability, by moving to a new place. We might lose the dream of a career, or even lose our sense of self when we are required to make big changes. It's okay to take time to acknowledge these losses. While I believe in fighting to get right back up after a fall, it's healthy to take the time to feel pain and grieve. Grief can help you become a more whole person and feel more compassionate for others.

When we carry unresolved grief, we might be tempted to use unhealthy coping mechanisms like denial, minimizing, rationalizing, distracting, avoiding, addiction, or becoming hostile. All these are ways of not facing the pain.

Years ago, I lost another close family member and did not process the pain of that loss properly. That experience prompted unhealthy behavior, and I was not even aware of the connection. I was trying to deal with my emotions and my pain, but the ways I chose were not productive—they were self-destructive. I have learned that there is no such thing as an unexpressed emotion. An emotion will manifest in some way, often a disruptive way, until it is acknowledged.

Do you have unexpressed emotions or unresolved grief? Could these be contributing to problems you experience in your life now?

Grief has many layers, like an onion, and no expiration date. Anything can remind you of a loss: a movie, a random comment someone makes, the weather, a certain place you visit, or many other things. Each time you discover another layer or grief, you'll experience another cycle of mental processing. You might need to revisit the cycle over and over.

A five-stage cycle—with the acronym ARNMA—can provide a loose framework for the way many people experience and process grief:

1. Avoidance – In this stage, you avoid the truth and focus on a false reality.

2. Rage – You recognize that your false reality is indeed false and become angry. You might have thoughts of blaming, unfairness, or self-pity.

3. Negotiation – You look for ways to avoid or minimize the severity of the loss.

4. Melancholy – You feel deep sadness and sometimes hopelessness.

5. Acknowledgment – You accept the loss and begin to realize you will survive it.

You may go through one or several of these stages. They don't always happen in order. The purpose of listing them here is to help you see that your experience is normal. Know that all these stages are common in people who experience loss.

Many cultures urge us to get over losses quickly, equating sadness with weakness. We need a new culture that says:

- It's okay to acknowledge our losses.

- Processing our losses is important for our emotional development.

- Accepting and grieving our losses helps us become more mature and compassionate.

I've been privileged to hold space with people who have experienced severe disappointments, traumas, and tragedies. I've had clients who lost a career after being with a company for more than a decade, or experienced divorce after 20 years of marriage, or lost a home and possessions in a fire. I've known people who experienced the loss of a child. Hearing their raw and honest stories about their process, and the kind of people they became after the trauma, gave me the courage to be honest about my own grief and pain. When we share our struggles, and not only our successes, we restore a greater sense of humanity in the world.

Many people were raised in homes where they were taught not to share their pain. They held their pain in silence to protect themselves from abusive, manipulative, or controlling family members. They lived with adults who broke confidences or used emotional blackmail to get their way.

In Chapter 33, I'll provide a framework for finding SAFE People to share with. Chapter 35 will deal with learning to be more assertive. Both are important in processing grief and loss. Once we have established that we can be safe with our pain, we can process our grief. Then we can begin to live and love again with a whole heart.

CHAPTER 32

Forgiveness

Unforgiveness is like drinking poison hoping the other person dies.

"IN ORDER TO MOVE ON, you have to let go."

I heard this in a Sunday sermon, and I never forgot it. Sometimes in life, you have to hear something a few times before you truly get it. I've heard close to 100 teachings on forgiveness, but this statement was what did it for me.

I realize that forgiveness is not an emotion. It's a *decision* centered in the will to let go of the need to get even and to cancel the emotional debt against the person who has hurt you. Forgiveness is a gift that you give yourself for the value of a relationship or for your desire to move on.

Forgiveness means you won't hold things against someone because of what happened. I've always considered myself to be a pretty forgiving person, just like I considered myself a patient person. All that went out the window when I encountered situations that tested the sincerity of my conviction.

I've had situations in my life where the weakness of the beliefs was tested. There were offenses against me that I did not let go of, and the longer I waited, the more I felt like I *could not* let them go. I held onto them for so long that the bitterness hardened my heart. It affected my language, my attitude, my trust in people, my vision, and subsequently, my relationships. It also affected my ability to use my talents and gifts freely.

Unforgiveness turned me into the worst version of myself. In addition to the unforgiveness I held against others—who needed to be released from my heart—I also held unforgiveness against myself. That needed to be relinquished as well.

I've done some really foolish things over the course of my life. Some of those mistakes may still be affecting people's lives today. For me to move forward with a spiritual and emotional freedom, I needed to come to terms with the mistakes I have made, grieve the pain I caused myself and others, and then *let it go*. This is the process, and it's necessary and worth the work for life to be lived greatly.

Forgiveness is a discipline that needs constant practice. In the same way that you go to the doctor to get a checkup, or see an accountant to get your taxes done, or visit the mechanic to get an oil change, you need to go to God to give you the strength to let go of the pain that you carry—both from the offense committed against you and from what you did to yourself.

The great news is that we all have a choice. No matter how long it has been since the offense, we can learn to let it go. We must come to see that forgiveness is not for the offender. It's for the offended. It frees us to move on and allows us to give up victimhood. We no longer have to be held hostage by the offense.

Forgiveness will give us emotional freedom. We will feel more alive when we unyoke ourselves from the burden of blame. It's certainly not easy to do. As a matter of fact, the forgiveness and the grieving process often go hand in hand, because many offenses come with a great deal of pain and sadness that can last a while. You have to pray for the strength and courage to deal with your pain. Don't run from it, as many people do. See Chapter 31 for tools on handling grief. Going through the grieving process, several times if necessary, is important.

Unforgiveness is ultimately selfish, because it causes you to see events through a lens of fear, anger, resentment, or even hatred. This distorted view robs you and the people you are here to help of the best version of yourself. Everything you create is influenced by your emotional and spiritual state. What you see with your eyes, hear with your ears, and say with your mouth is colored by the condition of your heart.

One great example of forgiveness is Nelson Mandela, one of my heroes. He was in prison for 27 years for fighting the brutal regime of *apartheid* in South Africa. Upon release from prison, he didn't go out seeking revenge and murder. Instead, he preached a gospel of forgiveness. He sought to forgive those who had imprisoned him, not just for him, but for the sake of the people of South Africa.

In a way, forgiveness means cutting your losses with a losing investment and re-investing in things that matter. The next time you are tempted to hold a grudge against someone, think of someone you may be hurting and what you will be losing by holding onto the grudge. Take time to journal your thoughts at the end of this chapter. Sometimes writing helps you to better process what you're feeling.

WHAT FORGIVENESS IS NOT

We need to discuss what forgiveness is *not*, to clear up any confusion on this important topic.

1. **Forgiveness is not reducing the impact of the wrongdoing.** "No one's perfect." "Worst things have happened." These statements, though well-meaning, do not reflect true forgiveness. They sound nice, but they fall short of actually being forgiveness. Minimizing the harm done can be a way to avoid dealing with major wrongdoings. Be mindful of the words you use. Speak appropriately and with the seriousness required.

2. **Forgiveness is not allowing wrongdoing to continue.** This is called *enabling*. Enabling is supporting someone in their irresponsibility or immaturity. Unfortunately, enabling can be confused with kindness, because the people who enable are usually sweet and nice people with good intentions. It's important to be able to be stern with people to make the wrongdoing stop. Protecting yourself might involve confronting someone.

3. **Forgiveness doesn't instantly end the pain.** Sometimes, you can be injured in a way that has lasting consequences and leads to ongoing pain. Still feeling hurt doesn't mean you haven't forgiven. It means you need time to heal.

4. **Forgiveness doesn't necessarily restore trust.** You can forgive someone and still decide not to trust them again. Trust should be given based on evidence, not desire. See Chapter 33 on Safe People.

5. **Forgiveness is not pretending the wrongdoing never happened.** "I just moved on." "I didn't let it affect me." While people do move on, it's not necessary to live in a state of denial, particularly if something really harmful was done to you. You don't have to avoid the full acknowledgment that something was wrong in order to forgive.

6. **Forgiveness is not waiting for an apology.** You might feel you need someone to say they're sorry. Some people will never be mature enough to admit their fault. Some people will die before they recognize their offense. Don't wait for anyone to seek forgiveness before you grant it. I know it's not the most comforting thing to hear, but forgiveness is not for them. It's for you.

7. **Forgiveness is not forgetting.** This might be one of the biggest myths in our culture. "Forgive and forget" sounds nice, but some offenses cannot be forgotten. Some *should not* be forgotten. If someone tries to kill me, you'd better believe I will never forget. I might forgive them, but I will remember their intention. If we ever cross paths again, wisdom will remind me to be cautious. We do not erase history. We free ourselves from the past, but we do not erase it.

8. **Forgiveness is not a one-time event.** Sometimes, forgiveness needs to be regularly chosen. Feelings of anger, resentment, and even revenge might keep popping up. Forgiveness will eventually banish them.

9. **Forgiveness is not neglecting justice.** Justice and forgiveness can co-exist. We must remember that what is sowed will be reaped. Actions have consequences. You can let go of the desire for revenge but ensure that there are repercussions for wrongdoing. Consequences help people learn not to do wrong.

10. **Forgiveness is not reconciling with the offender.** Forgiveness takes only one person: you. Reconciliation takes two people. I know people who have gone through divorces, bad business partnerships, fractured friendships, and family drama. These situations sometimes have ripple effects that keep people from ever being close again. Sadly, that is the reality of our world. Sometimes, it's best to have no contact with the person who has hurt you. You can still forgive them.

Steps to Forgiveness

1. **Recognition:** Is there someone you have not forgiven? How did their offense or perceived offense affect you? Grab a journal or start talking about this with a trusted friend. To forgive, you must first acknowledge what your betrayer has done to you and understand that you are holding onto anger or resentment.

2. **Release:** So many of us carry feelings of unforgiveness for so long that it almost feels normal. Give yourself permission to get release through the grieving process and working through the pain you still feel. Name the emotions connected with what happened to you. See Chapter 34 for a list of emotions. The stages of grief are avoidance, rage, negotiation, melancholy, and acknowledgment. If you're still experiencing these difficult emotions, keep working through them. Your goal is to develop the strength to let go. If you feel rage, work on that emotion until you can choose to give up the desire to see the other person suffer as you have. To forgive, you'll need to release all feelings of revenge and retribution.

3. **Remove:** Remove any people or things that reinforce feelings of unforgiveness during the process. Don't keep things around that provoke anger or bitter memories. Environment is an extremely important factor in becoming the type of person you want to become. (See Chapter 22 on Environment.)

4. **Remind:** Remind yourself why forgiveness is important. Look at who you have been and who you have become. Decide to walk in forgiveness from this day forth.

CHAPTER 33

Boundaries and Safe People

Givers have to set limits, because takers never do.

LIKE A LOT OF PEOPLE, I was not raised in a family that embraced emotional health. By emotional health, I mean feeling a sense of emotional security and positive well-being. A healthy family is free from tension and anxiety.

Growing up, we were so concerned with "making it" that we didn't take the time to learn how to set healthy boundaries. We didn't express our thoughts and feelings honestly, clearly, and respectfully. We didn't heal the emotional wounds of the past.

The movie *Fences* in some ways reminded me of my upbringing. It depicted a black garbage collector in 1950s Pittsburgh named Troy Maxson who felt that he missed opportunities in life due to racism. He took his frustrations out on his family. In one particular scene, Troy is having a heated discussion with his son about not expecting people to like you but to ensure that they are doing right by you. This certainly reminds me of the messages I received growing up. The actor's delivery was insensitive, but there is a lot of truth in those messages that people need to learn to have an overall healthy life.

Troy was teaching his son how he should be in the world—in a word, he was teaching him about *boundaries*. Boundaries are property lines that determine what we are and are not responsible for in life and relationships, as well as what's acceptable and what's not acceptable. Boundaries protect things that are valuable to us.

In a perfect world, we would be able to pursue our goals and dreams without any issues. Everyone would support us wholeheartedly and considerately. No one would disagree with our beliefs, values, or vision. But sadly, this is not a perfect world. Boundaries ensure that we are not living anyone else's life and it also protects what is most precious to us, which allows us to love well. We must continually set and defend our boundaries. And as we learn how to live, we must raise the issue of boundaries and learn how to apply them in a healthy way.

Over the years, I have heard countless stories of people who have been so emotionally, psychologically, or physically wounded that their lives become full of fear and controlled by the thoughts and opinions of others. These stories all tell the tale of poor boundaries, along with a poor sense of self and a lack of healthy self-regard. Many wounded people never learned how important it is to set boundaries.

Boundaries are interconnected. Just like sand castles or dominoes, the moment one falls, the rest come crashing down. As a result, people without boundaries are routinely victims of damaging relationships. Fortunately, it's never too late to learn these principles.

I would like to highlight four areas where it is extremely important to establish boundaries: time, talents, treasures, and thoughts.

TIME

The one commodity that cannot be replaced is time. I have a friend who says, "If you waste my money, I can make more. If you waste my food, I can buy more. But if you waste my time, I can never get that back." I take this warning very seriously because I've learned, over the years, of the devastating consequences of wasting time.

Boundaries around time are important because time is a finite resource. You only get so many hours in a day, and you can use that time toward something productive or waste it by not making a decision.

Here are several tools that can be used in protecting and planning your time.

1. **Annual calendar:** Know which important events that you want to anticipate and prepare for, such as conferences, holidays, birthdays, etc. When you have a sense of when things will be, you can better organize your activities and preparations.

2. **Daily/weekly calendar:** This list will help you to fine-tune your schedule in the more immediate time. If you don't have a sense of when you will get things done, you will constantly be a victim of circumstances. Set appointments with yourself when you have activities that require dedicated time. In writing this book, I've had to set very strict boundaries on my time to research, write, and edit.

3. **Phones:** I know many people who have to be close to their phone for work purposes. This is understandable, but it's important to also put it away sometimes. I have periods of time set aside when I do not answer my phone. For example, I know this is extreme, but I don't take my phone with me to certain places. At work, I might leave my phone in my car. Being without the distraction of my phone allows me to focus on being fully present at my job and able to provide the best service and do the best work. Your perspective might be different, which is fine. But I urge you to evaluate your phone use. Does it ever keep you from being effective in life, work, and your relationships? If so, see if you can put a system in place to help you manage the use of your phone.

Consider establishing assigned times to check your phone, such as twice a day—once in the morning and once at night.

See Chapter 18 for a helpful tool in naming and managing your priorities well, so you can use your time wisely.

TALENTS

A talent is defined as a naturally recurring pattern of thought, feeling, or behavior that can be used fruitfully. Everyone has talents, but strength is given to those who work for it. You develop strength by working on your craft. You have to practice persistently and consistently so you can stay within striking distance of excellence. Yes, this can be hard work! The important thing to remember is that you are responsible for the naming, cultivation, and use of your gifts and talents.

Here's a question that motivates me: If you have the ability to be better, then why aren't you? The benefits of working on your skills and talents are worth it. As the Scripture says, observe people who are good at their work. Skilled workers are always in demand and admired; they don't take a backseat to anyone. (Proverbs 22:29, MSG)

I see so many people who spend their lives living out someone else's script. They waste their time, investing it in wrong things or people, and they neglect to improve themselves. Boundaries will help you continue to love what you do and were made to do while you avoid taking on things you shouldn't. Boundaries remind us that there is a destination.

You have to remember one thing: You cannot please everyone. This is the biggest trap that people fall into, especially the "nice" people, who want to be people-pleasers. One speaker said, "I don't know how to be successful, but I do know how to fail. Try to please everyone."

Your life matters. Anyone who truly cares for you will want you to make the most of your life by taking the time to improve your skills and abilities. See Chapter 4 on finding your talents and Chapter 24 on using the 10,000-hour rule to achieve mastery of your gifts and talents.

TREASURES

Your treasures represent your money and other resources. I've not seen anything in my life that generates more conflict, and that affects more dimensions of life, than money. Whether it's not having enough money; having enough, but mismanaging it; lending or borrowing money; or having too much and losing sight of priorities—money affects everything.

Money boundaries are important because you need this resource to move through life with options. Please review Chapter 14's lessons on money. You'll find simple principles and tools in the management of funds and how to think about money and its use.

I also want to deal with the topic of borrowing and lending money. As the Scripture says, just as the rich rule the poor, so the borrower is servant to the lender. (Proverbs 22:7, NLT) This is an extreme picture of the relationship that money creates when that money is borrowed and lent.

LENDING

As a rule, I do not let people borrow money unless I'm ready to lose it. Over time, I have seen numerous examples of relationships in families and friendships destroyed because of unpaid loans and unhealthy ways of dealing with loan defaults. When funds go unpaid, it causes resentment, slander, factions over who's right and wrong, and a whole host of other issues. Lending money really doesn't become a problem until you don't have enough. I recommend that, if someone asks to borrow money and you do not have your emergency fund in place (which is discussed in Chapter 14), it would be wise to say you cannot help them. That being said, the circumstances of the situation can be more complicated, so you need to assess several factors, including:

- The financial responsibility of the person asking for money. Are they dependable and reliable when it comes to paying their debts?

- The circumstance of the loan. Is the person borrowing money because they want to go on vacation or because they need to pay for their rent or face eviction?

- Your current financial condition. Are you in a position to help someone financially? Are you struggling financially? Do you have your 3-6 months of emergency expenses in place?

These questions can help you decide whether to loan money.

Borrowing

Don't make a habit of borrowing money from others. If you're in such a tough situation that you must borrow money, do everything within your power to pay the funds back in the time promised. If you're managing your own money well, you should seldom find yourself needing to borrow. Do everything you can to put yourself on good financial footing, through strong financial disciplines such as budgeting, living below your means, and setting financial goals, which is discussed in Chapter 14. Establish an emergency fund so that in a time of crisis, you can borrow from your own savings.

Thoughts

When I was in high school, I heard a motivational speaker say, "If you don't know what you believe about a particular topic, read two books on it and make up your own mind." The message has stuck with me: Ensure that what you do is a product of your own research and your own conclusions. This practice helps you set reasonable boundaries for your thoughts. We need to *own* our beliefs and attitudes, because they fall within our property line.

As the Scripture teaches, the gullible believe anything they are told. The prudent sift and weigh every word. (Proverbs 14:15, MSG)

Three things that you should do to make the most of your thoughts:

1. Take the time to evaluate your beliefs and philosophies. When you feel pressed to make a decision, it's okay to say, "I don't know right now. Let me think about it." One of the worst things that I see happen is people rushing to a conclusion about serious life matters, due to outside pressure. Chapter 7 includes a tool you can use for this practice.

2. Continue to expand your mind by taking in new information, letting it renew and even transform you. See Chapter 16 for more on personal development.

3. Sometimes we all have what my counselor friend calls "stinking thinking." When your thoughts become distorted and unhealthy, they can lead to decisions that are bad for your life. Avoid black-and-white thinking, emotional reasoning, jumping to conclusions, minimizing, overgeneralizing, and more. I recommend sitting with a certified coach or licensed counselor to discuss the tools and how to apply them to your life.

SAFE PEOPLE

In life, you don't get to choose whether you get hurt, but you do have a say in who hurts you. Every close and intimate relationship will have its fair share of hurt, anger, sadness, and fear.

Often, there are "elephants in the room" of a relationship—factors that we should take into account, but that we pretend don't exist. If we don't acknowledge the elephants, they can get bigger and cause relational discomfort and turmoil. Deal with the obvious potential problems in a relationship as clearly and quickly as you can.

We should set standards for the people we allow into our lives. We should know the kind of people we want to become for our friends and our communities as we continue on the journey to honoring our calling. Personally, I've come to the point where losing friendships is not as important to me as losing my integrity. Unfortunately, most people have never learned the tools needed to find good friends and have never learned how to be good friends who protect one another's integrity. Hoping someone can meet your needs and trusting their capacity to do so are two different things.

Any healthy relationship must include safety and trust, both of which are built in moments. Trust is not something you can do or produce. Trust is the fruit of a relationship where you know you're loved by someone who has a history of helping you in a positive way. But how can you know whom to trust?

The way we determine trustworthiness has been broken down into six factors that form an acronym called CASUAL. I define casual friends as friends that provide a sense of comfort and safety, and allow you to be yourself.

CASUAL

Clear up assumptions and clarify expectations

It's common for people to misread someone else's intention. Read these questions and ask yourself what usually comes to mind:

1. I sent someone a text message, and they haven't texted me back.
2. Someone walked past me and did not say hello.
3. I looked in someone's direction, and there was a frown on his or her face.
4. I was on the phone with someone who promised to call me back and never did.
5. It's my birthday, and I have yet to receive a text or a callback from someone.

If you experienced any of these situations, would your take on it be negative? Would you believe the other party doesn't care about you or doesn't like you? Would you make assumptions about their motivations?

Consider how easy it is to get it wrong, in these situations. Instead of thinking, "Jon told me he would call me back and did not. I knew he didn't like me, and now he's trying to show me I don't matter to him," you could take a more neutral approach: "I wonder why Jon didn't call back." Instead of taking a position of moral superiority and concluding something negative, switch to an attitude of curiosity and compassion. When someone doesn't behave or react exactly as you expect, they might well have a reason—and it has nothing to do with you.

Let your favorite words going forward be "I wonder ..." instead of "I *knew* it!" We often don't know what we assume we know. See Chapter 35 on how to create valid expectations.

Admit wrongs and accept your individuality

I believe relationships would be less drama-filled if everyone would take responsibility for their own wrongdoings and hold themselves accountable. Using statements like, "I made a mistake. I'm sorry. How can I fix it?" help relationships grow stronger. Saying "It's not that deep. You're too sensitive. Just get over it," do the opposite.

When I think about accountability, I have to think about the intention or the motivation of the person being held accountable. In other words, do you care about someone enough to *own it* when you let him or her down? Do you trust them to do the same? Sometimes the answer might be no. Be as honest as you can when it comes to relationships, so you and your friends don't have mismatched expectations.

The truth is, all of us can be insensitive at times, but we still have a responsibility to be mature. Mature people don't let their insensitivity govern their behavior. Mature people acknowledge their insensitivity and put things into place to heal any damage they cause, so they can maintain a healthy sense of self. Only foolish people allow their insensitivities and unreasonable expectations to create conflict, alienation, and eventually a breakdown in a relationship.

We expect people to care about our feelings, but we also need to temper our expectations of how other people will behave. As you continue to build your friendship with someone, you'll begin to cultivate a certain consistency in your expectations—but be prepared to be flexible as life offers new challenges that require you to change those expectations.

So many of our judgments are relative. Have you ever noticed that, when you're driving, anyone going slower than you is a moron and anyone going faster than you is a lunatic? We compare all things to ourselves—but you and I are not the standard for friendship, and the world does not revolve around us.

I believe there is no such thing as "common sense." What's common to you and what's common to me might be very different, based on our upbringings and personalities. Don't think your expectations of others are based on some kind of uniform "common sense." We are all unique.

Your goal should be to have a healthy relationship where there is reciprocity and healthy and honest communication, in which both parties are honored as unique individuals.

Secret-keeping

Some years ago, I attended a special church service called the "Right Hand of Fellowship." This was the day when all the new members of the community were formally presented, prayed for, and welcomed into the church. The pastor stood up at the podium started by explaining what it means to be part of a community. In his own words:

"We appreciate the value of community and family and want our community and family to be healthy and strong. We will ask you to leave if you do this one thing. Adultery never destroyed a church. Drug abuse never destroyed a church. Alcoholism never destroyed a church. But gossip has. If you gossip, we will ask you to leave. Nothing has destroyed a community faster than gossip, because people no longer feel safe to be honest about their struggles."

This was one of the times when everything stopped, and I had to reevaluate my life and how I might have played a role in destroying community and family. Yes, I have been guilty. His words rang so true, I decided that day that I would become a secret-keeper—someone who could be trusted to hold on to your secrets.

The Scripture says that a gossip betrays a confidence; so avoid anyone who talks too much (Proverbs 20:19, NIV). A true friend is a vault; they don't share your secrets with anyone, and they don't share with you anything that's not theirs to share. There is nothing that makes me lose trust in someone faster than when they share with me private details of other people's affairs. Many people use gossip to gain social capital and to be liked, but this is unhealthy behavior that needs to end. Being a good friend means being a secret-keeper.

UNDIVIDED AND WORD-HONORING

People who are *undivided* have integrity. They choose what is right over what's easy. They don't just profess their values—they actually practice them. I give my highest level of respect to a man who lives what he says he believes. On the flip side, it's hard to trust people who aren't living according to the values they profess.

It takes true strength and courage to follow convictions in the face of criticism and opposition. It's hard to be honest, insightful, and thoughtful, and to have a conviction to honor your beliefs and values—even to the point of death. When I meet someone with such conviction, I want them in my corner because I know I can count on them to live what they say. If you have integrity only occasionally, people notice that and call it *hypocrisy*. If you have integrity all the time, people notice that and call it *honorable*. An honorable person is a safe person.

When an honorable person says that they will do something, they will try their best to do it; if they can't do it, they are honest about their limits. I appreciate it when I can count on someone to be there when it matters most, and also when they can be humble enough to say when they cannot honor an obligation. Can people count on *you* to live up to what *you* say? Take some time to evaluate your level of reliability in relationships. If you've noticed inconsistency, or you have often been unreliable, have the courage to confront this trait. Find someone you trust hold you accountable.

Avoid Judgment

Billy Graham and Bill Clinton and their families met after Clinton's scandal. Clinton had had an affair and lied to the country and the world about it. A media reporter ran to the front and asked Billy Graham how he could support a man who had this major moral failure. Billy Graham said: "It's the Holy Spirit's job to convict, God's job to judge, and my job to love."

It is very easy to judge another person's weakness by your strength in that area. But we are all weak in some part of our life. Never judge yourself or anyone else by a momentary mishap. Someone who is safe doesn't judge you when you tell him or her about your mistakes, struggles, or challenges. A safe friend is there to support you in the process of growth and healing, and tries hard to have empathy and get perspective of your situation by putting themselves in your shoes. A safe friend offers support and compassion instead of condemnation.

If you have been judgmental to someone, one of the most redeeming things you can do is go back to the person and apologize for your insensitivity. Doing so shows the person you valued them enough to right this wrong. We need to empty ourselves of the need to change other people, because others can never be where we are or think what we think.

Limits

Limits mean what's okay and not okay in a relationship with you. In the section above, we emphasized the 4 Ts—your thoughts, time, talents, and treasures—as worthy of boundaries and protection. You establish and maintain boundaries through conversation, sometimes confrontation, and conflict resolution, which will be discussed in Chapter 35.

Unfortunately, too many people allow themselves to be taken advantage of in friendships out of fear of losing the relationship. To them I say, you should never forsake or sacrifice your uniqueness, emotional safety, and mental judgment just to stay in a relationship where you are being held in contempt or disregarded. In other words, don't be a fool for anyone.

If you have difficulty in setting boundaries, it might be because of your upbringing and family of origin. You might have been raised to believe you had no personal rights, and that everything had to accommodate another family member. If you need help in setting proper boundaries, read about or take a class about codependency, or work with a coach or a therapist.

This CASUAL tool is about picking the right people to trust and also becoming a trustworthy person. Please keep in mind that everyone comes with "some assembly required." Use this tool to help you build loving and healthy relationships, families, and community. Remember, in the presence of true, unconditional love, you will need no defenses.

CHAPTER 34

Survivor or Victim

A MAN CROSSING THE STREET was suddenly struck by a speeding, drunk driver. He survived with serious injuries. Doctors assumed that the man would never be able to walk again.

The man had a wife and two daughters. He wept, picturing everything he would lose now: the ability to play sports, to walk his daughter down the aisle, and even to work to support his family. After many hours of crying, he realized that he might not have been responsible for what happened to him—but he was responsible for what happened next.

His healing and recovery were up to him. He could schedule physical therapy appointments and arrange for someone to transport him to and from the doctor. He could organize his life to be as productive as possible. While he had a great support system, his healing was his responsibility.

Instead of being a victim, he became a survivor, someone who functions and even prospers in spite of hardship. He chose not to remain helpless and hopeless.

When tough times hit, what mindset do you take on? Are you a survivor or a victim? How do you know which you are?

Nine Signs You Are a Victim

1. You complain rather than take action to improve your situation.

2. You discuss the same issues over and over, month after month, and sometimes year after year.

3. You receive solutions but always seem to find them unworkable or inapplicable to your circumstance.

4. You wait for a "superman" to rescue you.

5. You avoid taking responsibility for your actions. You look for people or circumstances to blame for your current condition.

6. You are a parasite. You take but don't give. You're more of a liability than an asset because of your selfish perspective.

7. You refuse to take care of yourself, to ensure that someone will take care of you.

8. You are constantly in "trouble" because you catastrophize situations.

9. You drain the people around you with your unwillingness to deal with your situations head on.

Nine Signs You Are a Survivor

1. You engage in behaviors to move you in the direction of improving your situation and restoring your sense of hope.

2. You are willing to fight the fear of change and make sacrifices to position yourself to grow.

3. You are patient because you understand that delayed gratification is a tool on your journey to reach your goal.

4. You fight your fears on a daily basis.

5. You make plans based on reality, not a fantasy world.

6. You embrace your circumstances instead of running from them.

7. You use all the resources at your disposal to bring about positive change.

8. You seek skilled help when you get stuck instead of spinning your wheels.

9. You stay prudent instead of being impulsive and reacting solely off emotion.

Shame

As I write this section, I am aware that our upbringing and family of origin is where we learn how to be a victim or a survivor. Our families are supposed to help us learn who we are and fortify our authentic selves. Unfortunately, many of us did not have this experience. In fact, many of us were conditioned to disconnect from our authentic selves and live out the lives of other people. In the process, we might have developed a *shame-based* identity. *Shame* is a feeling of being broken, shoddy, and unfit for connection and love from others. Shame says, "If you knew the truth about me, you would no longer love me."

Sadly, the feeling of shame has become a public health issue, as it is correlated with depression, anxiety disorders, and addictions.

Families that produce shame generally use these often unspoken commandments:

- Never ask for help, because people who ask for help are weak.

- Don't rock the boat as long as our image looks good. It's about perception, not reality. (This commandment encourages secrets, and secrets make us sick.)

- Don't trust anyone, because they will exploit your weakness and hurt you. (Reminder: We can set standards for the people in our lives. See Chapter 33's section on Safe People.)

- Don't question your parents, no matter what they do. You owe them your loyalty because they always know what's best.

- Find a "black sheep" to blame for all problems, because if we acknowledge our own mistakes, it will make us feel defective.

We all have, at one point or another, experienced shame. But if we grew up experiencing perpetual shame, we can now take steps to heal and grow into the persons that we were meant to be. Shame arises out of beliefs about ourselves and the world around us. It requires that we buy into the belief that we are alone.

When we get to the root of the beliefs behind our shame, we can start to question them, using our logic and reason. Once we start questioning them, we might realize that we don't actually agree with them and, from there, we can deconstruct those feelings and replace them with a more accurate and helpful view of ourselves.

One of the ways you can know if you're in shame is if you hear tapes playing in your head that say, "You're not good enough" or "Who do you think you are?" Without disclosing the names of individuals, here are some specific messages that people feeling shame have shared with me:

- "You failed the CPA exam five times! You're not really smart. You just got lucky."

- "Who are you to write a book? You didn't go to school for this."

- "You had a baby out of wedlock. Now you can never have a better life."

- "Your child is in prison. You must have been a terrible parent."

- "You've been used and abused. No one decent will want you now."

- "Why are you going back to school now? All you did before was fail."

- "You dropped out of school. You're not educated. No one cares about your opinion."

- "You had an abortion. This mistake can never be erased. This will haunt you."

- "You are not married yet. Something must be wrong with you."

- "You can't have a child. You are defective and worthless."

- "Why are you crying? Real men don't cry."

- "Why are you still unemployed? You should have finished college."

- "You're a felon now, an ex-con. No one will hire you."

I know these are difficult messages to read, but they are real, and we can't heal unless we bring things into the light and deal with them. Unfortunately, these messages can be planted into our minds and hearts from our upbringing, our families, friends, and our culture, which perpetuates a continuous sense of inadequacy instead of bringing about hope for redemption. We are not encouraged to learn from our pain. Some people spend their whole lives overcoming the negative messages from their past. So the questions become, what makes shame stronger and more powerful—and what weakens and eradicates it?

Shame is strengthened by three things:

1. **Secrets**: Shame is tough, but it's even harder to know that you are required to keep your mouth shut about something painful. We are as sick as the secrets we keep. It can be tremendously helpful to find a place where you can reveal everything—maybe a support group, a church meeting that focuses on your particular struggle, or a trusted and competent counselor/coach. The prior chapter shares a powerful lesson on how to evaluate safe people to speak to. Chapter 37 will also include pointers on choosing a counselor.

2. **Elephants in the room**: When we are not able to discuss tough issues like the scenarios mentioned above, their power to disrupt our emotional and psychological states grows. Ignoring the obvious also can destroy our ability to have true intimacy and community, and it sometimes leads to worse things, like medicating

your pain with food, alcohol, drugs, overspending, acting out sexually, and being around unsafe or unhealthy environments.

3. **Judgment or condemnation**: Attacking other people gives some people a false sense of superiority, which is really rooted in insecurity. It's easier to hurt others than to identify with them, because once you identify with someone, you are on equal ground. If you feel insecure about who you are and how important you are, see Chapter 13 for advice on how to begin to have a healthy self-regard. Many people who judge others say, "I'm just telling the *truth*." Word to the wise: Truth can be used as a sword or a scalpel. A scalpel is a medical device that cuts for the purpose of healing. A sword is used to bring harm. Be mindful of your intent and the effect of your words. Ask yourself, before you speak:
   a. Is it true?
   b. Is it helpful?
   c. Is it inspiring?
   d. Is it necessary?
   e. Is it kind?

Every day, I realize more the degree to which people were not affirmed, myself included. As a result, I am learning to develop the habit of being encouraging and speaking life, especially when providing constructive feedback. Speaking the *best* truth will help others overcome self-doubt and believe they are enough.

Shame can be removed using:

1. **Compassion and empathy**: Compassion is the ability to have concern for the suffering of other people. Empathy is putting yourself in someone else's shoes. Advice: The next time you see some type of abuse of a human being, take it personally. Refuse to tolerate abuse. The way to truly create a safe and healthy

community that fights shame is for everyone in that community to work together.

2. **Awareness of your triggers**: A trigger is something that sets you off emotionally. Everyone has different triggers. Your shame triggers might come from your childhood or from some difficult or traumatic experience in your past. For me, it's in the area of academics. I didn't feel smart as a kid, because of bad messaging from well-intentioned but unwise people who called me derogatory names, thinking their verbal abuse would motivate me to do better in school. Words do hurt, and they can affect the course of someone's life. The tongue has the power of life and death (Proverbs 18:21, NIV).

3. I walked around feeling dumb and destined to fail in school and, ultimately, in life. It took a lot of prayer, work in counseling, and self-awareness to realize this was not the case—but I am still sometimes triggered to feel that old lack of confidence. I have identified my shame triggers and I work to stay confident in my abilities and be honest about my weaknesses. I had to have compassion for myself and give myself room to be imperfect.

We all have areas where we feel shame. It's important to identify your shame triggers and being prepared to fight against them, so you can move through life without letting shame paralyze you. Common shame triggers involve body image or physical appearance, abuse, financial status, intelligence and academic strength, parenting, past sexual relationships, and a criminal past. You might be able to add to this list. The point is that these issues affect your life, but they should not affect your self-worth. That's where the work needs to be done.

Get aware. Get honest. Get healed and walk in freedom. I know it's easier said than done, but you have to get started if you want to achieve emotional freedom. Find a safe place, like a counselor's office or a support group, and work on dealing with your shame by affirming your value—apart from any accomplishment, position, possession, appearance, title, or skill. Get perspective on what you are here to do. I pray that God gives you courage in dealing with these issues and getting your life back from shame.

4. **Awareness of shame messages**. Certain aspects of our culture are designed to trigger shame. Authority figures might use shame to keep us from misbehaving. Advertising uses shame to prompt us to spend more money. Once you recognize these messages, you can take responsibility for which messages you hear and which you *push back* against. In general, we should oppose the views of the culture that perpetuate shame by evaluating these messages in three ways:

   a. Investigating why certain messages exist.
   b. Determining how these messages impact the community.
   c. Determining who gains from the messages.

Once we've done this work, we can boldly proclaim that we are not broken or defective. We are enough. From a sense of being enough, we can live more full, impactful, and wholehearted lives.

A word to anyone who works with people in any capacity:

Guilt and shame are two tools that are often used in working with people. Guilt says you did something bad. Shame says you *are* bad. Guilt focuses on behavior. Shame focuses on the person's intrinsic worth.

Shame is a dangerous tool to use to change behavior. It often causes more harm than good and perpetuates a negative culture where emotional abuse is used to achieve progress. Results may be achieved in the short term, but over time, shame has damaging effects on a person's soul and their community.

Guilt can affirm the dignity of the person while correcting mistakes or bad behavior. Shame destroys dignity. Remember to focus on guilt and not shame.

Always remember: *Be kind, because everyone is in a fight that you know nothing about.*

Examine the list on the previous page and write down the negative messaging about yourself that you might have received from your culture and your family. Use Chapter 7 on differentiation to help you in breaking down the different areas of beliefs:

Naming Emotions

I was tempted to not include this section—probably because this is the area that I struggled with the most and still struggle with today. Whether I am successful at it or stumbling my way through, I recognize how vital this lesson is and I understand its benefits over time.

Emotions are the language of the soul. I was raised in a home where healthy expression of emotions was not given much attention. At times, emotions were not allowed, not seen as important, or were acted upon with little regard. There were no "spaces" where I could pour out my heart and be honest, especially about my sadness. I never felt it was safe to work through my confusion and pain.

My life focus was more about moving along and making progress in whatever course of life that I was on—school, church, or work. In some ways, I was *crippled* in my emotions. At times, this made me an unloving person. This, of course, is not to blame my parents or my culture, but it does highlight a deficit in a much-needed area of my development as a healthy person.

In working with people over the years, I've observed that my experience was common. Most people were raised in environments where they could not comfortably talk about their emotions.

We now know that if you want to change people's behavior, you have to speak to emotions. The healthy expression of emotions is a skill that has numerous benefits. Emotions are not to be followed solely, but they are to be expressed and used in the process of evaluating significant matters in life such as job satisfaction, relational health, and determining your values.

Paying attention to your emotions is extremely important, because emotions that go unexpressed diminish your sense of self over time. Unexpressed emotions can turn you into either a zombie or a ticking time bomb. In my experience, the more difficult emotions—like fear, anger, or sadness—are the hardest to work through. Fear tells us to run away or confront the threat. Sadness tells us we've lost something. Anger can indicate an unmet expectation or the violation of a boundary and can be a healthy, natural reaction to injustice.

We all feel these things, yet naming our emotions is a skill that takes practice. Review the feeling charts on the next page. Make it a habit to routinely ask yourself the following questions and journal the answers. If you are like me, this will feel like hard work, because it has not often been done. But just like a new workout where you discover muscles in your body that you didn't know you had, this emotional workout will provide you with the tools needed to build your emotional flexibility and to aid you in your life.

Feelings can be expressed in multiple ways: writing, art, physical activity, prayer, or conversation with a trusted friend or counselor. But before you can express an emotion, the emotion has to be named.

Ask yourself these questions to get a feeling for what you might be feeling:

What makes me anxious?

What makes me sad?

What makes me angry?

What makes me happy?

What am I feeling? What am I feeling about the feeling? Use the list below to help you.

LIST OF EMOTIONS

Joy – Tenderness – Helplessness – Defeat – Rage – Cheerfulness – Sympathy – Powerlessness – Boredom Outrage – Contentment – Adoration - Dread – Rejection – Hostility – Pride – Fondness – Distrust – Disillusionment – Bitterness – Satisfaction – Receptivity – Suspicion – Inferiority - Hate – Excitement – Interest Caution – Confusion – Scorn – Amusement – Delight – Unease - Grief – Spite – Elation - Shock – Overwhelm –Vengeance – Enthusiasm – Exhilaration – Discomfort – Isolation – Dislike – Optimism - Dismay – Guilt – Numbness – Resentment –Amazement – Hurt – Regret – Trust – Loneliness – Ambivalence - Alienation – Calm – Stun – Melancholy – Exhaustion –Relaxation – Interest – Depression -- Insecurity – Offense -- Relief - Intrigue – Disgust – Indifference – Hope – Absorption – Sadness – Pity – Pleasure – Curiosity –Revulsion – Confidence - Anticipation – Hurt – Contempt – Bravery – Eagerness –Weariness – Comfort – Hesitancy –Boredom – Safety – Fear - Preoccupation – Happiness – Anxiety -- Anger – Love – Worry – Sorrow – Jealousy – Lust –Uncertainty - Envy – Insecurity – Anguish – Annoyance – Disappointment – Humiliation – Compassion – Horror - Self-consciousness – Irritation – Caring – Alarm – Shame – Aggravation – Infatuation – Shock – Embarrassment – Restlessness – Concern - Panic – Grumpiness – Trust – Disgrace – Awkwardness – Nervousness – Exasperation – Attraction – Disorientation – Neglect – Frustration

CHAPTER 35

Assertiveness

Staying passively silent in the face of oppression slowly corrodes the soul.

GROWING UP, I LEARNED QUICKLY that the kid in the playground who doesn't want to fight always leaves with a black eye. I witnessed a startling level of violence and aggression in my neighborhood. I had to learn fast to stand up for myself, or life on the playground would be a series of challenges by the neighborhood bullies. I had to be prepared, at any moment, to protect myself and those I cared for. This was difficult for me since I was naturally a friendly kid who valued relational harmony. Sadly, my value system and the Newark playgrounds did not mesh too well. I had to become tougher, because the environment called for it.

In our adult world, we meet people just like bullies on the playground. These people intimidate, coerce, manipulate, or harm weaker people with no consideration for their well-being. Their motivation is ignorance or selfishness. If you've been around long enough, I'm sure you've known a bully or two. They can be people in your community, your boss, friends, co-workers, and even parents. You might even *be* a bully, intentionally or unintentionally.

To defend yourself against people like this—and also encourage others to resist bullies—you have to develop the skill of assertiveness.

It's a skill that the world we live in calls for. There are three aspects to assertiveness:

Expressing your beliefs in a non-offensive way. See Chapters 3, 7, and 33 for guidance on how to come to a place of identifying and naming your beliefs and values. In this chapter, you'll learn why some people are afraid or unable to articulate their beliefs, and we'll explore some possible solutions for people with this problem.

Standing up for your rights and negotiating peace in close relationships. You'll be given a framework for having what is called a "clean fight." Most people do not fight in a respectful way, but if you understand how you developed your fighting style and you're motivated to let go of dirty fighting, you can learn to fight clean. Another word for clean fight is *negotiation*.

Expressing your feelings in a non-offensive way. See Chapter 34 for guidance on how to identify and process your feelings so that you can articulate those feelings clearly.

WHY ARE PEOPLE AFRAID TO SPEAK UP?

Over time, I've noticed several reasons why people have a hard time being assertive. This is not an exhaustive list, but it certainly covers a lot of ground for many people.

Reason #1: They lack information or subject matter expertise. Many times, we know what we want to say but we have not taken the time to put those ideas into words. I believe "think before you speak" can be applied in a general sense here. It's wise to anticipate that you might be asked to clarify your ideas and views to your coworkers or friends. I recommend reading or listening to a teaching on the subject. Take notes that can be easily recalled, and practice by envisioning yourself explaining your stand. I know it sounds weird, but this kind of practice helps you overcome nervousness and learn to speak clearly about important topics.

Assertiveness can open doors, professionally and personally. The ability to communicate an idea is just as important as the idea itself. If you have trouble ever speaking in front of others, enroll in a public speaking course at your local college or university or sign up for a Toastmasters club near you. (www.toastmasters.org). Toastmasters is a communication and leadership development organization that provides people with the opportunity and training to speak in public.

Reason #2: They are intimidated by authority figures. Many people find it hard to be assertive in front of their bosses or people who have more authority than they do. But this hesitation to speak truth to power also can be overcome.

Grab a journal or use the Notes section at the end of this chapter and write about the last three times you were passive in a meeting with a perceived superior. Brainstorm all the positive and negative results that could have occurred if you had been more assertive. What might you lose if you speak up? What might you lose if you don't speak up?

Remember, even people who seem supremely confident to you most likely had a moment in their life when they were intimidated by someone. They overcame their fear by making a choice to speak up rather than allowing someone else's presence to silence them. It's been said that courage is not the absence of fear but the judgment that something else is more important than fear. As long as you are confident in what you are saying and have done your homework, you can respectfully and clearly make your point in front of anyone. The best answer to fear and uncertainty is anticipation and preparation.

Being assertive might help you earn respect. People who get easily intimidated to the point of remaining silent don't get a chance to demonstrate value. Make a choice that you will speak, when prepared, in a wise and appropriate manner.

Reason #3: They are uncertain about their convictions. I believe the solution here is knowing and committing to your values and being differentiated. Values say what you are committed to and willing to pay the price for. Differentiation is the calm separation of your true self from the demands and voices of people around you.

Too many people allow their lives to be governed by the will of other people. They develop a low sense of self-awareness, which makes them unable to be assertive. Please go back to Chapter 3 on Values and Chapter 7 on Differentiation and review these lessons, which will help you to pinpoint what is most important to you, what you truly believe in, and what you are responsible for.

You want to be inner directed rather than outer determined. Once you know who you are, some people will be attracted, and others might be repelled. That's okay. The pleasure of approval and the pain of rejection never entirely goes away, but you can't betray yourself because of how others react to you.

At the end of the day, assertiveness is a skill that takes effort and practice, like any other skill. Make the commitment to work on this skill consistently. It'll change your life. If need be, get a coach who can help you walk through practice scenarios with you.

The Rights that People-Pleasers Need to Know
You'll never be loved if you can't risk being disliked.

I put together a list of the rights that people-pleasers need to know they have. Some people are inclined to let others govern their lives. They put other people's needs first, considering their second-place role as the price of admission to a relationship. If you are a people pleaser, let this list be a guide as you reclaim your life. If your direction has been fear-based, it's time to decide that from now on, you will act from a place of genuine self-motivation.

1. **The right to set boundaries.** People-pleasers believe that whenever someone needs, expects, or wants something from them, they must ALWAYS be available to accommodate. But they have the right to evaluate whether they have enough time, money, energy, and resources to meet the needs of others. See Chapter 33 on Boundaries.

2. **The right to make decisions.** People-pleasers believe that others need to agree with their decisions for their decisions to be valid. But everyone has the right to feel confident and happy about their decisions, even if others disagree. They also have the right to change their minds about a decision upon further consideration, without explaining their new decision (unless the decision affects others).

3. **The right to be imperfect.** People-pleasers believe they should never disappoint anyone or fall short of anyone's expectations of them. We will talk about valid expectations a bit later. We all have the right to make mistakes.

4. **The right to say how they feel.** People-pleasers believe they always have to be nice, upbeat, and never hurt anyone's feelings. But we all have the right to express our emotions, even if they might hurt someone's feelings. There's a difference between *hurt* and *harm*. *Hurt* is when pain is inflicted for someone's growth because the "wounds from a friend can be trusted" (Proverbs 27:6, NIV). *Harm* occurs when someone's well-being is damaged.

5. **The right to identify their responsibility.** People-pleasers believe they must have the answer to every problem in every situation for every person and take care of everyone, even people who aren't asking for help. We all have the right to determine if

we are responsible for finding the solution to a problem. We also have the right to say, "I don't know," "I don't understand," or "I can support you in solving the problem but it's not my problem." And everyone has the right to say "No."

6. **The right to ask for assistance**. People-pleasers believe that they should never bother others when they need help with their own needs or problems. But we all have the right to ask for what we need and to be taken seriously.

If you're a people-pleaser, I hope you recognize yourself here and this list serves you on your journey to getting your life back. Review this list regularly to evaluate your past and current choices and decide if you need to pull back and readjust how much you are giving.

If you are someone who manipulates and uses people-pleasers for your own benefit, let this be a moment of awakening for you. You might be robbing someone of their destiny. For a variety of reasons, people-pleasers feel they must give their power away. As a responsible, loving, and moral person, make sure that you are honoring the autonomy of others and ensuring that they are serving out of a genuine motivation—not being used.

EXERCISE FOR THE PEOPLE-PLEASERS

Practice saying a powerful word, a word that people-pleasers struggle with. It's a little, two-letter word, but it requires a backbone to say it and mean it. It's the word, "No."

Here is a set of scenarios that can come up over the course of your life that you may have to say *no* to:

1. *Scenario*: A financially irresponsible person who already owes you money asks, "Can I borrow some money? "

"No. I want to help, but I can't until I can be confident that you can pay me back."

I had someone in my life who would ask me for money constantly but never paid me back. Eventually, I realized I was enabling bad behavior. The next time they asked for money, I said I needed to see a budget of their expenses and a timeframe to pay it back. I even offered to help with the budget. Needless to say, it's been years since this person has asked me for money. It's funny what happens when you challenge people to be accountable for their decisions instead of enabling. This lesson is one that we should have learned growing up, but if you never did, it's not too late.

2. **Scenario**: When you have to study for a test, your friends ask, **"Do you want to catch a movie with us?"**

"No. I really want to, but the reality of my school schedule says no."

I remember failing exams because I spent time hanging out when I should have been studying. When I failed, some people felt sorry for me, but no one else was responsible. I carry that lesson until this day, and I hope you will too.

3. **Scenario**: It's against your values and beliefs, but your friends ask, **"Do you want to smoke with us?"**

"No. Thanks, but I'm just not into it."

I wrestled with these decisions in my younger days. Social pressure can be very difficult, even when you get older. But I remembered that, each time I did something contrary to my value system, it weakened my character—and that character would be the same one that I would carry with me into every situation for the rest of my life.

4. **Scenario**: Someone who always runs late asks, "Can you take me to the airport in 30 minutes?"

"No. I'm sorry, but I have a meeting at work."

I know this sounds cruel, but for all my last-minute people who live in their own time zone, time is the most precious commodity. It's irreplaceable. You can't make more, and you can't get it back. If you are someone who is always late to events, please review Chapter 18. One of my mentors said he could tell how much impact people will have in life by how they deal with time. I know things happen, but things don't *always* happen. It's better to learn about the importance of time when the stakes are low than to miss out on a major opportunity when they are higher. Your schedule affects your rhythm and pace. Your rhythm and pace affect the quality of your life.

In general, people want to be liked by others, but compromising your deepest values, mental judgment, or emotional safety to please people will only lead to frustration and regrets. "Yes" and "no" are two of the most powerful words in the English language. You might have to say "no" to someone so you can say "yes" to your values. Money, education, health, and time are valuable.

MIND READING AND EXPECTATIONS[5]

Assumption is the lowest form of knowledge.

People often make assumptions simply because they don't have the courage to ask questions. But what we assume about people and situations might not be true. Sadly, we might then pass around our assumptions on in the form of gossip, which can damages relationships and cause further confusion and conflict. The maturity of any relationship can be measured by your ability to have *uncomfortable* conversations, including finding out information to replace your assumptions. Let's look at some scenarios.

Common scenarios where people "mind read":

- You call someone, and they don't pick up.
- You send an e-mail and don't get a reply in twenty-four hours.
- You send a text message and don't get a reply.
- Someone walks past and doesn't acknowledge you.

These situations are common, but sadly, some have caused tremendous damage to relationships simply because people misunderstood and responded inappropriately.

Some common assumptions or "mind readings" conclusions:

- They must be mad at me.
- I knew they never liked me.
- They must think I'm not that important.
- They are trying to get back at me.

While these assumptions *might* be true, they are certainly worth having a conversation about, if you value the relationship. As a mature person, be the one to take responsibility for the issue. What's the real explanation?

Here are actual scenarios that I've experienced personally or heard firsthand accounts of. Think about these situations when you're tempted to assume you know why someone behaved rudely or indifferently to you:

- "I'm sorry Jon. My wife went into labor (this one really happened to me)."
- "My father was in the hospital."
- "My mom just died, and I just zoned out."

Exercise: Think of a recent scenario where you had an expectation of someone and they let you down. What story did you tell yourself about why that happened? Take time to think of the story and how long you held on to it. What was the real explanation?

EXPECTATIONS

In life, you are never disappointed by what you find. You are disappointed by what you *expected* to find. Unmet expectations are the cause of most frustrations.

But sometimes, those expectations are invalid. We need to recognize whether our expectations are fair.

Expectations come from a variety of places: school, church, TV/movies, family, friends, etc. Your expectations might be unspoken, and you might have no awareness of them until they are unmet—and by that point, anger or disappointment have moved in.

Remember: Your anger and disappointment are unwarranted if the expectations were not valid in the first place. So what makes an expectation valid?

A valid expectation has four traits (which form the acronym CARS):

C – Conscious: There's an awareness of the expectation by the other party.

A – Agreed Upon: Both parties agree to the expectation.

R – Realistic: The people involved have the ability and a willingness to do it.

S – Spoken: There has been a clear expression of the expectation.

Unrealistic expectations cause confusion in workplaces, families, neighborhoods, and churches. The violation of expectations can lead to divorces, failed businesses, family tension, and broken relationships.

Certain events seem fraught with expectations, including holidays, vacations, family functions, date nights, birthdays, household chores, and weddings.

Think about what you expect from the people around you. Use the list to go through your expectations and decide whether they are valid or invalid. Does everyone know what you expect and have the ability to do what you expect? Have you asked them clearly to do what you expect?

Albert Einstein said that the most incomprehensible aspect about the universe is that it is comprehensible. I believe that is also true about relationships. Many problems in relationships are preventable if we take the time to understand and manage our expectations. Unspoken agreements or expectations have the greatest potential to cause trouble.

I believe you can prevent half of the drama in relationships is by bringing those expectations to the light.

Exercise: Go through a recent, simple expectation you had that went unmet, which made you upset or frustrated. Maybe you didn't get a birthday card, or someone didn't return your text, or someone forgot to take out the trash. Ask yourself ...

Conscious – Are you aware that you had the expectation?

Agreed Upon – Did the other person agree to the expectation?

Realistic – Was your expectation reasonable? What evidence did you have that this person could or would do this?

Spoken – Did you clearly express the expectation—or did you just think "they should've known"? Note: The words "They should know" come from the pit of hell. Nothing destroys a relationship quicker than the mindset that the people in your life *should already know* what you believe, think, or feel without you informing them.

Exercise: Use a partner to practice saying these statements, which can help you clarify expectations and assumptions:

- "I'd like to clarify an expectation I have of you. Is this a valid expectation?"
- "I expect … because…. Can we agree to that?"
- "Can I check out an assumption I have of you? Is this true?"

Some examples of these statements in real life:

- "I'd like to clarify an expectation I have of you. I expect you to call me on my birthday and get me a gift or at least a card. Is this a valid expectation?"
- "I expect you to fill up my tank when you borrow my car, because I would do that for you. Can we agree to that?"
- "Can I check out an assumption I have of you? I'm assuming that you didn't respond to my text because of the argument we had … is this true?"

CLEAN FIGHTING

The more arguments you win, the fewer friends you'll have.

All close and authentic relationships will, at some point, be tested. Conflicts arise because of the different perspectives, values, and priorities that each person has.

Conflict is not a bad thing. It actually gives you the opportunity to learn about each other's values, priorities and concerns. Resolved conflict can further deepen the closeness of a relationship. I know I have grown closer to the people in my life when we have resolved conflicts.

Many people ignore or avoid the tension of conflict because they were never taught how to resolve the issues in relationships. Unfortunately, bad things grow naturally, while good things have to be planted. For most people, the lessons on how to deal with issues in a healthy way are learned too late or not at all.

I learned unhealthy ways of dealing with issues because of the environment I grew up in. But I consciously studied and learned better ways to handle conflict as an adult—and so can you.

The *worst* time to learn conflict resolution is in the middle of a conflict. I'd like to provide you with a set of tools that will help you learn how to fight "clean." A clean fight is the mature resolution of a conflict, in which both people involved take responsibility for the issues. A clean fight is a negotiation between two people to find a resolution that will help protect their relationship.[6]

Dirty Fighting Tactics[7]

True peace will never come by pretending that what is wrong is right.

Silent Treatment – Sarcasm -- Using "Always" or "Never" – Lecturing – Complaining - Anger/Rage -- Blaming/Verbally Attacking – Denying - Escaping – Indulging in Addictions – Condescending -- Walking Away -- Passive-Aggressive Behavior – Making Threatening Gestures – Placating – Lying - Name-Calling – Avoiding -- Hitting/Violence – Criticizing – Shouting - Showing Contempt

Exercise: Before we can walk through the steps of a clean fight, we need to raise our awareness of what dirty fighting looks like. Let's list the dirty fighting tactics that we might have learned. Use the section below to answer the following questions:
- What dirty fighting tactics have you used?
- Where did you learn these tactics?

Please be honest about this. By doing this work, you are trying to break generational patterns of unhealthy relationships and set the stage for a new way of doing things. This is one of the most powerful exercises I have ever done in my life. It changed my life and relationships for the better.

CLEAN FIGHT MODEL[8]

A clean fight is going to look and sound weird. You'll need to walk through the mechanics of this kind of negotiation over and over before you can get the hang of it. It's like riding a bike or driving a car. Once you've done it enough times, it becomes second nature—but first, it takes a lot of practice.

Remember, this work is about changing the unhealthy and dysfunctional ways that you may have done things in past relationships, so prepare for it to be uncomfortable.

1. State the problem. "I notice ..."
2. State why it is important to you. "I value."
3. Fill in the following sentence: "When you ... I feel ..."
4. State your request clearly, respectfully, and specifically.
5. Listener: Consider the request. In a few sentences, share your perspective on it.
6. Listener: Are you willing to do all of it, some of it, or none of it?
7. Speaker: Agree on the request.
8. Here's a practical example of how the clean fight is done.

"I notice that when you borrow my car, you tend to block the sidewalk and not pull the car all the way up. I value an unobstructed sidewalk. When you block the sidewalk with your car, I feel anxious. I worry that our neighbors will think we're inconsiderate. I would like to ask that you pull your car to the very end of the driveway when you arrive home first. If you forget, I would then like to ask that you take responsibility for moving both cars in all the way."

"I had no idea it bothered you. For me, it is no big deal to move the car. I am more than willing to do it. I have one adjustment, though. I would like to ask that you remind me nicely if I forget to do it within 30 minutes."

"It's a deal."

THINGS TO REMEMBER

If the other person offers an alternative, you can renegotiate—but not more than three times. If a proposal requires more than three adjustments, take a break, give it some thought, and try again. You might need to get someone more objective—like a coach, counselor, or a mature friend—involved in the negotiation.

This skill works best with things that are non-volatile. Here are a few examples:

- I notice you call after 11 p.m.
- I notice you leave dirty dishes in the sink for more than a day.
- I notice you rarely fill the car up with gas.
- I notice you don't answer my e-mails for at least a week.
- I notice when we are out together in a restaurant, you pick your cell phone up at least three times.

CHAPTER 36

Community Care

I can't say that I love people if I don't care about the issues that affect them.

WE ALL HAVE COMPLICATED LIVES and many things to deal with. Why should we care about our communities? The answer is simple: hurt people hurt people. Reducing the suffering around us helps lift us all.

As I see it, the issues facing our communities can be addressed if we prioritize our resources and commit to wrestling with difficult conversations. Many issues that are not being addressed carry a stigma of some kind. People feel embarrassed to talk about these problems and unequipped to handle them.

In some communities, it's not safe for people to share their pain and brokenness. We can help by *breaking the silence, removing the stigma*, and *offering resources* that bring healing to our communities.

Breaking the silence must be done in a few steps.

1. Get aware.
2. Develop empathy and compassion for others.
3. Research the available resources.
4. Become committed to being safe.
5. Stay hopeful.

GET AWARE

The first step to healing is becoming aware of what plagues our communities. What issues affect the environment around you? Life is so busy, we forget to pay attention to each other. We are so frantic and distracted—with social media, technology, work or school, and struggling to achieve that we simply don't always take the time to see each other. It's hard to pay attention to your community when you're going too fast and focused on too many things.

I have served both as an emotional intelligence and life skills coach for the last few years. In that time, I've noticed several patterns of important issues. These are things that affect people deeply and, in some cases, for the rest of their lives.

In the next five chapters, we'll discuss issues that are often stigmatized or ignored altogether in our communities, even though they have powerful, long-lasting, and insidious effects on people. I call these issues "Open Secrets" and, as the saying goes, we are as sick as the secrets we keep.

Many people operate on the premise that if something is never discussed, it doesn't exist. Sadly, that's not true. Our communities are riddled with secrets, and we cannot have healing (restoration to one's original purpose) unless people have safe places to talk about these struggles and their solutions. These open secrets are fatherlessness, colorism, sexual abuse, mental illness, and mass incarceration.

These five things plague our communities and affect people at a deep emotional level. The emotional struggles surrounding these issues affect behavior, and that behavior affects every aspect of life, including the ability to succeed in pursuing a calling. If we want to facilitate healing, we need to turn down the emotional noise in people's lives that distract them from their purpose.

Question: Which issue should you focus your energy on?

Simple answer: Whichever one you are most passionate about. We should strive to have a critical awareness of all the issues in our city, country, and world and support the work of others to tackle the issues you do not. But in your own life, address the issue that resonates most with you.

DEVELOP EMPATHY AND COMPASSION

Where you stand determines what you see. The goal of the next few chapters is to begin to change our perceptions of each other by placing ourselves in one another's shoes. We need to see not just the mistakes and bad behavior of other people, but also the conditions and circumstances that lead to that behavior. Only then can we develop the compassionate awareness needed to bring solutions to the table.

Think of empathy as "stepping into another person's reality." When another person's humanity is being assaulted, take it *personally*. Then you can fight to address your fellow man's needs and concerns with practical tools and solutions, and bring about significant change in our communities.

I believe that, when we get close to the issues that burden us, it changes us. Feeling what someone else experiences can stir our desire to love and serve others, as well as making us more effective problem solvers.

You can love others by letting people know they are not alone. My proximity to the lives and problems of other people completely changed the course of my life. My closeness to them meant I could no longer remain ignorant about these issues. It triggered in me a sense of calling to restore hope in and bring healing to people's lives, and to give people the tools to reach their destinies through my prayers, presence, and passion.

The truth is, we've all been called to serve our communities, but not in the same way. We have different individual callings as well as different responsibilities, desires, and visions. Each of us has a different pace of life and different manner of serving. I've always been drawn to hands-on service, whether it's in a group home, detention center, school, church, or a prison. I am most comfortable either speaking, coaching, or listening to people's stories and providing information on the resources available. But other people might find they deliver their most effective healing through prayer to tackle the spiritual realities affecting our lives, individually and corporately. Still others might find it best to give financial support, to undergird work that is already being done in their communities. Or they might want to donate a few hours a month to volunteer with organizations like Big Brother and Big Sister, Boys and Girls Club, or other mentoring programs.

We need to find ways to get close to the issues that burden us and ways to serve that fit our personalities, talents, temperaments, and limits. I believe that if you begin working on the issues that have affected you most profoundly, you'll find your own healing.

Solutions are possible in our communities if we can remove stigmas, cultivate awareness, and make resources available. People can be destroyed by a lack of knowledge—but people also can be saved through an abundance of saving knowledge that speaks to the deepest needs of their souls.

GET INFORMED

I am thankful for so many people who work, sometimes thanklessly, to build safe, healthy, and strong communities: the religious leaders, social workers, teachers, law enforcement agents, community activists, motivational speakers, school administrators, and many others. Their work is vital. I want to make a case for getting them more support.

One of the greatest enemies known to mankind is ignorance. Information is critical in helping us heal. We must commit to listening to one another in a loving and compassionate way as we journey toward our own healing.

A facilitated discussion in a small group can give people the space to be honest about their pain and brokenness in a family-like environment. Group members learn to be supportive of and hold space for one another in their vulnerability around topics that are not often discussed in everyday life. Such conversations can inform you on a personal level. In addition, you'll find a list of recommended resources at the end of the book that you can look into, to grow in your knowledge and ability to bring solutions.

BECOME COMMITTED TO BEING SAFE AND RESOURCEFUL

Decide to end all practices and behaviors that contribute negativity to our communities. If you don't believe that these issues are real or problematic, I probably can't change your mind. But if you have been one to stigmatize these issues, I want to challenge you to get close to people who have been affected by them. Take an objective and honest look. This will take some work, because empathy is a muscle that needs to be exercised. If you can't do this for someone else, do it for yourself. I believe other people's problems are our problems when they affect us.

My hope is that someday we believe that "if it hurts my brother or sister, it hurts me." I heard about a man who drove his car into a pole. He got out, dazed, and lay on the ground. A crowd gathered. After a few minutes, someone asked if anyone had called 911. No one had.

This often happens in situations involving groups of people. The idea to call 911 had occurred to nearly everyone, but each person assumed someone else made the call. When a great number of people are aware of a problem, no individual will feel *personally* responsible for solving the problem. Unless we assume personal responsibility, the problem might not be solved at all. Knowing that other people are aware or present can change our conviction that *we* need to take action—whether a situation is trending on social media or happening right outside your doorstep.

And this "group dynamic" doesn't stop there. When we see people walk away from the pain of others, it often gives us emotional permission to walk away as well. We start becoming accustomed to dysfunction—and once dysfunction is normalized, it can affect all communities.

I believe we have the power to change this.

I'm not making the case for everyone to become some sort of die-hard activist, but rather for recognizing our responsibility for doing everything within our power to help change our communities. We need to help create a culture where everyone does their part in solving problems and healing wounds. We can't do everything—but we can't let that undermine our determination to do *something*.

Every pain experienced deserves attention. We don't have to selectively compare pain to figure out who is more deserving of attention. Compassion and empathy don't run out. There's plenty to go around. If we want true community, we can't let anyone suffer alone.

Ask yourself these questions:

- How can I be an asset in solving communal concerns, within my sphere of influence?
- How can I be of benefit, within my limits?
- What role is each person to play?

I've facilitated small groups in many places during the last few years. I've come to one conclusion: everyone wants to feel SAFE. And when I have asked groups, "What is your greatest fear today?" without fail, they say they fear being judged. No one wants to be looked down upon or ridiculed when they share their truth. People want to know that, even if you see their failures, insecurities, and fears, you will still love them.

Every wound needs a witness and a validation to heal well. I believe, as simple as this sounds, we have the power to give each other the type of safety needed to heal from pain. We can help each other let go of the past and to begin to unlock our gifts and talents to pursue the future.

Yes, *it is possible*—but we will need to commit to changing our bad behaviors. We must become safe people to know, and stop gossiping, slandering, dirty fighting, and sharing things told to us in confidence. I've found that, once people have the space and support to be heard and to process their experiences, they often muster up the courage to solve their own problems.

STAY HOPEFUL

I stay motivated by feeding my belief in things I have only seen in my imagination. As intelligent and rational as we are, ideas alone cannot get us up out of bed every day. We need ideas that are fueled by convictions of the heart. Our conviction motivates us to not only pursue our own opportunities but also to sit with people through their difficult times and circumstances. When my own life gets dark, my faith in God gives me hope. This story gives me tremendous comfort:

"God can do anything, you know—far more than you could ever imagine or guess or request in your wildest dreams! He does it not by pushing us around but by working within us, his Spirit deeply and gently within us." Ephesians 3:20 (MSG)

> There was an old man who would plant an annual fruit garden. It was hard work. The man's only son, who used to help him, was in prison. The old man wrote a letter to his son and explained this situation.

> "Dear Son, I'm sad that you are not here to help me with my fruit garden. I'm not as strong as I used to be and the ground is really hard. I know if you were here, you would be glad to help me dig up the ground. Love, Dad"

> A few days later, he received a letter from his son.

> "Dear Dad, Don't dig up that garden! That's where the bodies are."

> The next morning, the police came to the old man's house and dug up the ground without finding any bodies. They apologized to the old man and left. That same day the man received another letter from his son.

"Dear Dad, Go ahead and plant the fruit garden now. This was the best I could do under the circumstances."

We can always find a way to offer our assistance, despite our limitations.

The community is as good as we bother to make it and we can always find a way to make it better, if we are committed and creative. We have to be able to see the worst from people and still believe the best for them. Maintaining this vision takes a tremendous amount of strength, love, and integrity. We know that healing will not be done perfectly, but we can fight for it faithfully.

CHAPTER 37

Mental Illness

To not have your suffering acknowledged is a devastating form of violence.

MENTAL ILLNESS AFFECTS ONE'S FEELING, thinking, or mood that inter-feres with our ability to function and relate to others. It's very common: One out of five adults suffer from some form of mental illness. One out of 17 adults lives with a severe mental illness like bipolar disorder or schizophrenia.

Mental illness affects not only the patient but also the patient's fam-ily, friends, and community. In my experience, most people dealing with a mental illness are suffering in silence because this condition carries a stigma. One therapist I spoke with described mental illness as a computer crashing, yet no one cares enough to stop and see what's wrong with the hard drive.

For those dealing with a severe mental illness, the most basic tasks can be difficult or even impossible. Yet the mentally ill person might never tell anyone, because they feel a sense of shame about the condi-tion. People who are not familiar with mental health often ask, "What does it look like to have a mental illness?" or "How do I know if I have a mental illness?"

The spectrum of mental illness is wide and includes depression, anxiety, post-traumatic stress, schizophrenia, bipolar disorders, and other conditions. It can be hard to know if some symptom you experience is mental illness: "When am I just having trouble sleeping, and when is it depression? Is the trouble I have focusing a type of attention deficit disorder?"

If you or someone you know struggles with mental illness, learn about their condition. Don't try to diagnose a mental illness in yourself or anyone else. Study the condition so that you can eliminate the stigma around mental illness and provide resources to begin seeking help.

My hope is that, when people begin to feel unmanageable difficulty in life due to their thinking, emotions, or mood, they will seek help. I hope they will find a trusted friend, a therapist, or a psychologist to guide them. But often, people who need help don't know how to ask. They might not even recognize that their sadness or anxiety can be helped.

Mental illness affects many different aspects of life. As compassionate people, our call is to remain mindful of our own well-being and be non-anxiously present and attentive to the deepest needs of others, as much as we can. This takes time and patience. Although I love coaching and facilitating small groups, I've had to slow my life down to remain fully attentive to other people. Taking time to listen and care will ultimately change our communities for the better, because so much healing depends on building healthy relationships.

MENTAL ILLNESS IN THE AFRICAN-AMERICAN COMMUNITY

"Therapy is for white people." This is what one of my mentees told me as he came back from his weekly visit with a therapist.

"Really!" I said. "So black people don't need to talk to people about their problems?"

"Nah," he replied. "Black people go to church and pray to Jesus. We got used to struggle, and it made us stronger. That's what I do."

I appreciated his honesty and candor. Struggle can certainly help to make someone strong, but it can also cripple people when the mental and emotional wounds from the struggle are not properly addressed. While I commend the desire to become spiritually richer, a strong faith doesn't necessarily mean you are mentally free. As one pastor said, preaching a sermon to a man with a broken head and telling him to be right with God is equal to telling a man with a broken leg to get up and run a race.

I grew up in a community where mental illness was rarely discussed. If it was discussed, in most cases, it was done to ridicule or mock, not to bring awareness, compassion, and healing resources. Fortunately, our culture around mental illness is changing for the better, as more people acknowledge that they and their loved ones experience mental illness. People have a better attitude now about seeking mental health services, but unfortunately, they still don't always seek the treatment they need.

I know this feeling. I struggled with bouts of depression due to poor self-care and unresolved grief for a few years. I remember the shame associated with feeling that I couldn't get up and go like other people. I had trouble thinking clearly. I had emotional struggles that felt shameful to even describe. So I simply faked it and suffered in silence.

I didn't have anyone I felt I could be honest with and didn't know there were mental health services that I could access. But the shame was the worst. I wasted so much time before I sought help, because of ignorance and shame, which I believe are the two biggest enemies in the fight to bringing healing to people's lives.

In a sense, this book was born when I sat down with a trained counselor and began dealing with all my issues. I began to feel better when I adopted healthier practices like exercising, getting adequate sleep, and being active in hobbies, I also began to take steps to find my calling.

By going to therapy, I gave myself a degree of love and attention that I had previously lacked. The Golden Rule is to treat others as you want to be treated. Well, I want to be heard and validated without being judged, and I want to return the favor and hold space for others in that way.

If you're like me—someone who is prone to solving everyone's problems—sometimes you might need someone to be there for you. If you're struggling with any type of mental illness, I hope you will reach out for help. There are trained people out there who know how to help.

Seeking mental health treatment doesn't mean you're crazy or weird. It means you're human. Don't feel ashamed, and don't let anyone shame you. It takes courage to ask for help, but you don't have to go through life fighting your battles all alone. Healing is available.

DEPRESSION

Depression is a common mental disorder and one that I've come across pretty often. It's a state of low mood where people lose interest in daily activities. Some people might experience depression as just "the blues" or a bad day. If these moods or bad days happen so often that they're interfering in your life, you might want to seek help.

Many times, people of faith are assumed to feel only joy—but joy is not the only human emotion. All people experience anger, frustration, and sadness. There's a book of the Bible called Lamentations. Two-thirds of the Book of Psalms are laments. Sad emotions are part of the human experience, even for the spiritually devout. Deep sadness can to hopelessness, a sign of clinical depression. Sometimes we have to recognize this condition in others, because they are unable to see their own mood or they have no hope that life can improve.

Mental health professionals use these symptoms to help identify if someone is suffering from depression:

- Changes in ability to concentrate
- Feelings of guilt or hopelessness
- Decline in interests
- Appetite changes
- Slowness of thought
- Reduction of physical movement
- Changes in energy levels

- Changes in sleep patterns
- Thoughts of suicide.

These signs are not to be used to make an official diagnosis for depression. They can, however, help you recognize whether it's time to reach out for help. If you are experiencing these issues or any other set of difficulties, mentally or emotionally, that last for more than two weeks, please seek help. If you're in school, locate the school social worker or mental health worker to schedule some time to speak with a counselor.

More than ever before, people are being open and honest about their mental health challenges. Please don't suffer in silence. Contact a trained and licensed counselor. Ask a trusted friend, physician, or clergy member to help you find someone. See the resources at the end of this chapter.

AREAS AFFECTING MENTAL HEALTH
The American Way of Life

Researchers have been confounded at the increasing rates of depression and suicide in western countries. One factor we can point to as contributing to emotional and mental breakdowns is the American Way of Life. This mindset that says progress is our primary goal.

In our desire to pursue more and more things, and live faster and faster lives, we have sacrificed our emotional health. We long to be productive, but it comes at a cost. As we strive for more, we might violate the natural limits on our time, energy, finances, and emotions—and then we're surprised when we break down.

To be blunt, we simply want too much: bigger houses, better cars, more expensive weddings, extravagant vacations, maxed-out 401k balances. We strive for these things by working two or three jobs, keeping insane hours. We take eighteen credits each semester. We lobby for promotions at work by skimping on other things in life, like marriage and family. In a sense, exposure to so much affluence and extravagant living has corrupted our pure value system.

High level executives at large companies have come to terms with the fact that their divorce rate will be two to three times the national average. Their career success comes at the expense of their personal lives. They go beyond their natural capacities and pressure their employees to do the same.

I won't pretend that shifting from this fast-paced culture of "succeed and achieve" is easy—but we must do what is necessary to get back to emotional and mental health. To be sure, there will be seasons of life where you have to pick up the pace and get extremely focused to accomplish a particular endeavor or pursue a meaningful goal. That can be a good thing. It can become a bad thing when each goal is rapidly succeeded by another, and there is no clear end in sight. An unbalanced life is unhealthy, mentally, emotionally, and physically. (See Chapter 12 on defining your success.)

We have to fight to be content but not complacent. We have to stop comparing our successes to what the next person is achieving or acquiring. Someone else's blessing might be your curse. Their success might be something that would derail you from the pursuit of your calling.

I have two antidotes to help in our fight against the American Way of Life:

1) Chase contentment and avoid negative cultural pressures.
The following Scripture gives a pretty clear admonition to us about the pursuit of more material wealth: "Don't be obsessed with getting more material things. Be relaxed with what you have. Since God assured us, 'I'll never let you down, never walk off and leave you,' we can boldly quote, God is there, ready to help; I'm fearless no matter what. Who or what can get to me?" Hebrews 13:5-6 (MSG) And this Scripture encourages us to be mindful of what we allow to influence us: "Guard your heart above all else, for it determines the course of your life." Proverbs 4:23 (NLT)

As a practical example, strawberries are a delicious fruit that tastes sweet, but when you eat a Snickers bar, the strawberries won't taste as sweet. With all the intensified sweetness in the Snickers bar, your taste buds become so excessively stimulated that the strawberries lose their appeal. Something that was meant to provide contentment and natural enjoyment loses its value because of excessive stimulation.

This same factor applies to lifestyle choices influenced by movies, TV, and music. An ordinary life seems dull when you expose yourself to the "made up" reality shown on entertainment outlets. Some people are tempted to make foolish choices with major financial implications in the pursuit of the "happiness" shown on TV—and when they discover they're still not happy, depression can ensue. I've seen it time and time again.

I believe it's possible to want so much that you cannot recognize the amazing life that can be enjoyed with simple pleasures. Be mindful of what you let influence you, because that will affect how you live and make decisions. To be free from excess desire is a good thing. It helps us to maintain perspective. If we live without envy, we have the freedom to decide on what we deem to be worthwhile goals and healthy lifestyle choices.

1. *Get counseling* from various sources and perspectives, but take everything with a grain of salt. Use your value system (Chapter 3) to sift the advice you hear regarding major life choices. Not all advice is good advice. Those advising you might not be familiar with or committed to your value system. Personally, as a man who wants his steps to be ordered by God, here are the Scriptures I use to anchor me and give me confidence to hold true to my core values:

    a. "Doom, rebel children!" God's Decree. "You make plans, but not mine. You make deals, but not in my Spirit." (Isaiah 30:1, MSG)

b. "Blessed is the one who does not walk in step with the wicked or stand in the way that sinners take or sit in the company of mockers, but whose delight is in the law of the Lord, and who meditates on his law day and night." (Psalm 1:1-2, NIV)

c. "If any of you lacks wisdom, you should ask God, who gives generously to all without finding fault, and it will be given to you." (James 1:5, NIV)

d. "The LORD directs our steps, so why try to understand everything along the way?" (Proverbs 20:24, NLT)

e. "Trust in the Lord with all your heart; do not depend on your own understanding. Seek his will in all you do, and he will show you which path to take." (Proverbs 3:5-6, NLT)

Technology

Technology exists for the purpose of making life simpler. Unfortunately, that's not always how it works. If you're chronically checking to see how many likes or followers you have on a Facebook, Instagram, or Twitter—or if you're constantly text messaging in group chats—technology has made your life more complicated and stressful.

Miscommunications or emotionally charged dialogue in text messages or on social media can harm or even destroy relationships. Because of technology, people can overthink situations, worry excessively, or misread a friend's feelings, which leads to relationship drama that affects emotional health. When troubles arise, people are less likely to pick up a phone these days or meet face-to-face to hash out differences.

In Chapter 35, there's a tool on clean fighting; Chapter 42 will discuss listening and healthy conversations that can help in these situations. But you must also be mindful of how reliant you have become on your cell phone and how tied up your well-being is with the number of followers you have on social media. Here's a challenge: Try leaving your phone in the car when you go to work. Try not using social media for one day. How hard will it be? Why not find out!

For some of you, taking a technology break is not even an option. If this idea alarms you, take time to assess your technology use. How tied is your cell phone to your well-being? Decide if you're satisfied with this and make whatever changes.

Financial Stress

Many people experience tremendous stress concerning money, partly because they lack knowledge on how to plan their financial lives. In Chapter 14, you'll find a conversation about how to begin DEALing with your money:

> **D***etermine what you goals are.*
> **E***stablish an emergency fund.*
> **A***utomate your finances.*
> **L***ive below your means.*

Perhaps you have financial obligations because of people you care for. These are difficult times, to be sure. Don't journey alone if you don't have to. Seek the help of experienced financial professionals with an official certification (such as a CFP, CFA, CPA, EA, etc.). I also recommend a class called Financial Peace University (www.daveramsey.com) to help you get a handle on your finances and to reduce stress in that area in your life.

Choosing a Counselor[9]

If your mental health is standing in the way of you living a happy life and pursuing your calling, it's time to find help. In choosing a counselor, always keep in mind that you are the consumer, purchasing a service from a professional. You have choices about beginning such a relationship and the form their help will take. These are some questions you might ask:

1. What are your techniques of training, experience, and specialization?
2. Which particular techniques do you use?
3. Will you discuss my treatment plan with me?
4. What happens if we disagree about my goals?
5. Are you licensed by or registered with the state?
6. Have you ever had a charge of unethical conduct brought against you?
7. For what length of time do you usually work with clients?
8. Is there anyone else with whom you will be discussing my case?
9. Have you had experience with other clients in my situation?
10. Do you charge for an initial consultation?
11. Do you charge for a telephone consultation?
12. How much do you charge for each counseling session?
13. Will my insurance pay for this counseling?
14. How long will our appointments be?
15. If I decide that I would like to work with you, are there any other interviews that you require me to complete?

Many therapists gain clients through word of mouth, and a recommendation can be valuable. But just as you won't necessarily like all your friend's friends, you won't necessarily "click" with your friend's choice of therapist, either.

A good therapist for you is one that you feel comfortable with. You need to like and respect your therapist, or you will not be open to what they say to you. You should also feel comfortable with your therapist and free to say anything to them without feeling they would judge you or think less of you. This is very important, since there might be things that you tell a therapist that you will never tell another person. You need to trust them and trust their judgment.

It is a good idea to give a therapist at least two sessions before you decide if you can work with them. If you still feel uncomfortable after the second session, it might be time to find someone else. You should be prepared to feel nervous and uncomfortable at times with your therapist. After all, they are not meant to be a friend who will nod and agree with everything you say. Sometimes, you might feel discomfort as your therapist slowly moves you towards areas in your life that are blocking you and things you don't want to deal with. This is why the trusting relationship is so important. When things start to get hard in therapy, you need to feel reassured that your therapist is there to help you and is ultimately on your side.

Occasionally, you might get angry with your therapist, and a good therapist will be able to cope with that and not get angry back at you. An angry therapist is not a good sign, and although rare lapses are acceptable, since we are all human, a therapist who routinely displays frustration at your slow progress or inability to move past a certain difficulty in your life, is not the right therapist for you.

The best client/therapist relationship is one where you are able to look back and see that, during the difficult times in your life journey, your therapist was there, like a patient parent—listening to you, and hoping for and watching your recovery. When you finally "get there," they are almost as pleased as you are!

RESOURCES

If you are having a mental health crisis, please seek help immediately. If someone you know is having a mental health crisis, please help them get help. Contact the following organizations for information about 24-hour crisis services in your area:

The National Suicide Prevention Lifeline's 24 hour toll-free crisis hotline, 1.800.273.TALK (1.800.273.8255) can put you into contact with your local crisis center that can tell you where to seek immediate help in your area.

The SAMHSA Substance Abuse Treatment Facility Locator and the SAMHSA 24/7 Treatment and Referral line at 1.800.662.4357 provide referrals to alcohol, substance abuse, and dual-diagnosis treatment facilities, including facilities that offer sliding scale fees and other special payment arrangements. Dual-diagnosis services provide integrated treatment for individuals who have both an alcohol or substance abuse problem and a mental illness.

The Child-Help USA 1.800.4.A.CHILD (1.800.422.4453) crisis line assists both child and adult survivors of abuse, including sexual abuse. The hotline, staffed by mental health professionals, also provides treatment referrals.

To locate therapists, you can go to this link: http://www.mentalhealthamerica.net/finding-therapy or www.mentalhealth.gov for referral services.

Do everything you can to seek help. Please don't hesitate to contact a trained and licensed counselor to help travel with you on your journey to recovery.

CHAPTER 38

Colorism

You're pretty for a dark girl.

IT'S BEEN SAID THAT IF President Barack Obama were a dark-skinned black man, he would not have been elected president. This is debatable to some, while others believe it wholeheartedly.

In comedy circles, President Obama has been referred to as someone who had "the complexion for the protection and the connection." The idea that there is prejudice or discrimination among same-race people—based solely on skin tone—is called "colorism." Essentially, it means that if you have a lighter skin tone, you're considered prettier, more valuable, and more successful.

The root theory behind colorism is the belief that beauty and desirability increase with the proximity to whiteness.

HOW DID COLORISM START?

I will speak to the issue of colorism from the vantage point of the African-American community, though the issue of colorism is not isolated to African Americans. Colorism occurs in many places around the world, including East and Southeast Asia, Latin America, the Caribbean, and Africa.

Colorism has a long-standing history dating back to the enslavement of the African people in the United States, which began in 1619. Colorism is a spinoff of racism and involves prejudice and power. White Europeans in power considered light-skinned people to be more valuable than darker-skinned people—possibly because light-skinned slaves were often the illegitimate children of the slave masters, who would want to keep their offspring close by placing them into service in the house.

Some families believed their homes could be run better if those slaves were given an education, so it was more likely that light-skinned house slaves were taught to read and follow the customs of upper-class, white society. It was also believed by most white people at the time that, if slaves had white blood, they had a greater intellectual ability and subsequently, a greater capacity to be "civilized."

Sadly, many light-skinned slaves internalized these assumptions and developed a sense of superiority to darker-skinned slaves, which eventually lead to distrust and resentment by darker-skinned individuals. Colorism became an instrument used by slave masters to divide and conquer their own enslaved persons, by extending to light-skinned slaves more privileges. This would often pit light-skinned slaves against dark-skinned slaves, and make the light skinned slaves more loyal to their owners in the event of a slave rebellion.

To make the impact of colorism clear from a time standpoint: Black people in America were enslaved from 1619 to 1865. For those 246 years, the humanity of black people was assaulted, disparaged, and dismissed. They were often treated like animals and beasts. Families were ripped apart, identities stripped away, and trauma was inflicted through torture, rape, and public displays of slave lynchings.

After the Civil War, in 1865, the slaves were emancipated—but they were not helped to integrate into society. They did not receive services from therapists with licenses in social work or marriage and family therapy. There was no life coaching and no plan to rehabilitate this large group of people. There were no slavery support groups.

For about another 100 years, from 1865 to 1964, black people in America faced tremendous legal barriers at state and local levels. They were prevented from voting. They were routinely attacked, lynched by the KKK, and discriminated against via the Black Codes, which were an attempt to re-enslave black people through vagrancy laws and disadvantage black people through Jim Crow laws.

That's 346 years of oppression and a little more than 50 years of so-called freedom for African-Americans. For this entire span of time, black people were being told the color of their skin was connected to being ugly, immoral, unintelligent, unethical, and of low value. For the last 100 years of it, they were fighting for the right to participate in the political process while being beaten publicly, attacked by police dogs, and sprayed with fire hoses if they attempted to vote. That's a long time.

Slavery created this mentality. The system of slavery is gone now, but the mindset created by the system is still here. It does not automatically change. You can't just flip a switch and remove all feelings of inferiority from black people. As a matter of fact, a sense of identity is more like an autopilot mechanism, which can only be changed through the hard work of reconfiguring the mindset.

Many people fail to realize that generational trauma has been passed down from one generation to the next. Until history is acknowledged and taught, and the pain of the past is fully grieved, these issues will continue. Colorism is a good example. Unfortunately, many black people are guilty of reinforcing the same ideals of colorism imposed during slavery. This needs to stop.

From the media to politics to my immediate community, the effects of colorism are alive and well. I am not a psychologist or psychiatrist. I am a coach, and many of the people I work with are people of color who highlight this issue as one they personally deal with in their community. If we don't talk about an issue, we never heal from it.

It's important to begin by acknowledging the wounds we carry and how their impact shows up. Colorism manifests in many different ways that hurt people's well-being, oftentimes long term. It affects self-esteem and their ideas about what they can do and become in life. It affects ideas about worth and value. It divides families and communities.

By influencing what's believed to be beautiful and desirable, colorism affects marriage and relationship trends. Love and compassion demand that we become concerned and fight to change this through healthy and honest conversation. Honest, compassionate conversation raises the consciousness from which people make judgments and decisions. It can be the catalyst for change in our communities and in people's lives.

Healthy and honest conversation about colorism can create a healing presence, in which people can let their guards down and show others their wounds. It can be the start of a process of empathy, compassion, and healing.

Am I biased?

This might be one of the hardest questions to answer. We all develop biases as part of the human experience. Explicit racial prejudice has diminished, although we certainly have more work to do on that front. But implicit bias or prejudice still needs to be addressed.

Implicit bias occurs when our subconscious thoughts or feelings drive how we think, feel, and behave. We might not have the power to get rid of all of our prejudices, but we can acknowledge them. The first step is to turn a hidden bias into a visible one—a process that requires honesty and humility.

Do you have negative associations with certain people based on skin color or skin tone? Find out by taking the implicit bias test through Project Implicit, a non-profit organization and collaboration between researchers whose goal is to educate the public about hidden biases. Project Implicit was founded in 1998 by three scientists: Tony Greenwald (University of Washington), Mahzarin Banaji (Harvard University), and Brian Nosek (University of Virginia).

Here's the link to the test –
https://implicit.harvard.edu/implicit/takeatest.html

or you can go to www.google.com and in the search bar, type in
'Project Implicit – Harvard University'

The test will assess your skin-tone bias. The test results are not meant to be accusatory or condemning, but to bring awareness to how you see others. With this information, you can better honor your intentions as you interact with and relate to people with different skin tones.

HOW DOES COLORISM MANIFEST TODAY?
Race Bias in Children

Drs. Kenneth and Mamie Clark created "The Doll Test" in the 1940s to study the psychological effect of segregation on children. The test was actually used in the 1954 *Brown v. Board of Education* Supreme Court case that made it unconstitutional to segregate students in public schools by race. The test involved presenting a child with two dolls—one white and one black. Researchers then asked the child questions:
- Which doll was the nice one?
- Which doll would you play with?
- Which one looks bad?

The findings showed that most black children preferred the white doll, which researchers felt indicated self-hatred and internalized racial inferiority, which helped win the landmark case.

Fast forward to a new doll test in 2010, in which children of various races were shown five images of dolls ranging from dark-skinned to light-skinned. Most of the children again showed a bias toward whiter skin, showing that this preference has been perpetuated. Researchers interviewing the children's parents found that African-American parents prepared their kids for diversity and the potential of discrimination, while many white parents believed that discussing race would contribute to the bias problem.

While I understand the motive of being "colorblind," children discover race very early on their own. It's not healthy or safe to refuse to acknowledge someone's racial difference in a world where race has implications.

What are the implications of race today? While racism used to show up primarily in lynchings, the KKK, racial slurs, and hate crimes, today it is reflected in the mass incarceration of people of color, racial profiling, police brutality, redlining, housing and hiring discrimination, judicial bias, and implicit bias. Failure to discuss race is not a solution. Healthy and honest conversations between parents and children—and between all people of every race—will help bring awareness. We must acknowledge this bias and begin to explore ways to compensate for it, to eliminate prejudice in the next generation.

Messages from Media

We must not underestimate the tremendous power of advertising and media to influence our perceptions of beauty, particularly images in magazines, music videos, TV shows, and movies. Marketers put tremendous thought into how to get consumers to respond to an image, and they use the prevalent bias toward lighter skin to help sell their products. Most lighter-skinned people shown on TV and in movies are held in higher esteem than darker-skinned people.

Because of this messaging, many people of color aspire to be lighter. People spend hundreds of millions of dollars each year on skin-bleaching products, throughout the world, to help work this bias in their favor. The exportation of American media to foreign countries has spread the bias. In American TV, movies, and advertisements, a white or lighter-skinned person is depicted as the protagonist, the good guy, or the more desirable person. Widespread awareness that this is happening can begin to reverse the trend, but that is only the beginning.

Messages from Family and Society

Our families are our primary source of messages about our value. Sometimes those messages are good, but sometimes they're not so good. It is important for each of us to acknowledge the messages we've gotten from our families and decide which were prompted by love and helped elevate our self-esteem—and which messages we might want to leave behind. Unfortunately, family is where many of us first learn to demonize black people and deify white people.

My family members have all different shades of skin, yet I was raised believing that folks with lighter skin were more desirable. This message was taught covertly and sometimes overtly. Our families of origin play a huge role in teaching standards of beauty—and if beauty preferences have been learned, they can be unlearned.

The notion of lighter skin being more appealing is prevalent in American culture. It shows up in several ways. Many of the black women in my life have been candid about their love for former President Barak Obama's wife, Michelle Obama. Many have said that seeing a dark-skinned lady in the White House boosted their self-esteem, because dark-skinned women are not often seen in positive roles on television.

Movies have been slightly better at depicting dark-skinned women in a positive light: Viola Davis won an Oscar for the 2016 movie *Fences,* and Lupita N'yongo won one for her role in the 2014 movie *12 Years a Slave.* Both women possessed both visible beauty and talent, and their inner beauty also needs to be acknowledged and recognized.

A question still looms: Are we beginning to accept dark-skinned people as part of the tapestry of beauty, or are we trying to over-correct for the legacy of white supremacy without acknowledging white supremacy still exists? How can we ensure that women of all shades are given an opportunity to share movie screens and magazine covers equally?

How does it end and how do we bring healing?

We must remember that we are the keepers of our souls. We must guard our hearts against allowing unrealistic and imbalanced standards of beauty to enter our consciousness, even when they are pushed forward by the media. Conversations create fertile ground for change. Listening to one another's stories is pivotal to creating a community that fosters healing. What would this look like in your life?

Talk about it. I am a fan of people sitting with a coach or counselor who is familiar with the issue of colorism. Each of us is affected uniquely. You can begin by becoming aware of your baggage regarding standards of beauty that are unhealthy and unrealistic. Personally, I'm still unloading this baggage, but it's getting easier. The more you learn to love yourself, the less you'll buy into any standards of beauty that say you're less valuable and the more you'll accept yourself as God made you. Change your awareness of yourself, and you can no longer be brainwashed.

Evaluate. Evaluate the skin tones you see on the TV programs, commercials, and movies. Take a critical look going forward and take steps to challenge any imbalance you see. Societies that perpetuate color bias have a responsibility to self-correct. We need to affirm the beauty of black people of all shades, particularly black women. Media outlets should have casts of people representing all shades of black. Is this what you observe?

Listen. We need to hear the stories of people who have experienced colorism and empathize with them instead of invalidating their experience. I'm not unaware that these conversations are delicate and can get unhealthy very quickly. We must remember that the issue of colorism affects everyone, not just those who experience it directly. Our job must be healing wounds, not pouring salt on the wounds. Healthy, healing conversations begin and end with a posture of listening and understanding without judgment. Everyone needs space to share, be heard, and critique without being attacked. Otherwise, it will only do more damage and perpetuate pain and separation in the community. Use the tools in Chapter 34 on Shame and Chapter 42 on Listening to help you on this part of the journey.

Appreciate. Study history to understand the pain and the trauma of black people in America. Don't stop there. Recognize the resilience of black people, so you can begin to know that there is a fight, a grit, and something special about black people that cannot be oversold. Appreciating this fact will help to reframe your perspective of people of color in healthy ways.

Go deeper. Elevate the colorism conversation to a more general examination of beauty: hair, facial features, weight, etc. What is considered beautiful today in your country, and who has determined what beauty should mean?

We can fight to right the wrongs of the past and move forward with a greater consciousness and a clear intention of bringing healing. Let's start with healthy and honest conversations, and then take an active role in promoting and supporting positive change in our world.

Chapter 39

Sexual Abuse

I am not what happens to me. I am what I choose to become.

SEXUAL ABUSE IS UNWANTED SEXUAL ACTIVITY. Abusers might use force or threats, or simply take advantage of victims not able to give consent.

According to child advocacy experts, about one in six boys and one in four girls are sexually abused before the age of 18. Social workers and therapists I've spoken to believe the numbers are probably higher. Many victims choose to not say anything out of shame and fear.

From personal experience and from countless stories, incidents of childhood sexual abuse are buried so deeply out of shame and fear that the issues are not dealt with it until the emotional turmoil begins to re-surface. I learned that emotions are like a "Jack in the box." They can be suppressed for a long time, but they will eventually find their way out.

After this abuse, my life became consumed by fear. I felt unable to trust anyone and was afraid I'd never be able to be mentally or emotion-ally stable enough to pursue my calling. Like many abuse survivors, the pain of loss was so great that I suppressed it for many years and put on a happy veneer to avoid the pain that I felt.

After a number of emotional breakdowns, I knew it was time to come clean and stop lying about what I was going through. Everyone thought all was well with me because I had graduated with honors, gotten my CPA license, and was working for a reputable company. But I dealt with secret addictions and emotional and mental battles.

I experienced bouts of anger that led to disrespectful confrontations and misunderstandings. When I suppressed the anger, it caused depression. These issues kept me from having healthy relationships and were robbing me of the fullness of the calling that God had placed on my life. Fortunately, I had a great support system around me. They helped me find a competent counselor, so I could begin to deal with the pain of losing my innocence at such a young age.

There is no such thing as an unexpressed emotion. For me, emotion surfaced through paranoia, bouts of anger, and moments of depression. I remember watching an interview with the retired NBA player Keyon Dooling. I'm an NBA basketball fan, so I was familiar with his career. Dooling suddenly retired and later revealed that he had been sexually abused as a child, and he'd kept the information from his own wife. All of the memories from his past came to the surface following a random incident. Hearing his story gave me hope that I wasn't weird or alone in what I was experiencing, emotionally and mentally. I have learned that many people hold on to secrets like this for years. Eventually, some work up the courage and break their silence.

I was fortunate to hear stories of these celebrities—Tyler Perry, Tom Arnold, Dax Shepard, Sugar Ray Leonard, Todd Bridges, Lewis Howes, and Pastor John Gray—describe their stories of sexual abuse. Their courage helped me find my own courage and enabled me to talk to someone safe and knowledgeable about what I experienced as a child. You never know who you might be helping by telling your story.

People not familiar with the topic of sexual abuse might ask, "What happened?" A better question is, "How has it affected you?" The details of an incident are less important than the impact.

I want to share an excerpt from a book *The Color of Pain* by Gregory Reid, someone who works with at-risk youth. Many people have given me the privilege of holding space with them and trusting me with their stories of sexual abuse; this is one of the best descriptions I've seen about what sexual abuse does to someone. Several pieces of this commentary resonate with me and so many others.

V. What Being Molested Cost Me[10]

The cost to a kid who gets molested is higher than most people know. It's too easy to minimize the damage by saying, "It's just one of those things," or "Get over it." Sexual violation is a violent thing, even when it's not violent. It takes so much inside. After many years, I've taken notice of the losses (much of which has been healed and restored), and I want to tell you about it, so you'll know.

It cost me my childhood. Repeated molestation blocked my memories, and what I did remember was covered with a haze of physical illness, stalking fear, repeat nightmares, and deep loneliness.

It cost me my ability to trust. I resented authority and feared adults so much, I wouldn't go anyplace like a public restroom or swimming pool locker room because I'd get sick from the fear of what might happen.

It cost me my ability to be spontaneous. I kept such rigid control over my emotions, my body, and my mind, that I couldn't laugh, I couldn't play, and being around kids could made me feel sullen, angry, depressed, alone, left out.

It cost me my sanity. Shortly after the initial abuses, I was in a complete emotional dead zone; and one night, as I sat alone in a chair, my mind filled with filth and blasphemy, and tears streamed down my face, because I loved God and I couldn't stop this mental

*rape, and I just snapped after several days of this, and I started
cursing and smoking and drinking, and I told God to give up on
me because I was evil. I was eleven.*

*It cost me my education potential. I was a brilliant child. Being
molested cost me my ability to think without confusion, trance
outs, and frustration. I couldn't concentrate. I could have been
a straight-A Valedictorian. Instead, by the time I finished high
school, I was taking four basic classes and barely passed.*

*It cost me my identity. Being molested created such sexual and
emotional confusion that I was an old man before I was fifteen and
still a boy at thirty. I felt numb and removed, like I was not there,
just a piece of property for others to use and discard.*

*It cost me my adolescence. Being molested made me afraid of adults,
men, women, crowds, public places, challenges, fights, and almost
everything else—including being scared to death I was gay and
scared of all my emotions, including anger and joy. I couldn't date,
I didn't go to the prom, and alcohol was my only "friend." Being
a kid is screwed up and scary enough, but I carried enough guilt
and fear to take down ten normal adults.*

*It cost me time. Being molested started me running, and I ran and
kept going until I crashed in my late twenties, and then it cost me
time in recovering, facing hard truth, and healing.*

*It cost me my family. Being molested crippled my heart enough to
destroy any potential marriage or children. God has restored most
of what was taken, and more. But you need to know, being molested is not a "get over it" thing. It's an evil robber whose damage
goes deep and keeps taking until we can face it and start to heal.*

Gregory Reid knew there was life before the trauma and there would be life after the trauma, if he found the courage to heal. If you've been victimized in this way, you have wounds that need to be healed and lessons that need to be learned on how to heal. Don't let what someone did to you rob you of your destiny. They say time heals all wounds—but in this case, if not dealt with properly or at all, the wound remains. It can make people bitter, caustic, and angry.

Are you a sexual abuse survivor? Here are a few things I recommend:

Break the silence. I know I have said before that we are as sick as the secrets we keep. For some people, simply speaking to a safe person about their experience is all that is needed. Sexual abuse survivors often feel alone. For all survivors, I want you to know that you're *not* alone. Chapter 33 includes information on how to evaluate SAFE people to talk to. See the resources below to find the next steps.

Consider the impact. Ask yourself the hard questions about how abuse affected you. What negative thinking styles and unhealthy habits or addictions have you adopted? Review chapter 34 on Survivor or Victim.

Get informed. Below you'll find several resources that have been a benefit to many others and me. Please take the step. Recovery requires that you pick up the pieces of the past so that you can see yourself more completely and enjoy a freedom to make choices that are not determined by what happened to you.

Find support. Skillful, trusted therapists or support group members can make your journey to healing more successful.

Help someone else. I believe that, once you start to get healing from the pain of your past, your purpose will begin to reveal itself. You have the power to change someone else's life by sharing what you've learned.

Redeem your pain by turning it into a means of serving your community and the world. Don't let it keep you from your calling; make it a steppingstone instead.

RESOURCES

1. RAINN (Rape, Abuse & Incest National Network) is the nation's largest anti-sexual violence organization. RAINN created and operates the National Sexual Assault Hotline (800.656.HOPE, online.rainn.org y rainn.org/es) in partnership with more than 1,000 local sexual assault service providers across the country and operates the DoD Safe Helpline for the Department of Defense. RAINN also carries out programs to prevent sexual violence, help victims, and ensure that perpetrators are brought to justice. Visit www.rainn.org.

2. The mission of *1in6* is to help men who have had unwanted or abusive sexual experiences to live healthier, happier lives. They also serve family members, friends, and partners by providing information and support resources on the web and in the community. Visit www.1in6.org.

3. These books and DVDs, available at www.amazon.com, www.audible.com, or your local Barnes & Noble bookstore, can help to guide you on your healing journey.

Books:
Courage to Heal by Laura Davis
Beyond Betrayal by Richard B. Gartner
Victims No Longer by Mike Lew
Uncaged Project by Sallie Culbreth M.A. and Anne Quinn
When A Man You Love Was Abused by Cecil Murphey

Not Quite Healed by Cecil Murphey
I Thought It Was Just Me by Brene Brown

DVDs
Boys & Men Healing from Child Sexual Abuse
The Healing Years – A Documentary About Surviving Incest and Child Sexual Abuse

CHAPTER 40

Fatherlessness

It's much easier to become a father than to be one.

MY FATHER WORKED A LOT when I was growing up. He was a hard worker who provided for his family, but he didn't have much time to come to my extracurricular activities.

I played basketball in high school. I remember seeing my father walk into a game just as I was being substituted in. The referee blew the whistle. My teammate inbounded the ball to the point guard, and the point guard passed it to me. I was supposed to pass the ball back to the point guard, but my heart said, "No thanks, Coach. You can bench me for the rest of the season, but I have to show my dad I can play." This was my opportunity to show my dad that I had value.

I drove to the basket like there was no tomorrow. I jumped as high as I could, like I was Dwayne Wade with a resolve to score. I scored!!! I had two points for the whole game. My coach took me out, but it was complete. My dad knew I could play. That one moment was cemented in my heart and mind forever. It highlighted the power of a father's approval and a child's desire to prove their worth and value.

Fathers are able to make emotional investments in children that children can withdraw for the rest of their lives. That day boosted my self-esteem, and I walked with a little more confidence. It sounds silly, but it is amazing to me how motivating and empowering a father's approval is to a child.

Kids want to know they are wanted, that they have value, that they matter, and that they are loved. Fatherless children can be devastated by not having that validation and sense of belonging.

Fatherlessness is an issue that is plaguing our country. One in three children in America grows up without a father. The reasons vary. Fathers die, divorce their wives, get sent to prison, or abandon their children. The particular details surrounding each situation can be complex, but the results are the same. Fatherlessness causes emotional pain and leaves scars.

Many times, it's not what happens that hurts (abuse, trauma, witnessing addiction/dysfunction in the family, etc.) but what *should have happened* or what was missing (love, appreciation, teaching boundaries, healthy praise, etc.) that causes pain.

WHAT ARE THE EFFECTS OF FATHERLESSNESS?

1. **Self-esteem/self-worth issues**

   Sons and daughters react to the pain of fatherlessness in different ways. For sons, an absent father means a missing role model. Sons never see a benchmark or barometer for manhood. For daughters, an absent father affects self-worth. Overall, fatherlessness can leave a child feeling defective or inadequate. These children grow up to experience continual patterns of insecurity, confusion, and sadness.

2. **Relationship issues / Fear of rejection, abandonment, commitment**

A father teaches a daughter what to expect from men. A father teaches a son how to treat women. People who don't learn those lessons can make serious relational mistakes. One young man told me that his standard of how to treat women came from what he saw in movies and TV shows. In light of what's on TV these days, that's pretty scary. One woman told me that she would not have dated half of the men she'd dated if a good father had shown her how to spot nonsense from a mile away.

Fatherless children grow to be adults who fear commitment, because the feeling of abandonment and rejection is known all too well. Some of them are uncomfortable with the vulnerability of an intimate relationship, so they might sabotage a connection or leave abruptly, because it's better to leave than to be left. Both men and women might avoid close relationships to avoid pain.

I recently read a book called *4 Things Women Want From Men* by A.R. Bernard. It's written to give women a standard for evaluating men and men a framework to determine how they are doing in the area of manhood. The premise is that, when a man becomes the kind of man that a woman can respect and admire, it liberates her to be the kind of woman she was meant to be. That's the foundation of a healthy relationship. Even if you grew up without a father, you can learn to evaluate and trust relationships in your life. See Chapter 33 on Boundaries and Safe People.

3. Anger

Fatherlessness children might be sad and fearful, but they also can grow up to be angry. Anger is more socially acceptable for men to demonstrate, but women get angry, too. Anger generally manifests itself in either rage or depression, depending on whether the anger is externalized or internalized. Social media has made us all more aware of violence. Whenever a fight breaks out, cell phone cameras come out. The depression that happens when the anger becomes internalized is harder to record.

4. Addiction

A fatherless child has a hole in their soul that is the shape of their father. That child can grow up trying to fill the void with negative things like drugs, alcohol, overeating, overspending, etc. Fatherless young people have a higher risk of substance abuse.

5. Promiscuity/Teenage pregnancy

Teens without fathers are twice as likely to become involved in early sexual activity; fatherless girls are seven times more likely to get pregnant during adolescence. Through my experience as a life skills coach and my discussions with educators, therapists, and social workers, I have seen the role fatherlessness plays in promiscuity. Young girls without father are often left without guidance on the decision to be sexually active.

6. Academic performance/Dropout rates

Students living in fatherless homes are twice as likely to repeat a grade in school. More than half of all high school dropouts come from fatherless homes. Conversely, when a father is involved in a child's academic life, the child is more likely to stay in school and perform well academically. A good father can provide structure and discipline to keep a student on track.

EXERCISE: FATHERLESSNESS IN YOUR LIFE

If you can, find a safe place like a support group or a session with a trained and experienced counselor to hold space with you when you complete this important exercise. The question to answer is, "How has fatherlessness shown up in your life or in the lives of people you know?" Don't feel restricted to the list of symptoms above. Truth is vitally important here, because without truth, there is no healing, change, or freedom.

Ways to Heal from and Deal with Fatherlessness

1. **Grieve.** Find safe places to acknowledge your fatherlessness and grieve the loss of your father. You might have to see yourself as a victim before you can see yourself as a survivor. You were victimized by your father's absence, and you might have been ignoring the pain it has caused. It's preferable to work on your grief in a support group or with a counselor who understands the issue of fatherlessness. Use Chapter 31 as a guide for grieving.

2. **Forgive.** Remember that your father's absence had nothing to do with you. The reasons for a father not being there can vary, but it has nothing to do with the worth or value of their children. You might need to forgive your absent parent, but absolve yourself from guilt. You can become a survivor. See Chapter 32 on Forgiveness, and Chapter 34 for what it means to be a survivor.

3. **Achieve.** Be the best person you can be, in spite of not having your father. Identify the deficits of fatherlessness in your life and put things in place to deal with what you didn't get. For example, if you never learned how to manage money, take a class on money management. If you don't have healthy relational skills, see a coach or a counselor. Books, classes, and therapy can help fill in areas of your life where you should have received guidance.

4. **Reconnect** with yourself. It's a great and important step in the healing process to learn to face yourself—both your best self and your broken self, your bold self and your bruised self. See Part 1 on Self-Awareness is a great starting point for discovering or rediscovering who you are.

5. **Help others**. Do the work above, and if you feel comfortable, use your experience of fatherlessness to provide the support and affirmation to others. Fatherlessness leaves a yearning for relationship. When I first started mentoring, I noticed that my mentees didn't just want information—they wanted relationship. They wanted to talk about how their first interview went. They wanted someone to show them how to budget their money and talk about their experiences with money, not just walk them through the mechanics. Within the relationship—when people can be honest about their fears, pains, frustration, hopes, and joys—healing takes place. Some ministries have been founded by fatherless people to help give other people what they didn't get growing up. Find a way to serve as a surrogate father for someone who needs one. You can mentor and coach through a lot of different programs like Big Brothers Big Sister or the Boys & Girls Club. Go to www.bbbs.org or www.bcga.org.

FOR FATHERS WHO WANT TO GET BACK INTO THEIR CHILD'S LIFE

I empathize with fathers who have not been there for their child for many different reasons. I understand that it's hard to be what you haven't seen. Life isn't always fair, and it's truly not always your fault.

Many men who leave their families come from fatherless homes and eventually succumb to the fear of not being able to be a good father. A difficult relationship with their child's mother can make it almost impossible for a father to see his child. I write this not to beat you up or to berate you, but to encourage you to take the opportunity to get back into the life of your child—even if you have to fight for it using every legal and emotionally healthy avenue available. Stay in touch with your child and if possible, with the child's mother.

Our society sometimes sees the role of the father as providing financial support, but being a father is more than that. Being a father is about nurturing, guiding, protecting, and building up. It's not about the *presents* but the *presence*. At the end of this chapter, I will share some resources to help support you as you prepare to re-enter the life of your child.

These action steps can serve as a ramp to get back on the road to a wholesome relationship with your child:

ACTION STEPS FOR RECONNECTION

1. **Forgive your mistakes**. Give yourself the space to honor your mistakes and their consequences and your separation from your child. We are not perfect people, but mistakes don't define you. Grieve them and forgive yourself so you can get on to the work of reconnecting with your child. See Chapters 31 and 32 on Grieving and Forgiveness.

2. **Take responsibility**. Be ready to acknowledge your role in creating the problem, so you can learn how to pick up the pieces. Don't beat yourself, but do take time and effort to seriously take responsibility for the damage that was done.

3. **Manage your anger**. Find a safe place to work through your anger around the circumstances of your separation from your child. You need to talk about the portions of the situation that were not your fault, or you risk becoming depressed or letting your anger lead you to make unwise choices. A support group, a wise and trustworthy friend, or a professional counselor can

help you work through your own pain and anger over becoming disconnected from your child.

4. **Stay connected**. If the communication lines are open, seek out the opportunity to speak with and if possible, be with your child. If distance is an issue, use technology that allows you to see your child while you communicate. Be careful about what you say you will do during these conversations, because children will take every word seriously.

5. **Demonstrate your love**. Tell your child that you love them, but also reinforce your words with actions. Be consistent, to help establish a foundation of trust. You have to work to understand that your child also might be frustrated with the situation. Try to learn about the person they've become without you, so that you can support the person they will become with you there.

6. **Continue to grow**. Focus on your own growth and development, because you cannot give what you don't have. See Part 1 on Self-Awareness and Part 2 on Self-Development for a good place to start. You cannot give what you don't have. Begin to develop your sense of self and build on it.

RESOURCES

CUNY Fatherhood Academy: This free program was designed to promote responsible parenting and economic stability for unemployed and underemployed fathers ages 18-28, through education, employment, and personal development. The program provides a range of academic and personal supports including TASC (High School Equivalency test) preparation classes, tutoring, individualized counseling, parenting seminars, MTA Metrocards, and job preparation.

Phone: 718-368-6784

Website: http://www.laguardia.edu/cunyfatherhood/

National Fatherhood Initiative: Mission: Creating a world in which every child has a 24/7 dad. NFI is the nation's leading non-profit organization working to end father absence by offering an online community and other resources.

Phone: 301-948-0599

Website: http://www.fatherhood.org/

CHAPTER 41

Mass Incarceration and Reentry

Let the one who has never sinned throw the first stone!
John 8:7, NLT

IN THE 1970s, THERE WERE 300,000 Americans in prison. Today, that number is 2.3 million. There are several reasons for this dramatic increase, including legislation that aimed at being "tough on crime." In the process, the U.S. has not been "smart on crime."

Michelle Alexander, in her critically acclaimed book *The New Jim Crow,* describes how the 1970s War on Drugs left many Americans as second-class citizens with felony records. Racism is also a factor in the criminal justice system. We will need to have conversations about this issue and take action to bring about change.

In 2017, the state of New Jersey, where I was born and raised, leads the nation in racial disparity between white and black people in the prison system. For every one white adult incarcerated in a NJ prison, there are 12 black adults. For every one white youth incarcerated, there are 30 black youths—even though studies show that white and black adults and youths commit crime at about the same rate.

This is the same system that criminalized crack cocaine users, most of whom were black, and now welcomes opioid users with compassion and treatment. The startling and remarkable reality is that criminal justice decisions are often not based on guilt but on wealth, connections, and race. If you want to learn more about this, I have listed other pioneering works on criminal justice reform and changing the legacy of racial hatred and hierarchy at the end of this book.

Eventually, most incarcerated people will be released. People coming out of prison need strong support. In my experience, most ex-convicts have high hopes of doing the right thing and becoming positive members of society. Unfortunately, they are at a tremendous disadvantage, partially because of the stigma of being an ex-convict. The sense of shame experienced by those coming out of prison makes it harder for them to reenter a forgiving society with the necessary resources to be successful.

Society is likely to treat ex-offenders as hopeless cases, saying things like, "You know life is hard with a record, so do what you can, but don't expect much" or "That's what happens in this system. It's never going to change" or "Most people end up going back to prison anyway. Why bother?" These are not unchangeable facts. People who have spent time in prison will encounter obstacles in their reintegration, but they should be met by a society that is hopeful that they have a significant chance of successful re-entry.

One of the ways to ignite that hope is by creating a resourceful environment of forgiveness and grace that makes redemption possible. People might say that those who have committed a crime deserve whatever they get. But if someone violates the social contract by committing a crime, and then pays their debt to society with incarceration, do they deserve to have that mistake held over their heads for the rest of their lives? Most Americans have, at one point or another, broken the law. Most simply were not caught, or they had access to competent legal services to secure their freedom.

In some communities, it's easy to get caught up in the criminal justice system because of the powerful, negative influences in the environment. This is not to excuse personal responsibility, but to highlight how important environment is. The community I grew up in was like that. I could have easily run with the wrong crowd and made one dumb decision that took away my freedom. We must begin to develop empathy and compassion for those coming home from prison by remembering how easily we might have ended up in their shoes.

About 700,000 ex-offenders are released from prison every year. Just as parents need to tailor ways to meet each child's individual needs, society must offer different paths for people coming out of prison—but they do have common issues and needs that must be addressed if they are to successfully transition back into society:

1) Legal challenges

One key factor to help people attempting to change their lives is to assist them in having their records expunged. An expungement is a court-ordered process in which the legal record of an arrest or criminal conviction is "sealed" or erased in the eyes of the law. Taking away someone's criminal record gives them an opportunity to get a job without having their past mistakes used against them. In New Jersey, ex-offenders with a drug conviction who graduate from a specialized program can have their records expunged. For information on expungement eligibility, instructions, and free legal services, go to:

https://www.njreentry.org/about/resources

2) Case management (including jobs, housing, substance abuse treatment, mental health services and legal assistance)

Ex-offenders need meaningful economic and social opportunities to make a successful transition back into society. Every state has its own reentry programs for ex-offenders that vary in the scope of services they provide. Your state's official government website is a starting point to locate the reentry services available to you and those in your community. If you keep searching, you'll find many organizations willing and able to help ex-offenders.

Some states have established special programs that can serve as models for other states.

- In 2015, the New Jersey Opportunity to Compete Act went into effect. The law makes it illegal for an employer to inquire about an applicant's criminal record during the initial job application process. This gives an applicant the opportunity to come in for an interview and tell own story, and gives the employers the opportunity to objectively evaluate prospective employees. This is an example of a step in the right direction that can be duplicated in other states.

- The New Jersey Reentry Corporation can assist their clients with issues ranging from employment skills training and job search guidance, substance abuse, mental health issues, unstable housing, and legal assistance. Their administrative office is based in Jersey City, NJ. There are other NJ locations in Newark, Paterson, Toms River, and Kearny. You can visit the website www.njreentry.org to learn more. You can submit a referral today for yourself or someone you know who is a returning citizen at www.njreentry.org/referrals, via e-mail to intake@njreentry.org, or call 551.222.4323. Their address is 398 Martin Luther King Jr. Drive, Jersey City, NJ 07305.

- New York's Osborne Association offers opportunities for individuals affected by crime and the criminal justice system to transform their lives through innovative, effective, and replicable programs that serve the community by reducing crime and its human and economic costs. The association offers job readiness training and employment services, alternatives to detention and incarceration, healthy parenting and relationship programs, substance use disorder treatment, supportive services for people living with chronic health conditions, housing placement services, mentoring, community reentry services, case management, senior services, children, youth, and family services, video visiting, social enterprises in janitorial and food services, and computer and hard skills labs. Visit their website at www.osborneny.org.

3) Emotional stability

Incarceration can strain family relationships. The first thing that I recommend for anyone who is coming home is that they take some time to come to grips with themselves and the kind of person they want to be going forward. Part 1 on Self-Awareness and the first five chapters of Section 3 on Self-Care include information that might help. Chapter 31 on Grieving and 32 on Forgiveness also hold important information.

Re-entry for ex-offenders might involve grieving a number of losses, including lost time spent in prison, people who passed away while you were in prison, and relationships that changed during your incarceration. It's vitally important to forgive yourself and others for these losses as you start the journey to successful reentry. A therapist or social worker or a support group can help give you space and emotional support to deal with the challenges of reentry.

4) Education

In addition to jobs, housing, and overall case management, ex-offenders who want to re-enter society need education. There are people coming out of prison who have aspirations and gifts that they might never have gotten to chance to explore. Here are two programs that help people in prison and coming out of prison to have access to higher education to develop their gifts. (Please also see Chapter 4 on Gifts and Talents.)

- The New Jersey Scholarship and Transformative Education in Prisons Consortium (NJSTEP) is an association of higher education institutions in the state working in partnership with the

State of New Jersey Department of Corrections and New Jersey State Parole Board, to provide higher education courses for all students under the custody of the State of New Jersey while they are incarcerated, and to assist in the transition to college life upon their release into the community. Their vision is that every person in prison who qualifies for college should have the opportunity to take college classes while incarcerated and continue that education upon release. You can learn more about the program at http://njstep.newark.rutgers.edu/_or by calling the Mountainview program at 888-445-9251.

- The Prisoner Reentry Institute of John Jay College in New York City offers a program called College Initiative. CI's mission is to create pathways from criminal justice involvement to college and beyond and to establish and support communities invested in their own success. Their work reflects a deep passion and strategic commitment to empowering men and women involved in the criminal justice system to become stabilizing forces in their communities, advocates for change, role models, and engaged citizens working for a safer New York City. You can contact the director Ann Jacobs at ajacobs@jjay.cuny.edu or visit http://johnjaypri.org/educational-initiatives/college-initiative/getting-started/.

People who have committed crimes and paid the price with incarceration need a great deal of support in their journey to reenter society successfully. If you are an ex-offender, find that support. If you are not an ex-offender, think of ways you can lend that support.

At the end of this book I'll list more resources to learn about the criminal justice system and efforts to bring about positive change.

Chapter 42

Listening

My dear brothers and sisters, take note of this: Everyone should be quick to listen, slow to speak and slow to become angry. James 1:19, NIV

OVER THE LAST FEW YEARS, a word has been circulating in our society: "woke." "Being woke" became widespread after the 2014 deaths of several unarmed African-American men and women who were killed by police officers. Important details began to emerge about our criminal justice system, specifically the mass incarceration of people of color.

To be "woke" is to be critically conscious of the systemic institutional practices that promote and perpetuate racism, sexism, classism, and other forms of discrimination. In short, it's about an awareness of issues of social and racial justice. I am appreciative of this movement and the people who work hard to bring about true justice to our world. It's important to be woke and to move out into the world with a heightened social awareness, because that awareness informs your important judgments and decisions.

For the purpose of this chapter, I want to discuss being *woke* or critically conscious of our relational practices, specifically the practice of listening and the manner in which we dialogue with each other. The topics in this book, particularly the last few chapters, can prompt important conversations. The way we have these conversations will play a huge role in the progress we make.

A major cause of human problems is how people behave when we strongly disagree. When emotions and stakes run high, people often revert to an unhealthy type of conversation. Most of us have not learned healthy ways to disagree.

In Chapter 35, there's a discussion on how to resolve conflicts through negotiation or "clean fighting." Its goal was to teach us how to stop unhealthy behaviors like silent treatment, sarcasm, passive aggressiveness, hitting, etc. While learning how to negotiate is important, we also need to learn how to listen better—not for the purpose of responding, but so we can truly understand a message someone is communicating.

Listening at the heart level—without making judgment or assumptions—is a mark of maturity and a vital step in building communities that can heal the wounds of the past and bring about true reconciliation. We need to hear the stories of those who share a different perspective. We need to practice *incarnational listening*—listening from the heart and trying to become fully immersed in the perspective of the speaker.

The goal of effective incarnational listening is not agreement or winning a competition. It is understanding without making judgments or assumptions about the person. Another way to look at incarnational listening is that it's like playing charades, not playing chess. Chess is about the next move. Charades is getting attuned to what someone is saying and the heart behind their message.

I'm under no illusion that this practice is easy. To some, it might even sound ridiculous, but I believe this is one of the most important lessons in this guide. In our society, we suffer from an inability to love, and one of the best ways to show love is to listen. Until you sit down and hear someone's story, you are not qualified to judge their situation.

Most people, myself included, come from families where we were never truly listened to, nor were we taught how to listen at the heart level. I know that when I wasn't listened to, I felt unloved, unwanted, and dismissed. This kept me from wanting to be close or share anything with others, because I knew that what I conveyed would not be valued.

In families, friendships, marriages, and communities in general, if people aren't being heard, they are developing an emotional guardedness that breeds a dysfunctional and even toxic environment. Poor listening breaks up marriages, churches, businesses, and friendships. I heard one marriage counselor say that when a married couple stops listening to one another, they will have to listen to the therapist—and if that doesn't work, they will have to listen to the divorce lawyer, or ultimately to the judge who helps divide their assets. This was a sobering picture of the importance of listening.

When we don't discuss serious topics, they become "the elephants in the room." Elephants grow as they feed on avoidance. If we are to move forward as a community, and even as a family, we need to have these conversations and work hard to listen and understand one another. Can listening really make a difference? Let me assure you, it absolutely does. I believe that by learning to listen to each other and validate each other's experiences, we can turn our communities around.

Listening helps us develop empathy and compassion for one another, which changes our perceptions and the decisions we make based on those perceptions. Finding a way to discuss our differences will determine our future as a people, because true listening creates the environment that breeds change. We might never achieve agreement across the board, but we can find a greater sense of compassion and reduced sense of superiority. "I am right, and you are wrong" conversations don't lead to unity. Instead, they breed shame, hatred, and increased division.

I've participated in several support groups over the years where we were asked, at the first meeting, to write down our fears about being in the group. About 80 percent of the people in every group said they feared being judged. No one wants to be judged. No one wants to have their deepest beliefs, thoughts, vulnerabilities, and pain dismissed.

With complex topics, it's harder to feel safe enough to say how we feel. But when the necessary tools are available, the group can start down the road to healing and reconciliation. I know that healing as a community will require many uncomfortable conversations.

What causes this discomfort? Our beliefs are not always rooted in logic. Sometimes, they are rooted in deep emotional pain. We need safe places where we can explore, question, critique, listen, and be heard, where everyone has a willingness to learn and not a desire to accuse.

It's easy to get lost in the theoretical, so let's use a practical tool to evaluate how we behave when it comes to having critical conversations. Let's figure out how to create a space where hearts and minds are changed through expanded understanding. We must learn how to create safety before we speak the truth. We can deal more effectively with the content of an important conversation when we've acknowledged and processed the related emotions, which takes time and patience. It might even require a new level of strength and maturity.

Exercise – Listening Test: What are the ways you interact in conversation?[11]

It's important to remain civility when talking about race, class, sexuality, gender equality, and religion. This last election cycle demonstrated how poorly we handle disagreements. Some conversations require emotional maturity, and not everyone involved in the conversation is at the same level of maturity. If you find you are unable to stay civil, take a step back to process your strong emotions so you can re-enter the conversation without being easily triggered. I say this as a man who is passionate and often says something unwise in conversations about controversial topics. I share this not because I get it right, but because I get it wrong and need to hold myself accountable.

Lack of civility breeds defensiveness and creates an environment that feels unsafe. This kills the hope for unity and reconciliation. When people don't feel safe, the conversation loses its genuineness and ultimately, its ability to affect change in a positive way. It's hard to change the way you speak to and listen to others, particularly if you've grown accustomed to having conversations that are contentious. We have to humbly ask ourselves: Has the way we've done things been effective in building strong communities, where people can have disagreements without being disagreeable?

Our goal is a community that fosters love, healing, safety, and truth through listening, which is the currency of community. It's impossible to incarnationally listen to someone without being changed. Listening is the most important part of a crucial dialogue. We have to always remember our purpose as we engage in conversations. Let's roll up our sleeves and get to work.

The goal of this exercise is to help you evaluate your maturity level.

Directions: Circle all the statements you can affirm.

1. My close friends would describe me as a responsive listener.

2. When people are upset with me, I am able to listen to them without being defensive.

3. I listen not only to the words people say but also to the feelings behind their words.

4. I have little interest in judging other people or quickly giving my opinion to them.

5. I am able to validate another person's feelings with empathy.

6. I am aware of my defensive tactics in stressful conversations (e.g. appeasing, ignoring, blaming, distracting).

7. I understand how the family I was raised in has shaped my present listening style.

8. I ask for clarification when listening rather than "filling in the blanks" with assumptions.

9. I don't interrupt to get my point across when another is speaking.

10. I give people my undivided attention when they are talking to me.

11. I don't overemphasize facts to promote my agenda.

12. I don't change the subject to avoid acknowledging my ignorance or my wrong information.

13. I acknowledge when I don't have enough information and need to research and reflect to have an informed answer.

14. I invite dialogue instead of debate. Dialogue encourages a free flow of information, while debate is about defending your position, with no desire to consider if the other side's perspective has some value. The desire to win drives us away from healthy dialogue because we point out flaws in the other person's argument instead of looking for value.

If you circled ten to fourteen statements, you are an outstanding listener. If you circled six to nine, you are very good; and four to five, good. If you circled three or fewer statements, you are a poor listener and might be in trouble trying to work things out through discussion.

If you want to be really brave, after you score yourself, ask your spouse or someone close to you to honestly rate you as a listener. Be grateful for the insight you receive from this exercise, and if necessary, decide to improve your listening skills.

CHAPTER 43

Living a Life That Matters

The unexamined life is not worth living, but if all you're doing is examining your life, you'll never live it.

EVERYONE HAS A PART TO play in bringing healing and reconciliation to our world. While individual instruments produce incomplete melodies, taken together, they can play a symphony. The story of our lives can be a beautiful orchestra when everyone focuses on their PART—Priorities, Actions, Regrets, and Thoughtfulness.

PRIORITIES

We are all called to serve, but not in the same way. I've been around a lot of different kinds of people over the course of my life, and the most opinionated, I call "What we need to do" people.

"What we need to do is make sure literacy rates are up."

"What we need to do is strengthen the family."

"What we need to do is focus on entrepreneurship."

"What we need to do is change the laws to make a fairer world."

All of these are important and necessary priorities, but each of us can only have so many areas of focused effort. What should your focus be in this season of your life? Part 1 on Self-Awareness and Chapter 17

(One Major Focus) were written to help establish your priorities. I believe that, to live an impactful life, you must be willing to bravely ask the hard questions about priorities and work diligently to find answers, individually and communally.

Living a life that matters means you focus on your areas of greatest commitment. Those areas will be informed by your wiring, your beliefs, and your personal convictions. You need to honor your strongest inclinations, because where you are most passionate is where you are most powerful. You won't need anyone to motivate you in those areas, and you'll be able to invest the energy of your passion and personal sense of mission.

Actions

Martin Luther King, Jr. and his family faced many death threats over the course of his life as a civil rights leader, yet he continued to work. He believed that, no matter how deeply someone sank into racial hatred, that person could be redeemed. King's deep faith and spirituality led him to act with courage.

The basic measure of courage is action. Courage is when you are shaking and fearful of taking the next step, but you do it anyway. This is how you do your part. Whether it's retaking a class you've failed, applying for another job after you were fired, or pursuing your dreams despite experiencing failure, courage is taking the next step.

One thing I've come to realize is that the place where you will receive the most compliments will be at your funeral. You'll be looking up, and the pastor will be looking down at you, and you'll be able to say one of two things about your life: "I wish I had …" Or I'm glad I did… ." Which sounds better? "I wish I had written that book. I wish I had started that business. I wish I'd forgiven that person. I wish I had asked for help sooner."

Think this through carefully. To live a life that matters, you have to begin with the end in mind, and that end is shaped by your values. Let your destination guide for your steps, starting today. We don't always need to learn new lessons. Sometimes, we need to be reminded of the old ones—and then take action.

REGRETS

We all have regrets, and they have lessons to teach us. Reflecting on your regrets is a tremendously important practice because it can help you choose your next steps. To say you have no regrets means you have no restitution to pay, nothing else to learn, and no way that you could have been more courageous with your life.

We all fall short of the standards we've set for our lives, but we can own up to our mistakes and self-correct. If you spent your life living irresponsibly or without a plan, choose to spend the next few years and beyond living responsibly, with a strong sense of mission. Stay determined to figure out life, even when you feel confused and lost.

If you spent the last few years in a career that didn't fit you, decide right now that you'll spend the next few and beyond repositioning yourself, so that you can be where you're called. See Chapter 1 on Calling. If you spent the last few years full of hopelessness and living like a victim, spend the next few years and beyond taking responsibility for transitioning from a victim to a survivor. See Chapter 34 on being a survivor.

Don't just consider what you may have done or not done. Think about the kind of person you have become. Your character determines your actions, so the type of character you cultivate matters.

Acknowledge your regrets, but then let them go. While you can't change the past, you can break its power. We've all made and will make mistakes. I know I've made my fair share. We all have an opportunity to let the past teach instead of letting it bring us pain.

You are here to do something—but even more importantly, you are here to *be something*. Honest reflection—coupled with a resolve to learn from your past regrets—can be the catalyst to a better future.

THOUGHTFULNESS

To be thoughtful is to give something careful consideration or attention. Just as football teams huddle before a play to go over their strategies, we need to take time to develop the tactics that give us an advantage over any obstacles that would stop us from fulfilling our calling. We can learn from the last play without dwelling on the failures or basking in successes. All that matters is what we will do next, based on where we are on the field.

Stay mindful of the outcome you're pursuing, and go play by play. Think things through with the best strategies on hand and a full commitment to execute at your highest level. Take time to think about the path that you are carving out for yourself. Chapter 12 (Define Your Success) includes important information to help you see the outcome, and Part 2 features some strategies for running the play effectively.

Keep the big picture in mind. Nothing is worse than crossing the finish line only to realize you were in the wrong race. Make your decisions from a place of reflection and awareness. People who are effective and make an impact not only review their lives at the end, but also track their progress along the way.

Focusing on your PART is a process, and you will get out of the process what you put into it. If you invest your time, money (books, classes, conferences, therapy, etc.), and energy, change and growth will come—but you will discover that success is a journey and not an event. Be patient in the process. You don't have to be perfect, but you have to be committed.

My faith in God supports my ability to play my part. Jesus said, "The thief's purpose is to steal and kill and destroy. My purpose is to give them a rich and satisfying life" (John 10:10, NLT.) My faith empowers me to live wholeheartedly and abundantly. It levels the playing field of all my experiences and has served as a source of strength in moments of weakness. It has brought me hope in times of hopelessness and clarity in times of confusion.

Our common enemy—in our day and age, when the world is full of confusion and harsh disagreement—is hopelessness. And the answer to hopelessness is a restoration of faith, hope, and love. These qualities can help you move forward despite internal and external resistance.

It is my hope and prayer that this book will serve as one of the tools to restore courage in our personal lives, our communities, and ultimately, in our world.

I'll end with a passage from the Bible that speaks to what we need to truly live a life of significance: Love.

If I speak with human eloquence and angelic ecstasy but don't love, I'm nothing but the creaking of a rusty gate. If I speak God's Word with power, revealing all his mysteries and making everything plain as day, and if I have faith that says to a mountain, "Jump," and it jumps, but I don't love, I'm nothing. If I give everything I own to the poor and even go to the stake to be burned as a martyr, but I don't love, I've gotten nowhere. So, no matter what I say, what I believe, and what I do, I'm bankrupt without love.

Love never gives up.
Love cares more for others than for self.
Love doesn't want what it doesn't have.
Love doesn't strut,
Doesn't have a swelled head,
Doesn't force itself on others,
Isn't always "me first,"
Doesn't fly off the handle,
Doesn't keep score of the sins of others,
Doesn't revel when others grovel,
Takes pleasure in the flowering of truth,
Puts up with anything,
Trusts God always,
Always looks for the best,
Never looks back,
But keeps going to the end.
Love never dies.

Inspired speech will be over some day; praying in tongues will end; understanding will reach its limit. We know only a portion of the truth, and what we say about God is always incomplete. But when the Complete arrives, our incompletes will be canceled. When I was an infant at my mother's breast, I gurgled and cooed like any infant. When I grew up, I left those infant ways for good.

We don't yet see things clearly. We're squinting in a fog, peering through a mist. But it won't be long before the weather clears and the sun shines bright! We'll see it all then, see it all as clearly as God sees us, knowing him directly just as he knows us! But for right now, until that completeness, we have three things to do to lead us toward that consummation: Trust steadily in God, hope unswervingly, love extravagantly. And the best of the three is love.

1 Corinthians 13 (MSG)

Recommended Resources

These can be found on www.amazon.com, www.audible.com, or your local Barnes & Noble.

Chapter 16 – Personal Development
Leadership
Books:
21 Indispensable Qualities of a Leader by John Maxwell
Strength to Love by Martin Luther King, Jr.
Failing Forward by John Maxwell
Boundaries for Leaders by Henry Cloud
The Emotionally Healthy Leader by Pete Scazzero

Finances
Books:
Think and Grow Rich by Napoleon Hill
Think and Grow Rich – A Black Choice by Dennis Kimbro
Rich Dad, Poor Dad by Robert Kiyosaki
Total Money Makeover by Dave Ramsey
The Richest Man in Babylon by George S. Clason
Personal Development
Books:
I Quit!: Stop Pretending Everything Is Fine and Change Your Life by Geri and Pete Scazzero
7 Habits of Highly Effective People by Stephen R. Covey
The Secret to Success by Eric Thomas

As a Man Thinketh by James Allen
No Excuses!: The Power of Self-Discipline for Success in Your Life by Brian Tracy
A Whole New Mind by Daniel H. Pink

Career Development
Books:
Mastery by Robert Greene
48 Days to the Work You Love by Dan Miller
Entreleadership by Dave Ramsey
Start by Jon Acuff
Finding Your Element by Ken Robinson
Daring Greatly by Brene Brown
Rising Strong by Brene Brown

Relationships
Books:
Safe People by Henry Cloud and John Townsend
Boundaries by Henry Cloud and John Townsend
4 Things Women Want from a Man by AR Bernard
How to Avoid Falling In Love with a Jerk by John Van Epp
The Gifts of Imperfection by Brene Brown

Part 3 – Self-Care
Books:
Sleep Smarter: 21 Essential Strategies to Sleep Your Way to a Better Body, Better Health, and Bigger Success by Shawn Stevenson & Sara Gottfried, MD
Exercise Every Day: 32 Tactics for Building the Exercise Habit by S.J. Scott
Best Strategies to Cure Emotional Eating by Joy Marenski
Total Money Makeover by Dave Ramsey
Rich Dad Poor Dad by Robert Kiyosaki
Rich Habits by Thomas C. Corley
Margin by Richard Swenson

Fast Food Nation by Eric Schlosser
Documentaries:
Fully Charged by David Martin and Tom Rath (authors of *Strengths Finder 2.0* and *Eat Move Sleep)*
Food Matters by Andrew W. Saul, Charlotte Gerson, James Colquhoun
Fat, Sick, and Nearly Dead by Joe Cross and Amy Badberg
Fork Over Knives by Lee Fulkerson
Fully Charged by Brian Wasniak and Tom Rath
Audiobook:
Nutrition Made Clear by the Great Courses

Chapter 37 – Mental Illness
Books:
When Someone You Love Has a Mental Illness: A Handbook for Family, Friends, and Caregivers, Revised and Expanded by Rebecca Woolis
The Family Guide to Mental Health Care by Lloyd Sederer
But You LOOK Just Fine: Unmasking Depression, Anxiety, Post-Traumatic Stress Disorder, Obsessive-Compulsive Disorder, Panic Disorder and Seasonal Affective Disorder By Sahar Abdulaziz and Carol Sveilich

Chapter 38 - Colorism
Documentaries:
Dark Girls by D. Channsin Berry and Bill Duke
Good Hair by Chris Rock
Books:
Same Family, Different Colors – Confronting Colorism in America's Diverse Families by Lori L. Tharps
Blindspot: Hidden Biases of Good People by Mahzarin R. Banaji and Anthony G. Greenwald
The Hidden Brain: How Our Unconscious Minds Elect Presidents, Control Markets, Wage Wars, and Save Our Lives by Shankar Vedantam

Chapter 39 – Sexual Abuse

Books:
Courage to Heal by Laura Davis
Beyond Betrayal by Richard B. Gartner
Victims No Longer by Mike Lew
Uncaged Project by Sallie Culbreth M.A. and Anne Quinn
When a Man You Love Was Abused by Cecil Murphey
Not Quite Healed by Cecil Murphey
I Thought It Was Just Me by Brene Brown
DVDs:
Boys & Men Healing from Child Sexual Abuse by Big Voice Pictures
The Healing Years – A Documentary About Surviving Incest and Child Sexual Abuse by Big Voice Pictures

Chapter 40 - Fatherlessness
Books:
Fatherless Sons – Healing the Legacy of Loss by Jonathan Diamond, PhD
Whatever Happened to Daddy's Little Girl? by Jonetta Rose Barras
The Fatherless Daughter Project: Understanding Our Losses and Reclaiming Our Lives by Denna D. Babul and Karin Luise
Being the Dad I Never Had: Lifelong Lessons For Fathering After Fatherlessness by Dr. David R. Inniss

Chapter 41 – Mass Incarceration
Books:
The New Jim Crow by Michelle Alexander
Incarceration Nations by Baz Dreisinger
Just Mercy by Bryan Stevenson
Writing My Wrongs: Life, Death, and One Man's Story of Redemption in an American Prison by Shaka Senghor
Post-traumatic Slave Syndrome by Joy Degruy
The Miseducation of the Negro by Carter G. Woodson
Letter to a Young Brother by Hill Harper

About the Author

JONATHAN FREJUSTE IS THE CREATOR OF TheBridege330, a mentoring program whose mission is to provide quality mentoring tools and resources to underserved, under resourced, and vulnerable communities in ways that support sustained social change, a restoration of hope, and an avenue to emotional health. He is also an Associate Coach with The Center for Emotional Development. He is certified in the emotional measures EQi and EQ 360. He has coached leaders ranging from directors of law enforcement agencies to senior spiritual leaders. He worked as an auditor with Deloitte and Touche where he earned his CPA (certified public accountant) license and serves as a senior financial planner with Ernst and Young where he earned his Series 65 Registered Investment Advisor License. He served as a life skills coach at the Somerset Home for Temporarily Displaced Children and was certified as a behavioral assistant with the state of New Jersey's Children's System of Care. He serves schools and non-profits as a speaker, workshop facilitator, and a coach using the skills he's acquired through his diverse background to provide people with tools and resources to promote and support individual and community well-being.

FB: Jonathan Frejuste
IG & Twitter: @thebridge330
Website: www.thebridge330.com
E-mail: jon@thebridge330.com

Endnotes

1   Alboher, Marci, "When It Comes to Careers, Change Is a Constant" *NY Times*, 1 May 2007, http://www.nytimes.com/2007/05/01/business/smallbusiness/01webcareers.html

2   Scazzero, Pete, "The False Self", *Emotionally Healthy Spirituality*, 23 May 2014, http://www.emotionallyhealthy.org/the-false-self-2/

3   Scazzero, Pete and Geri. *Emotionally Healthy Skills 2.0: Transform The Way You Love God, Yourself, and Others.* Zondervan, 2012

4   Ibid

5   Ibid

6   Ibid

7   Ibid

8   Ibid

9   Mchugh, Beth, "Finding a Good Therapist," *Your Online Counselor,* 2007 http://youronlinecounselor.com/Articles/finding-good-therapist.htm

10 Gregory Reid, "What Being Molested Cost Me," Lighthouse Trails Research, 19 August 2013, http://www.lighthousetrailsresearch.com/blog/?p=12947

11 Scazzero, Peter, "Great Leaders Are Great Listeners," *Emotionally Healthy Spirituality*, 28 May 2017, http://www.emotionallyhealthy.org/great-leaders-great-listeners/

Made in the USA
Middletown, DE
19 July 2020